AN EXISTENTIAL PHILOSOPHY OF LAW

and

Other Essays

Published by Diviacchi Promotions, Inc.

Boston, MA. 2022

All Rights Reserved

Table of Contents

		Page
Abstract		1
I.	**Introduction / Prologue**	1
II.	**The Existential Problem of Law and Its Philosophy of Law**	7
	A. Existential Guides for this Contemplation	11
	1) The Power of Aesthetic Verbiage and Nominal Truth.	11
	2) Ultimately, the Existential Language of Law Is Normative.	14
	3) The Existential Reality of Law: It May Kill Me.	20
	4) Law as Unopposed Normative Violence in the Past and in Technological Society.	21
	5) Existentialism Must Have a Philosophy of Language with Truth Being Pragmatic.	23
	B. The Existential Choice in the Reality of Law	26
III.	**Plebeian Existentialism with and without Nihilism**	32
	A. The Existential Leap to Social Constructs	34
	B. Our Heart of Darkness: Accept It as a Necessary Part of Existential Reality and the Material Progress of Humanity	41
	C. The Reality of Which the Individual Is Conscious	49
IV.	**Ultimately, All Truth in Existential Language Will Be Pragmatic Truth**	54
	A. Existentially, There Are Right Answers: Ugly Ones	56
V.	**An Existential Theory of Language**	59

	A.	*The Existential Basics of Language and Meaning in Language*	64
	B.	*So, Existentially What Are Words?*	66
		1. The Problem of Universals in Interpretive Language.	70
		2. For an Existential Leap to Morality to Act as a Counterbalance to Law, the Meaning of Universals and Words Cannot Be Simply a Matter of Power.	73
		3. Interpretive Wordgames.	76
		4. Existential Wordgames.	81
		5. Ockham's Finger.	84
	B.	*Existential Scientific Language*	91
		1. Existential Universals in Science.	96
	C.	*Existential Language Of Law*	98
		1. So, for the Hermit To Use and Find Law Would It Be Enough To Meet One Other Person?	101
		2. Would More Than a Couple of Persons Lead to a Law?	107
		3. Law As a Universal or Even as a Meta-language.	110
VI.	The Nature of Law and Its Inherent Need for a Monopoly on Violence		112
	A.	*Morality, Ethics, and the Law*	114
		1) A Primitive State Analysis.	115
	B.	*Universals in Law Kill*	119
	C.	*Ockham's Finger in Reverse: Legality and Illegality and Their Unopposed Power of Violence upon Execution*	122
	D.	*Law, Its Truth, and Its Legality Are Distinct Wordgames that May Be But Are Not Necessarily Logically Related*	133
	E.	*Indeterminancy in the Language of Law Does Not Existentially Derive from Indeterminacy of Language But From Individual and Social Construct Will To Power*	135
VII.	Unnecessary Verbiage and Objections		139

    A.   *Legal-Positivism*   **142**

          1)   Morality and Ethics Are the Fuel of the Fuel Cell Container that Is Law.   144
          2)   Objections.   146
              a)   *Mob Island*.   147
              b)   *Ephemerally Non-Violent Law.*   148
              c)   *Who Are the Powers-that-be?*   148
              d)   *The Status of Legal Duties Are Not Dependent on the Monopoly on Violence, the Monopoly Is the Legal Duty.*   153
    B.   *The Hart-Fuller Debate*   154

VIII.   The Power of Nominal Aesthetic Meaning for Truth   156

IX.   Omnipotent Moral Busybodies, *Hoi Polloi*, and Nihilism   164
    A.   *If Your Nihilism Is Something You Can Talk and Write About, It Is Not Nihilism*   169
          1)   "My Dear Fellows, This Is Our Punishment for Associating with *Hoi Polloi*".   170
          2)   Science and the Cuckoo Clock.   174
          3)   Fear of Lawlessness Should not Hinder Nihilism in Western Civilization.   177

X.   Nihilism, Legality, and Illegality   181
    A.   *The Number One Rule for Existential Nihilism to be a Counterbalance to Law: Look Through the Aesthetics to See the Existential Ugliness of Unopposed Power*   184
          1)   No One Really Knows or Cares about Legality or Illegality Except In Relation to Their Will to Power.   185
    B.   *To Counterbalance the Law, the Nihilist*

		Must Be Rationally Opposed to All Legality or Illegality in the Law Not Just Acceptable Opposition	191
XI.	Legal Duty Is a Gun Pointed at Your Head		195
XII.	Am I Being Hegelian?		197
	A.	*Questions Asked and Answered*	202
XIII.	Conclusion		210
Appendix			213
	A.	*Why Tolerate Law?*	214
	B.	*Summary of my Meta-Ethics*	269
	C.	*Sound Generalization or Unsound Stereotype*	274
Bibliography / References			280

Abstract

This is a contemplation of the meaning of the universal "law" in its modern sense of nonscientific law: in the universe of language discourse that results in decisions of legality and illegality. It further contemplates whether this universal can be naturalized to scientific law and seeks to determine whether such meaning and naturalization are or can be an existential philosophy of law. This contemplation will require contemplating the attributes of existentialism as they exist in plebeian lives that includes nihilism and not solely from the more popular academic patrician existentialism that excludes nihilism. Law and its decisions of legality and illegality existentially exist in the universe of normative language in the same way that mathematics and numbers exist in scientific language: decisions of legality and illegality as are numbers are as particular and as real as any bricks or stones thrown at us, yet law as is mathematics is an abstract universal. However, unlike mathematics using rationality to go from aesthetics to particular and empirical pragmatic truth, the aesthetics of the universal law becomes particular and empirical as a social construct by irrational decisions of legality and illegality with their rationality running backwards from their pragmatic truth to aesthetics. The only descriptive "is" in law consists of the pragmatic truth of the empirical execution upon law through decisions of legality and illegality. The universal law is used and is useful as a universal to describe a social construct that is an unopposed normative language with a monopoly on violence to enforce its normative statements. It is the final arbiter through violence of all morality and ethics within the social construct that created it; it is essentially an unopposed ethics with a monopoly on violence whose goal is the survival of the social construct that created it in its struggle with the universe to survive.

I.   Introduction / Prologue

"A slave begins by demanding justice and ends by wanting to wear a crown. He must dominate in his turn" (Camus, 1991, p. 25).

This is a contemplation of the meaning of the universal "law" in its modern sense of nonscientific law: in the universe of language discourse that results in decisions of legality and illegality. There seems to be more to the meaning of law than simply a set of rules. For one, calling something a rule instead of a law requires knowing the difference between rules and laws. Second, unlike most sets of rules such as games, one can leave the game to make other games. This option does not exist with law; if one leaves the law or legality, one is either in lawlessness or illegal. I will further contemplate whether this universal can be naturalized to scientific law and seek to determine whether such meaning and naturalization are or can be an existential philosophy of law. This contemplation will require contemplating the attributes of existentialism as they exist in plebeian lives that includes nihilism and not solely from the more popular academic patrician existentialism that excludes nihilism. I do not want this contemplation and any existential philosophy of law to be just another academic '-ism', it must have pragmatic value for the plebeian portion of the class struggle that is history.

    Existentially, life will always be meaningless and whatever social meaning it has will be forced upon the many by a few. For those few with the power to make their meaning in life the meaning of the group's life, existentialism gives their Nietzschean Will to Power freedom to act and makes their struggle existential and aesthetically beautiful. However, for the many upon whom the few force their meaning, existentialism not only fails to give their Will to Power this same freedom but instead binds it and leaves their struggle to be existential and ugly. Patricians have the luxury to pine for meaning through their aesthetics and then violently either through law or directly to force that meaning on the remainder of humanity, but the plebeian existential absurd hero must not only fight and survive the Absurdity of the universe but also this patrician Will to Power that forces the meaning of their patrician lives upon the universe and all outside their class. For all known history and at present, both struggles eventually involve use of violence, but at least for the moment, the violence aspect is hidden in the behavior modifying techniques of Technological Society. As the plebeian existential absurd hero Don "Wardaddy" Collier through the actor Brad Pitt ad-libbed in the Movie *Fury* (2014): "ideals are peaceful, history is violent". Empirically, given that class struggle is an unavoidable inherent attribute of all social constructs, plebeians must ask whether it is better to suffer an existential struggle with the universe while governed by the few while living in material poverty in pre-Technological Society or to live comfortably in Technological Society with free time for contemplation of philosophy?

If an existential leap from Despair to morality is made, eventually that morality will run into the status of law as an unopposed normative power in the West as the present reality that must be confronted and then accepted or opposed as a good or an evil.

I do not intend to promote or criticize any particular social construct of Technological Society, either political (so-called conservative or liberal versions) nor any of the countless academic myopic constructs pretending to be history varying from feminism to classism to libertarian to post-structuralism to race studies and so forth nor its economic constructs such as capitalism, socialism, and so forth. My contemplation is only to describe the social construct called law that is a universal in all social constructs as a final arbiter of their normative statements. From the plebeian perspective, criticism would be stupid. Modern plebes irrespective of their status as wage slaves or not, of all sexes, kinds, and lives in Western Technological Society, live the finest material and least violent lives in known history. Money may not buy happiness but it buys everything else. At the same time, however, it would be stupid to promote Technological Society because it still maintains the same class distinctions and unequal Will toPower that all social constructs throughout known history have maintained. Patricians will promote it on their own without my or any phebian help — despite their pretending to despise it. However, patricians despite complaints to the contrary, will promote it as a static condition to remain forever as the ultimate social construct meaning for life in the same way they promoted chattel slavery, feudalism, bullionism, mercantilism, and all the other -ism's that came before capitalism and socialism and any other social constructs they presently promote. If there is a next progression for Technological Society, it must come through plebeian existential struggles with patricians and not from any patrician existential struggle among themselves. Regardless of whining about Despair, patricians are just fine as they are, were, and will be.

In Technological Society the need for efficiency by necessity demands not the irrational human freedom and responsibility of existentialism and its leap to morality, immortality, or amorality but the rational unity of thought and action of the present unopposed normative power of law with its monopoly on violence. As an unopposed normative power, using historic evidence to predict the future as any existentialist story-telling naturalized to science must do, law will eventually reach perfection as a tyranny no longer existing as a means to promote and motivate the pragmatic goals that created Technological Society but only as an end in itself. When it reaches this perfection, perhaps it already has, its normative language as with any unopposed normative language stops being pragmatically true but instead gives only aesthetic truth as justification for its power. This is not a problem for patricians because they can seek meaning in aesthetics and sit in their Inner and Outer Party neighbors admiring the art they create in their self-image. For *hoi polloi* however, once the will to power in Technological Society becomes an aesthetic end in itself, the usual options of work or go to jail become just one option: jail, either physically or metaphysically. Work will simply be wage slavery nominally different but substantively the same as the chattel slavery the law in its wisdom universally enforced throughout known history.

Should an existential absurd hero who has made a leap to meaning in life oppose, struggle, and fight tyranny of law or join in its power as an end in itself for meaning in life? Though existential philosophers and their patrician worshipers spend most of their time pontificating about the Absurdity, meaninglessness, and Despair of Technological Society while worshiping and enjoying the protection of its law, its material wealth, and the resulting aesthetic truth for their lives, very few have actually lived lives of Absurdity, meaninglessness, and Despair and thus usually have no or little clue about what they are talking about — they leave that to the plebeians they ridicule as failing to live "authentically" in their struggles with the universe. It is time for the absurd hero of existentialism actually to become a hero by choosing a side in the omnipresent existential struggle for power that is history and human life in Technological Society — either on behalf or against existential freedom and thus either for or against the unopposed normative power of law and its monopoly on violence.

It is time for existentialists to pick a side in humanity's struggle with the indifference and antagonism of the universe to our existence or to stop whining about it. Without doubt, there is an entire universe out there waiting to be discovered, explored, and conquered and this conquest requires actual physical problems to be solved using science and technology. While our existential patricians waste valuable time and resources generating never-ending circular verbiage on word puzzles that have no pragmatic purpose other than aesthetically to reflect their demigod image of themselves, the Orwellian *1984* O'Briens of the world have already chosen law as the means to create a world in their image that does not include existential freedom.

Reason is a tool for fighting the struggle but cannot be its motivator. To any existentialist who has rejected suicide and made a leap to morality, immorality, or amorality or even to nihilism, their existential struggle in Western Technological Society will unavoidably involve struggling with law and the Orwellian *1984* O'Briens of its Inner and Outer Parties who disguise their Will to Power and moral need to create a world in their image as law and its unopposed normative power in the Western world.

What about the rest of us who lack the Will to Power necessary to make a world in our image — assuming there are any rest of us who care? Because law gives meaning to the lives of those who decide by a monopoly on violence what meaning life is to have — regardless of whether they call themselves conservative, liberal, or whatever — and then to force it upon the rest of us, it should be a concern to the rest of us what law is. The communal normative force of law now decides who or what we can love or hate; if or when either is allowed; what gender is; what religion is; what marriage is; what work we are allowed to do and how; what worlds, if any, we can explore, discover, and conquer; who we can employ; who are customers are to be; with whom we can do business; it controls the education of our children; decides if children are to be born; begins documenting us at birth and continues to do so until our death; separates patrician from plebeian; brings back slavery in the form of wage slavery; and decides what the past was and what the future will be. "Who controls the past controls the future. ... Who controls the present controls the past" (Orwell, 1977, p. 44). Existentially, law is a Sword of Damocles hanging over our head every moment of our lives.

It took a few millennia of history for humanity to get to our present Technological Society with its material power over the indifference at best but usually the antagonism of the universe to our existence; yet, humanity's present material power is diminutive and minuscule in comparison to the universe remaining to be discovered, explored, and conquered by any existential absurd heroes who want to do so. Qualitatively, individuals are no different now than they have been throughout known history: we still have a Heart of Darkness that at best can be controlled sometimes but never eliminated. We all have a Will to Power over ourselves and the universe. Since God appears not to be here with us, maybe God is out there somewhere waiting for us to find Him. Will the law allow us to go and look for Him, Her, or whatever God is despite its claim to having killed Him or at least replaced Her with the demigods of law?

Unavoidably, once suicide is rejected, part of any existential struggle with life will involve the law. Part of this essay is to contemplate whether existentialism can and ought to make a leap of faith to social constructs so as to act as a counterbalance to the present existential status of law as the unopposed normative power of the Western World. Such a leap will in turn require dealing with the denial by most philosophers of law that law is an unopposed normative power. To be naturalized to science, this contemplation also requires contemplating an existential philosophy of language that essentially will be a pragmatic theory of language and an existential theory of aesthetics as truth.

II. The Existential Problem of Law and Its Philosophy of Law

"A man thinks that by mouthing hard words he understands hard things" (Melville, H. 2022. p. 1).

After a lifetime of philosophical contemplation, after over twenty-five years of practicing law in the trenches, and after all my graduate studies, my conclusion is that philosophy of law is neither philosophy nor law.

In one end of the spectrum of modern philosophy of law we have natural law theorists. Consistent with Western Law's hijacking of Christian dogma only without the Christianity, these philosophers try to hijack the *lex iniusta lex non est* of St. Augustine and St. Thomas Aquinas only without their Divine Law. Through the delusion of treating words as more real than reality, they argue that the meanings of morality, good, evil, and justice in an indifferent universe are not simply social constructs but things-in-themselves, and the universal "law" denotes the means by which the true meaning of morality is empowered in human society through social governance searching to accomplish justice among the good and the evil. Using "... a substantive makes us look for a thing that corresponds to it" (Wittgenstein. 1965. p. 1). Somehow, the arbitrary and random violence without meaning that is the existential substance of life has not led them to conclude that natural law and law might instead be the source of evil and injustice in life not the source of good and morality. They pay no attention to the existential warning from Albert Camus that "law, by definition, cannot obey the same rules as nature" (Camus. 2020. p. 58). None of this natural law version of philosophy of law has any predictive value: its hypotheses never seek to comply with Ockham's Razor and are logically and empirically unable to make any quantifiable, parameter controlled, repeatable, falsifiable predictions of what law will be descriptively; at best, it can only state what it ought to be in an evaluative and perspective normative sense. To their credit, at least natural law theorists do not claim nor pretend to be able to do any of these scientific tasks nor to be a science or even to be naturalized to science.

Supposedly directly contrary to this natural law view, we have legal positivists at the other end of the spectrum who according to them have given up on using words such as morality, justice, good, and evil or any normative concepts to describe law or any necessary attributes of law. To them, law is a social construct created by social practices, tolerations, decisions, orders, and other nonlegal obligations that are not moral obligations. The existence of a universal called "law" is dependent not on the merits of any law nor on whether it is justice but on rules of recognition, rules of change, and rules of adjudication and the separability thesis. The social construct universal law is bound by attributes consisting of "rules" and the values of these rules. Where are these rules? Everywhere and no where. How do they know the difference between a rule and a law if they did not know what a law is? By the power invested in them through the delusion of treating words as more real than reality, these rules exist everywhere around us in our actions, customs, traditions, and all social constructs yet they are in no particular place nor time. Are morality and law really separate? Not really, because lawgivers can consider morality when creating law. Actually, lawgivers can consider anything they want when creating law. Thus, must not the word law be purely nominal; it is what those with the power to name law say it is? No, because they can only name law if law gives them the power to name law. It is analogous to arguing that the social construct game of basketball is a universal created by the NBA and its fans issuing rules of basketball except there are no NBA nor fans unless the rules of basketball create them but there are no basketball rules anywhere to be found without the NBA and fans creating them. That legal positivists have gotten away with this nonsense for almost a century while claiming to be a science or of wanting to be naturalized to science shows the power of modern law. As the lead *consigliere* of Western Law, legal positivists can say almost anything as long as it sounds pretty. Worse, unlike natural law theorists, they do claim to be a science or naturalized to science though their hypotheses never try to comply with Ockham's Razor and are unable to make any quantifiable, parameter controlled, repeatable, falsifiable predictions of what law will be descriptively. Further, they cannot even state what law ought to be in any evaluative and perspective normative sense, but supposedly they are able to "interpret" law. That they are able to interpret "law" without preconceived notions of evaluative and perspective interpretation norms is assumed. What nonsense.

In between we have hydrids such as patricians Ronald Dworkin and Hans Kelsen who insist law is not just rules but a system of rules that derive from basic presupposed transcendental normative statements that at least for Dworkin include morality. So, what are these presupposed transcendental normative statements? They do not say. Doubt if Kelsen had a clue. In the finest tradition of Kant and Hegel, Kelsen was a virtuoso at throwing out categorical imperative and idealist verbiage so that the artistic beauty of the verbiage created a language reality or universe of discourse as some academics like to call it that became an end in itself more real than reality. For Dworkin, as a patrician who spent his whole life concerned only with achieving prestige and academic power within his patrician class, throwing the word "morality" into his social construct philosophy of law was simply a nominal *noblesse oblige* to justify his power and privilege. These two exemplify the modern philosophies of Arthur Schopenhauer and Friedrich Nietzsche — and even of Ayn Rand — predicting that aesthetics will one day become the meaning of truth. They claim to be naturalized to science even though their hypotheses never comply with Ockham's Razor and are unable to make any quantifiable, parameter controlled, repeatable, falsifiable predictions of what law will be descriptively. At best, some can only state what it ought to be in an evaluative and perspective normative sense while others interpret law by again assuming they have no preconceived norms of interpretation.

None of these philosophies defining law by reference to rules they create explain how they differentiate between a law and a rule without first knowing the difference between a law and a rule. None of these philosophies, as is true of lawyers, judges, and law schools in general, have no basic concept of history.

Supplemental to this philosophy of law mix are other great masters of the lawyerly art of shoveling smoke calling themselves schools of jurisprudence such as law and economics, critical legal studies, critical legal realism, critical race studies, and many others and their many academic progenies who have made philosophy of law into a formulaic zero sum patrician wordgame. Their wordgames, through aesthetic verbiage that annuls and contradicts, serve to cloud the thought and intellect of law students to con them into accepting dishonest and fraudulent thought as morality and ethics while at the same time giving unsophisticated non-lawyers a facade of intelligence for the law so they will also accept dishonest and fraudulent thought as morality and ethics with the law being the cathedral of the ultimate fraud called justice. Law wants to be a science without contemplating let alone understanding what science is. It ignores the one universal attribute of science the law most desperately needs: the use of Ockham's Razor as both a heuristic requirement for its technique and as an epistemological attribute of its truth. It does not use Ockham's Razor because its use would reduce philosophy of law, jurisprudence, and the practice of law to a craft and trade which philosophers of law, judges, and most lawyers would find insulting and dismissive of their skills in generating and shoveling smoke made up of aesthetic truth.

Philosophy deals with the fundamentals of reality but philosophy of law deals with the fundamentals of ignoring reality. It wants to contemplate law while avoiding the law except for the <1% of it that is published appellate decisions. Apparently there is an implicit assumption present that like sausages the less that is known about how particular law is made the more respect there will be for the law and their so-called profession. The little actual practice experience that the vast majority of philosophers of law have or contemplate almost always involves representation of patricians or the law itself as attorneys for the government. They deal in language but have no philosophy of language; they just assume everyone should assume they know what they are talking about because the talk is in the required formulaic verbiage. An existential philosophy of law must avoid these errors, assumptions, and lack of reality and above all its patrician arrogance.

A. *Existential Guides for this Contemplation*

For now, unless my contemplation leads me to contradiction of these guides, only the following seem to be existential descriptive certainties in philosophy of law and law — whatever law may be. I must examine these certainties as part of my contemplation of law and a philosophy of law and decide if they are actually certainties, attributes, or something else in whatever law turns out to be.

Following the contemplation of these certainties, I next will proceed to state a clear description of existential reality, and then the next step is having a philosophy of language before I can develop an existential philosophy of law.

1. The Power of Aesthetic Verbiage and Nominal Truth. In popular culture, Albert Einstein is popularized as saying that he studied physics because "I want to know God's thoughts — the rest are mere details." If this was his reasoning, it goes to show how even the most intelligent are often fools existentially. If one wants to know God's thoughts, mathematics and the sciences are the last place one would find them because they are too finite and limited by the need to actually solve problems and provide hypotheses subject to Ockham's Razor that are falsifiable by quantifiable, repeatable, parameter controlled experiments. In scientific thoughts, there are limits; there are even limits to the concept of infinity. In science, the infinite becomes just another number. In mathematical and scientific thoughts, $2 + 2 = 4$ and must equal 4 in all possible worlds in which mathematics and scientific thoughts exist. Such is not true for aesthetics.

In aesthetics, the artist can make $2 + 2 = 5, 4, 3$, or whatever the artist wants $2 + 2$ to equal. "Sometimes they are all of them at once. You must try harder. It is not easy to become sane" (Orwell. 1977. p. 316). This is truly the thought of God, the ultimate Power in the universe. "God is power" (Orwell. 1977. p. 333). Mathematics and logic would be trivial to the mind of God. "I fear that, to a mind of sufficient intellectual power, the whole of mathematics would appear trivial, as trivial as the statement that a four footed animal is an animal" (Holt. 2013. p. 183). In the wordgame of aesthetic truth, unlike science, one can say "there is no truth" or "all truth is relative" and not once notice the contradiction that disproves the statement. Not only can one say it without anyone noticing or commenting on the contradiction of stating absolutely there is no absolute truth, but one can write libraries on it, call it post-modernism, critical legal studies, critical race studies, post-structuralism, and other nice sounding nonsense and earn great esteem and a decent living by stating it in as much verbiage as possible. Aesthetics is truly the language of God, or at least of human demigods.

I do not mean to ridicule or denigrate aesthetic truth. Its power must be recognized as perhaps the ultimate means by which reason creates truth including those of science and social constructs. Scientific statements having descriptive and predictive value providing pragmatic truth are almost always truly beautiful. If they are not beautiful, it is a sign they are wrong or grossly incomplete. Aesthetic truth is the ultimate goal especially of social constructs involving normative statements because through the descriptive logic — not normative — logic of Hume's Law there is no way rationally to create them from descriptive statements; one must aesthetically create normative statements and thus all normative social constructs irrationally but beautifully from descriptive statements. Existentially, we must also recognize the other side of the coin by which aesthetics giveth it and taketh it away: the power of aesthetics is often also the means and sometimes the only means by which normative social constructs are destroyed. "But if thought corrupts language, language can also corrupt thought" (Orwell. 2009. p. 282).

Such destruction is not necessarily bad but is often a good. Such is the existential reality of plebeian life.

Plebes must be just as willing to destroy as to create and to confront as equals both creation and destruction in their existential struggle. For example, during the first three years of the Second Punic War when the Roman Republic was primarily a power only of the Italian Peninsula and the Balkans, it was made up of hundreds of separate tribes, cultures, societies, languages, religions, and federates. In the first three major battles of that War (Trebia, Trasimene, and Cannae) around 218-216 B.C., the Roman Republic lost 20% of its adult males. At present, that would be the equivalent of losing 20,000,000 males in war on the continental United States — not on foreign shores. These types of losses destroyed cultures in antiquity and in modern times (Western or Eastern) and it most certainly would destroy us. Not only did Rome continue to fight that War for another ten years, it eventually won and went on to create the *Pax Romana* and to become a dominant power in the West for the next fifteen hundred years eventually leading to modern Western Civilization. However, it was not the Roman Republic that dominated during all those years. No, despite the normative and social construct power of the Republic that allowed it to survive and flourish after losing 20% of its adult males in three battles, in just more than 200 years after the end of the Punic Wars, the Republic was abandoned by the descendants of those Honored Dead who died to defend it so as to move onto the Empire in order to continue discovering, exploring, and conquering. Through violence using the aesthetic beauty of the law combining Republican legal fictions such as tribune, consul, dictator, censor, and others into new legal fictions such as *Princeps Civitatis* ("First Citizen of the State") for Augustus Caesar and through the willing and knowing assent of the plebeians, the Republican social construct was socially converted into the new legal fiction of a *Principate* — what we call the Roman Empire and the first Emperor.

    It was the creative and destructive struggles of their civil wars that created the aesthetics of the Roman Empire and made its law an acceptable normative social construct. The struggle from Kingdom to Republic to Empire was a plebeian struggle for power with patricians. Patricians always win the war for power eventually, but plebeians start it and win the initial paradigm changing battles.

    The existential challenge for plebeians is to get the creative power without the destructive or to minimize greatly and substantively the destructive.

I want this contemplation to serve not as a patrician philosophy of law as is universally the case for all philosophy of law — and often philosophy — but as one to serve plebeians, even though unfortunately they are the last to deal with philosophy of anything. Based on my 25 years of practicing trial work in the miserable trenches of the American system of injustice, I know for a fact that present philosophy of law has no practical effect on life in the trenches. Except for the few patricians at the top getting rich off this trench warfare for whom philosophers of law act as *consigliere*, the existential reality of the practice of law is similar to a Samuel Beckett or Italian existential play or movie: a bunch of clueless persons staggering around trying to survive arbitrary and random events occurring around them. Present philosophy of law primarily acts as the aesthetic justification for the patricians being patricians. Nineteenth Century law school pedagogy treating law as a deductive science was at least able to teach law students how to think critically and logically, but it no longer serves even this simple task. Instead, law school pedagogy has replaced logic with the art of creating beautiful thick clouds of fraudulent verbiage to hide the shallowness of thought and the ambition for power of the wizards behind the smokescreen. An existential philosophy of law must give the plebeians still in the trenches a philosophical understanding of their struggle, a struggle that often by necessity is or involves illegality, so as to improve their lives in the trenches and out.

2) Ultimately, the Existential Language of Law Is Normative. This is not a contemplation of scientific "law" with its descriptive and predictive meanings but law with its conclusions of legality and illegality. Even if it can be argued that some particular law or law has some descriptive or other value, existentially, regardless of the extremes to which modern philosophers of law go to hide its nature, ultimately when law or any particular law or aspect of law is logically analyzed as far as logic can take the language of law, it is a normative language: it states what ought to be not what is. Unlike scientific predictive and descriptive statements nominally called "law" and hiding as "ought" statements because of leftover meanings from the days of divine and natural law, in pure normative language there is no reality separate from the normative language. In science, if one descriptively or predictively calculates what *"F=ma"* ought to be and then decides not to use the answer when intending to send a rocket to the moon, your intention will fail. If one normatively states what *"F=ma"* ought to be and then one ignores it when attempting to send a rocket to the moon because one normatively concludes *"F"* ought not be a certain value because it is evil or it is good that rockets cannot go to the moon, the result is still normatively true in relation to your normative statement regardless of whether the rocket makes it to the moon or not.

"Truth" in normative discourse has nothing to do with anything outside of the normative language. If something ought to be, it does not matter whether it really is or is not what it ought to be; what matters in the normative discourse and its normative truth is that it ought to be. Individuals are not being irrational when they have irrational normative beliefs, they are simply being existential humans.[1] All normative beliefs, statements, and truth are irrational: they make an existential leap to meaning in a meaningless universe.

Existentially, there is no justice, fairness, rights, duties, obligations, or anything of an evaluative or perspective or any normative meaning in the benign indifference of the universe to our existence despite the fact that sometimes the universe is antagonistic to our existence. (Why the universe hates the poor is a theological question for another day that is not at issue in this contemplation of a philosophy of law.) "'Everything is permitted' ... is not an outburst of relief or of joy, but rather a bitter acknowledgment of a fact"

---

[1] As I contemplated in my Meta-ethics *Masters' Thesis*, there is nothing fallacious or illogical in the proposition: "it is snowing outside but I do not believe it is snowing outside." *See* **Appendix**.

(Camus. 1955. p. 50). Thus, existentially, anything such as law that deals in words such as rights, duties, obligations, protections, fairness, justice, and other evaluative or perspective normative language regarding social interaction or even personal life, it must be either normative or just nominal and aesthetic. The law often hides its normative nature through statements, rules, and procedures that appear to be benign statements of what "is", such as wills, stocks, corporations, municipal bonding, probate, and so forth. However, ultimately all these benign statements of what is have meaning only because they are evaluative and perspective of what "ought" to be done. When the law says something "is", it means it is or else — or else there will be punitive consequences forcing what it says ought to be actually to be.

There need not be any connection between what the law says ought to be and what actually is in reality. If you do not agree with its statements of what is, ultimately there will be violent punishment for anything not being as the law says it ought to be. All meanings in the law are subservient to the normative meanings of the law. Presently, the violence will be unopposed by anything but law.

I must not allow this normative nature of the language of law to be hidden by smokescreens such as law and economics that pretend to give the law descriptive and predictive value by after-the-fact rationalizations, by hidden theories of interpretation by which descriptions are created, and its scientific behaviorism aspect that allows for predictive marketing and outfight brain washing on behalf of its hidden theories of interpretation. Economics can talk all they want about universals and fictions such as rational choice theory and other assumptions of Hegelian rationality in life just as the law casually talks about "legal person", "reasonable person", "reasonable parent," "reasonable landlord," "fair-minded and informed observer," "person having ordinary skill in the art," and so forth going back to the majesty of Roman law. These are all after-the-fact rationalizations of previous normative decisions. None of these carry the predictive value nor pragmatic truth of the universals and fictions of science.

At best, all such hidden normative meanings intermixed with descriptive and aesthetic meanings create helpful observations in the same way good fiction such as Herman Melville, *War and Peace*, and so forth contain helpful observations. They are not the descriptive predictive "law" of science. Ultimately, a "reasonable person", a "rational choice", or any such universal or fiction in economics or law trying to create a descriptive or predictive truth for law is circularly defined after-the-fact by both economics and the law simply as one that acts reasonably and rationally and not by any hypotheses subject to Ockham's Razor that are able to logically and empirically make quantifiable, parameter controlled, repeatable, falsifiable predictions for experiments.

Law and economics as with psychology and many other wannabe sciences are great at after-the-fact descriptions and as does good fiction give observations with aesthetic truth about humanity's Heart of Darkness without having to suffer its physical pain, but that is all they do. To the extent something such as pretend sciences such as economics and other "social" sciences are able to give pragmatic knowledge about normative statements, it does so by hidden behaviorism: assumes certain acts ought to occur; then creates incentives for those acts to occur; and then hides the assumptions by describing after the fact how the incentives must be the cause of the acts; and there we have law and economics. Economics is even willing to define "rational person" by irrational acts if they happen so often enough that they cannot be ignored in after-the-fact economic descriptions of acts assumed to be rational by hidden assumptions.[2] No philosophy of law especially an existential one should be allowed to play such a sleight-of-hand with the meanings of words.

Without doubt, through assumptions of randomness and scientific mathematical probability theory using universals and other

---

[2] For a rather dark humorous example of this rationalization at work in the economics of pirate tortures, *see* Leeson. 2009. pp. 107-133.

fictions used to interpret the use of randomness and probability theory, economists with or without law can use their descriptive Monday morning quarterbacking observations of what a reasonable person or rational choice or whatever they want to call it should have done and then create arguments for what the world ought to be; they can irrationally jump from what is to what ought to be as do all other normative statements. However, logically, what normative changes to make and whether they ought to be made are questions that can only be made not by assumptions of randomness but by assumptions of what ought to be. A normative ought statement does not become a descriptive statement simply by hiding or ignoring the assumptions. "Sanity is not statistical" (Orwell. 1977. p. 274).

Just because something works and solves a problem does not necessarily lead to the conclusion it ought to be and the reverse: what ought to be does not necessarily solve the problem. Executing all criminals will significantly if not entirely eliminate all crime; does not mean this ought to be done. Personally, I think dueling among consenting adults ought to be legal; to my knowledge, however, this will not solve any problems of violence in society. This is one of the problems with having the normative power of law be unopposed with a monopoly on violence to enforce itself: even if a solution is known — which usually it is not, what solves a problem or does not solve it does not matter to the law and is often irrelevant to its need for normative statements. In addition, the law defines what is or is not a problem in the first place. A social group can be in full agreement as to the facts of an event and still be in disagreement as to whether those facts ought to be considered illegal murder or legal homicide.

As an example for contemplation dealing with normative statements generally, we can descriptively say that modern baseball with its sabermetrics is without doubt a different game than it would be without it. In modern Major League Baseball, they is a distinction between teams that have won its championship Pennant and those that should have won it according to the statistics — the latter are called Pythagorean Pennant winners (Gibson, 2021). For those baseball teams with the money to fully use and apply it, it can make the difference between losing and winning. The Boston Red Sox with a $200,000,000 payroll after spending $2 billion in 15 years used sabermetrics to win the Pennant. *Ibid.* However, the Oakland A's with their $100,000,000 payroll and less than $1 billion in total team value have not been able to do so. *Ibid.* So, what about those that do not have the money to fully use and apply it? What ought to be done, if anything, to allow them to fully realize their Will to Power? Further, what kind of game ought baseball to be? Saying it ought to be the game sabermetrics says it ought to be is the law and economics delusion used to hide the non-random assumptions used to hide the normative foundation of both economics and of law and economics.

In the reality of law dealing ultimately with what ought to be and with what ought to be enforced by violence, the Is-Ought logical necessity distinction of Hume's Law, also known as Hume's Guillotine, will always be a certainty and must be contemplated and a necessary attribute in the language of any existential philosophy of law:

> In every system of morality, which I have hitherto met with, I have always remarked, that the author proceeds for some time in the ordinary way of reasoning, and establishes the being of a God, or makes observations concerning human affairs; when of a sudden I am surprised to find, that instead of the usual copulations of propositions, is, and is not, I meet with no proposition that is not connected with an ought, or an ought not. This change is imperceptible; but is however, of the last consequence. For as this ought, or ought not, expresses some new relation or affirmation, 'tis necessary that it should be observed and explained; and at the same time that a reason should be given, for what seems altogether inconceivable, how this new relation can be a deduction from others, which are entirely different from it. But as authors do not commonly use this precaution, I shall presume to recommend it to the readers; and am persuaded, that this small attention would

subvert all the vulgar systems of morality, and let us see, that the distinction of vice and virtue is not founded merely on the relations of objects, nor is perceived by reason. (Hume. 1739. pp. 469-70).

Because law existentially is by necessity a normative language then regardless of how badly I and philosophers of law might want law and its philosophy to be a science with its descriptive "law" stating what is, it never will be and we never will be scientists. The law will provide descriptive meaning only by at best nominally putting law in quotations (*i.e.*, according to statute, "the speed limit is 65 mph") but will never provide predictive value except nominally at best: the law will be what lawgivers are quoted as saying the law is or will be.

At best, it may be that for an existential philosophy of law, we can be naturalized to science only by accepting its truth as our truth: pragmatism. The problem with accepting pragmatic truth as truth for the present unopposed normative power of law however is that law will decide what problems ought to be solved thus it will decide the problem whose solution makes its pragmatic truth to be pragmatic truth — *a la* the law and economics and critical legal realism crowds.

So, as part of this contemplation on the nature of law, I must contemplate whether existentialism must accept pragmatism as truth in law as it must for science: truth means something works, it solves a problem or gives us useful consequences. With pragmatics as truth, all truth will have to be revisable upon new experience. Problem is what experience, if any, changes normative statements? If a descriptive statement cannot logically create a normative statement, how can a normative one logically create a descriptive statement?

3) The Existential Reality Of Law: It May Kill Me.

Because law is just normative — or in addition, nominal and aesthetic — by the necessary logic of Hume's Law that is descriptive of all logic, there is no logical way to go from what is to the normative ought language of law nor anyway to go from what ought to be to what is. Existentially, we can irrationally and rationally reject all of the absurdity of the universe: all that is and all that anyone including the absurd hero says it ought to be.

Contemplating such issues as philosophy is itself in many ways aesthetic and therapeutic of the physical pain and ugliness of reality, however it is important not to lose sight of reality. Though the normative statements of law are not logically related to any descriptive statements, the existential reality is that its monopoly on violence or existential need for a monopoly on violence does have one unavoidable empirical descriptive reality: execution upon its normative statements — it may kill me. Regardless of their aesthetics, the power of the normative statements of law supposedly dealing with justice, fairness, and other such well marketed words do not derive from aesthetic descriptive experience but through the ugly execution upon law through its monopoly on violence. This empirical sense experience will most definitely have empirical descriptive effects: death, destruction, and ruin for some; life, power, and success for others.

Execution upon law is associated with particular empirical experience but not necessarily. Even a normative statement with a monopoly on violence need not become an actuality: no one need do what they ought to do, just ought to do it.

Thus, in law, we might be faced with the problem of two separate distinct languages or universes of discourse — as some say — with no logical connection. I must contemplate whether it is possible to contemplate and to describe a normative language and a descriptive language as one language of "law".

4) Law as Unopposed Normative Violence in ihe Past and in Technological Society. As argued in my *Why Tolerate Law?, w*hile explicitly and implicitly subsuming Christian Divine and Natural law dogma into its jurisprudence while also denying it has or is doing so, Western law has successfully dogmatically rejected as its equal any normative opposition to its power from Christianity's dogmatic hope of rationally knowing God through human reason in the form of divine and natural law. Instead Western law has successfully claimed the absolute power to define and resolve whatever and everything it wants to define as good or as evil varying from ageism to Zionism while it gives religion only nominal toleration — despite the fact that historically any "-ism" is usually only pragmatically evil if it is enforced by the violence of the law. In the present and for the foreseeable future by the necessary rationality of Technological Society, Western law has replaced and superceded religious dogmatic normative power with the unopposed normative power of its own secular dogma enforced by a monopoly on violence.

      Historically, the fact that a power such as law needed others to execute upon its judgments was usually a weakness that exposed the violent nature of law and thus weakened its aesthetic truth. From Alexander the Great to Napoleon, the Inner Party was expected to lead from the front or risk the ability to execute upon their law. This is no longer true. Popular mainstream history easily forgets and distorts history; in the process, it has forgotten that only a short time ago, the Inner and Outer Parties of the law in order to execute upon their paradigm shifting normative statements and social constructs, such execution required actual execution of violence by the police and the military to enforce their irrational normative creations. Just as the so-called politically conservative needed the police and military to bust up working class unions and made May 1st International Workers' Day that is instead celebrated as Law Day in the United States, the so-called politically liberal needed the 101st Airborne Division, National Guard, and armed police to force integration upon the same working class — while of course leaving conservative and liberal patricians to live their sheltered culture of segregation free of such violence.

      At present and for the foreseeable future, the need to rely on the violence of police and military force for execution upon the law is no longer a weakness for the law that gives away its violent nature. The law's monopoly on violence is so dominant, fear of it so omnipresent, and its aesthetics so mind-numbing that patricians regardless of their pretend Inner and Outer Party persuasion (conservative or liberal) can now issue such social construct paradigm shifting decisions as *Roe v. Wade* and its progeny, *Citizens United,* and *Goodridge* and many more without fear of opposition. The law can now expect and assume that all individuals will conform and surrender to law regardless of morality. *Hoi polloi* do so and must so conform and surrender by the modern Slave Morality of the law expected of them even for a case such as *Roe v. Wade* in which the decision may involve infanticide. The power of the law for execution upon legality and illegality will only grow stronger in Technological Society as the human factor in execution diminishes with the Inner and Outer Parties gaining the ability to kill others actually and figuratively by algorithms and by imprisonment, personal, economic, and other sanctions through technology without getting their hands dirty.

Thus, even the check upon the violence of law created by the fact that its patricians needed plebeians to enforce execution upon the law is gone.

Though law constantly talks about morality, ethics, justice, and other such fictions; and philosophers of law dispute whether morality is or is not included in the universe of discourse of law; it is just talk. Whatever morality may be, as a purely individual construct it has long ago become submissive to the power of law. Law gives nominal toleration to morality in the same way it tolerates religion: it will tolerate it when it wants to do so and will kill it otherwise. No individual construct such as morality supported only by the Will to Power of an individual can become a counterbalance to the social construct power of law — unless it is the Will to Power of a tyrant. In the latter case, for all practical purposes it has become law anyway and we are back to one of the motivations for this contemplation: how to counterbalance the power of law?

5) Existentialism Must Have a Philosophy of Language with Truth Being Pragmatic. Since I do have a philosophy of language argued in my previous writings that I intend to contemplate at least in part in this essay, from the start I will not pretend as philosophers of law pretend that language is anything other than a pragmatic attempt to describe and solve a problem. Whatever law may turn out to be may not require accepting pragmatism as its truth, but any existential philosophy of law must accept pragmatism as its truth. Existentialism does not really care about law, social constructs, or any degeneration or devolution of Technological Society unless an individual existentialist wants to care or by circumstances is forced to care. At which point, once the leap to caring about the problems of life is made, the only truth that matters consists of solutions to the problems and the question must be asked whether the unopposed normative violent power of law will be a source of meaning in a Technological Society for its Will to Power over the universe or will it be just a tyranny of power as an end in itself? With its present monopoly on violence, the whatever to which the universal word "law" refers has become the religion and god of the Western patrician class. Actually, more of a cult of power than a religion — assuming there is difference. It gives meaning and power to patrician lives and thus to their intelligentsia who therefore expend great effort to give the word "law" philosophical meaning as a marketing tool to justify to the plebeian classes its monopoly on power. Most of this effort is exerted on the creation of aesthetically pleasing verbiage giving an aura of rationality to what substantively and essentially is an irrational norm creating process.

  I will not pretend this is a scientific or objective contemplation of the concept of law because there is no such thing nor of anything of which we can speak when dealing with normative language. Science and scientific language are "objective" in the sense that it describes by means of hypotheses subject to Ockham's Razor and makes quantifiable predictions that can be tested and falsified in repeatable parameter controlled experiments. Its truth is pragmatic: its truth is ontologically real as long as the words of its truth work to solve the described problem. "Certainly the answer is not provided by the semantical formula 'To be is to be the value of a variable'" but the subsequent famous motto "To be is to be the value of a bound variable" (Quine. 1980. p. 15). If existentialism wants philosophy of law to be naturalized to science as modern philosophy claims it must be, all its truth must be defined as either pragmatic or aesthetic. All reasoning of which we can speak is limited by its language that is in turn limited by its use and usefulness to that use.

    My existential leap to meaning consists of wanting to protect, promote, and flourish Technological Society into discovering, exploring, and conquering the universe. I do not want to leave my fellow plebeians behind in a world in which the end comes with a whimper of self-centered moralizing and Will-to-Power shallowness created by patrician *1984* O'Briens admiring their god-like images in the aesthetics of telescreens. If the meaningless universe is destined to kill us, in unity with the souls who struggled and fought it before us, we must go out fighting. As existentialists and as the first official modern existentialist Kierkegaard argued, we cannot and shall not decide which life fights the good fight most easily, but we reject Despair and we all agree that every human being ought to fight the good fight (Kierkegaard, S. 1993). This fighting "ought" is about the only "ought" we have in our normative language and from which no one is shut out. Thus, this contemplation is founded upon and intended to solve a problem: the unopposed normative power of law with its monopoly on violence. Solving this problem involves contemplating what normatively ought to be and thus the problem and its solution cannot be "objective" problems. As with all normative language, this contemplation involves a description of the problem and eventually what ought to be to resolve the problem. However, this "ought" is existential and thus does not involve morality, amorality, or immorality but an existential leap to what ought to be.

    If an existentialist makes a leap to law as the only normative source of meaning in life, then its unopposed monopoly on violence is not a problem. If one does not make such a leap or one makes a leap to a different normative language, it is a problem needing to be solved. Before I can argue for what ought to be, I must have some sense of what is: what "law" is in relation to what existentially "is". Part of this descriptive reality of what law is will unavoidably involve my individual existential leap to meaning and its Will to Power because otherwise I would not care and thus existentialism would not care about what law is.

It is clear from the vast amount of verbiage that philosophy of law issues with no predictive or descriptive value but only "interpretive" value circularly defined by its own interpretations of its own normative statements that philosophy of law is unconcerned with the limitations of language. It has no problem talking about that of which "one cannot speak, thereof one must be silent" (Wittgenstein. 2009. Prop. 7, p. 9). Actually, it does not even know or at a minimum does not acknowledge it is doing so. In the empirical tradition of Thomas Hobbes, modern philosophy of law assumes that any law is better than no law but unlike Hobbes sees this reality through a metaphysically idealist lens. Modern philosophy of law essentially is a naive belief in law as a rational world spirit in the Hegelian sense. For all modern philosophers of law, from natural law theorists to the most empiricist legal positivist, law is seen as the means by which human social groups express rational order in a universe otherwise dominated by irrationality. None of them see it as a source of irrationality nor as a source of domination of individual rational will to power by the irrationality of the universe. As a Hegelian would say, law is worshiped as the rational spirit of a society coming to self-consciousness through reasoning.

B. *The Existential Choice in the Reality of Law*

Because of this Hegelianism, existentialism should immediately be suspicious of philosophy of law. Not only because of its blind fanatic Hegelian faith in verbiage and rationality as powers without limit but also because its empirical reality has clear values and attributes with existential consequences: it will kill me. Law requires an existential leap of faith to acceptance of its unopposed normative power as a necessary value for Technological Society superceding all other normative powers including individual morality, but it does not admit to such leap. Again, if an existentialist also makes such leap and becomes a *1984* O'Brien for

Technological Society, then its unopposed monopoly on violence is not a problem. If one leaps to different meaning in life, it is.

As descriptive existential reality, one thing is certain: Western law for the present and the foreseeable future is the only normative power in Western Civilization and of our present and foreseeable Technological Society. For the present and the foreseeable future, it has defeated, negated, made obsolete, and superseded its usual opponent Western religion as a normative power and any other opponents such as morality. As the victor, Western Law and those who make law have a monopoly on violence to enforce their norms limited only by the willingness of those who execute their norms to execute them — a willingness that at present and for the foreseeable future seems to be limitless. While the remaining religious in Western Civilization contribute to social construction of normative social constructs by spending a few hours each week hugging, talking about spirituality, and singing Kum-ba-yah, with the advent and availability of drones and other robotics and artificial technological enforcement of law's monopoly on norms, even the execution limitation will gradually disappear as humanity becomes accustomed to technology becoming both the creator of normative language and then judge, jury, and executioner of the violence to enforce those norms. "Not even the moral conversion of the technicians could make a difference. At best, they would cease to be good technicians. In the end, technique has only one principle, efficient ordering" (Ellul. 1964. p. 97).

By historical evidence, Western Civilization had its Renaissance, Enlightenment, and Scientific Revolution because of the freedom resulting from, associated with, and created by the struggle between the Will to Power of secular law and the Will to Power of Christian dogma stating God and creation can be known by and through human reason through Divine and Natural Law. This dogma of being on this earth but not of this earth acted as a normative power equal in opposition to secular law with its emphasis on earthly power — but no longer.

Existentialism knows religious dogma to be false as is the equally delusional dogma of secular law summarized by the word religious word "justice". As the old trial attorney adage usually attributed to Clarence Darrow says, "there is no justice in life, in or out of court".

However, because existentialism is based on reality including historical reality, the existentialist absurd hero who makes a leap to a morality, immorality, or amorality that is naturalized to science cannot ignore the freedom created by the struggle between Christianity and secular law that allowed human reason to grow into modern science and modern Technological Society.[3] Without this struggle between Western religion and Western law as equal normative opposing dogma, we are left only with our Heart of Darkness acting through the normative power of law in which eventually power will simply become an end-in-itself. With power becoming an end-in-itself, both master and slave will be equal before the law in their Will to Power "demanding justice" by which they mean Camus' "[we] must dominate in [our] turn" (Camus. 1991. p. 25). However, this equality will not change the necessary existential descriptive law of life and the universe that there will always exist some who will be masters and others who will be slaves; the existentialist absurd hero who rejects suicide must leap to the freedom of the master or leap to a struggle to free the slave to become master and thus to renew the existential fight with absurdity.

As I contemplated in *Why Tolerate Law?*, as history's first sociologist Plato accurately predicted two thousand years ago would always occur and has occurred, historically all democracies eventually deteriorate into anarchy and then tyranny and then Plato's cycle of five regimes restarts. He hoped to stop this cycle not by the rule of law — which he ridiculed as being too rigid and

---

[3] See generally, Numbers, R.L. (2003). *Science without God: Natural Laws and Christian Beliefs. When Science and Christianity Meet* (D.C. Lindberg, R.L. Numbers, Eds.). University Of Chicago Press.

unable to deal with the dynamics of ruling a state — but by the rule of the best ruling by or through law. Having the rule of law replace the rule of the best — which has its own problems — is a relatively modern political concept for avoiding Plato's regime cycle that at present shows no sign of being any better at avoidance then previous attempts. As I have pointed out before in *Why Tolerate Law*, though philosophers of law like to trace the rule of law as a modern concept back to the *Magna Carta* they all seem to forget that it was Archbishop Stephen Langton of the Catholic Church who came up with the idea of this document in an attempt to force the King to admit submission to Divine Law. As seen by the transition of the Roman Republic into the Roman Empire, law does not prevent transition into tyranny but is simply the means by which it is formalized. Law is the means by which mob law becomes just "law" or the rule of law:

> Remember, democracy never lasts long. It soon wastes, exhausts, and murders itself. There never was a democracy yet that did not commit suicide. It is in vain to say that democracy is less vain, less proud, less selfish, less ambitious, or less avaricious than aristocracy or monarchy. It is not true, in fact, and nowhere appears in history. Those passions are the same in all men, under all forms of simple government, and when unchecked, produce the same effects of fraud, violence, and cruelty. When clear prospects are opened before vanity, pride, avarice, or ambition, for their easy gratification, it is hard for the most considerate philosophers and the most conscientious moralists to resist the temptation. Individuals have conquered themselves. Nations and large bodies of men, never. (Adams, J. 1814. p. 1.)

Furthermore, as historians and philosophers from Plato in his idea of a *Republic* to T.S. Eliot and his *Idea of a Christian Society* have noted, a society lacking the equal normative power of a successful religious tradition emphasizing spiritual concerns to counterbalance the worldly ambitions of secular law will degenerate into tyranny, social and cultural dysfunction, and fragmentation. In such degeneration, eventually, scientists motivated by a moral belief in rationality and its power as a good by which they can come to know the universe will get disillusioned by their lifetimes of work: work resulting only in falsified versions of truth or of pragmatic truth that will never satisfy anything but an amoral need for power as an end in itself. At which point, science will lose the existential leap to morality that motivated the scientific revolution and created modern Technological Society but will not have Christianity's dogma to fall back upon by which to renew its spirit and motivation. Yet, there will still be a universe out there waiting to be discovered, explored, and conquered. Since no one takes the risk of discovery, exploration, and conquest of the existential indifference and antagonism of the universe based on purely rational concepts such as the Ontological Proof, the only options to fall back upon as motivation for this discovery, exploration, and conquering will be either the amoral Orwellian tyranny of a need for power as an end in itself or the dogma of law — but are these two motivations the same?

Are there existential alternatives to such a monopoly? Ought there be? Of course, as always, our patrician class has much more power than the vast plebeian and wage slave majority struggling against the universe, and patricians ridicule as absurd the plebeian struggle to survive and give meaning to their lives by religion. The Inner and Outer Parties of our patrician class control the law as the means by which this class creates a world in their image, but it always has been that way and always will be. As Orwell writes in *1984,* we always have had and always will have a patrician class or High as he calls them with their Inner Party and Outer Party. Is the law the Outer Party enforcer of the Inner Party of our present and future Technological Society?

What is "law" when used in its nonscientific sense? Is this word a universal something that has universal attributes present in all social constructs that can be philosophically studied and contemplated? If so, what are they? Are they useful for anything other than nominal meaning? Or, is "law" a word used simply as shorthand for the millions of individual uses of the word "law" and determinations of what is "legal" occurring each day in courts and other government entities entitled to make useful the word "law"? In either case, is law a hindrance or an asset to allowing, fostering, and motivating Technological Society to discover, explore, and conquer the universe? Does this word "law" include "ethics" and "morality"? Does it matter what law is? In an existentially meaningless universe, what difference does it make — one god is the same as any other as long as the gods and their worshipers leave me alone?

Through the sound footing in empirical reality of existentialism, this contemplation and essay should also serve as a pragmatic attempt to create an existentialist philosophy of law to help Technological Society avoid, skip, or at least minimize substantially the harm to humanity of the tyranny portion of the Platonic regime cycle so that it can continue its material progression to a Brave New World — whether it be utopia or dystopia or whatever it may be.

By definition, such an existential contemplation is meaningful only if an absurd existential hero makes the initial leap to caring about what happens to humanity overall or in the regime cycle; a leap not everyone need or does make. Without such a leap, a philosophy of law is probably a waste of time but not necessarily. Even if the meaning of one's life is a nihilistic "fight the powers" including whatever the law is or whoever it may be — a fight that is an end itself — in order to make it a good fight, one must know the opponent.

If history continues as a guide with some predictive value, consistent with historical evidence, the United States as a republic form of democracy is at present or at some point will be doing the usual Platonic transition into anarchy and then into tyranny before starting the five regime cycle again with some form first stage monarchy. Historically, in Western Law this transition has not been a bad thing. It has happened before in Western Civilization as part of our path of human material progress. The question for present existentialists who make the leap to caring is whether such transition in a Technological Society will continue to be a path of human progress? Will a tyranny with a monopoly on violence through law in a Technological Society become omnipresent state worship similar to the tyranny of Islamic law, other Eastern state worship, or Hegelian state worship? If the latter, do existentialists care if it is the end of history?

If so, will this result in the Western World finally losing its War with the East that began with the Battle of Marathon? By such loss, we will then join the secular theocracy culture of the East with its regime cycle of state worship, stagnant human culture, conformity, and a herd mentality and thus end our Technological Society? For a nihilist who wants to fight the good fight, there would be no joy nor Will to Power joy in a nihilistic struggle against an opponent who does not fight back. If an omnipresent stagnant secular theocracy regime is to be our existential future under the law, might as well join Nietzsche and live in our room having our mother take care of us — in our case, having our Big Brother take care of us.

III. Plebeian Existentialism with and without Nihilism

"If I thought of God as another being like myself, outside myself, only infinitely more powerful, then I would regard it as my duty to defy him" (Wittgenstein. 1984. p. 5).

Existentialism deals with the absurdity of individual human existence. Its mantra is "existence before essence"; it reverses the Cartesian "I think therefore I am" to "I am therefore I think". For patricians and academics, this reversal results in existentialism concentrating its descriptions on interpretations of the word "individual" and of individual sense experience or consciousness whose only value is its own existence in a meaningless reality of which the individual is conscious. As a result, it is easy to fall into the modern self-absorbed versions of existentialism viewing and arguing about reality and its social constructs as if it and they can all arbitrarily and randomly be changed to fit self-centered individual need: sexual preference, feminism, sexism, gender, race, racism, self-identity, sexual identity, and much more. When existentialism does get into social constructs, because of its emphasis on a self-centered view of reality, the result should be nihilism but most often it is just a shallow form of nihilism such as post-modernism essentially serving to make the aesthetic value of verbiage generated by intelligentsia be an end in itself and the meaning for life — even academic existentialists are in denial as to absolute nihilism being the only consistent conclusion for old school and new school existentialism. Therefore existential contemplation usually has little value for anyone but patricians and academia and it has little need to go on to contemplation of social constructs such as law as anything more than a random and arbitrary creation of the conscious mind.

    Law may be an arbitrary and random creation of the conscious mind just as the universe may have arbitrarily and randomly created small pox, syphilis, various plagues, polio, and much more, but just as these arbitrary and random creations will kill you and me, so will law. Historically, as with smallpox and other creations of the universe, law will kill arbitrarily, randomly, and indiscriminately: regardless of sex, gender, race, self-identity, feminism, racism, sexual orientation, and so forth if I or anyone oppose its normative statements. Thus, an existentialist who has rejected suicide and wants to live the life to which they have made a leap of meaning, at some point they will have to deal with law in the same way they deal with small pox: rational description; understanding it as best as reason will allow; and then either Will to Power join it, control it, or oppose it.

    Nominally changing "small pox" to "butterfly bumps" or "God's Will" makes its reality more aesthetically pleasing and this aesthetic truth may make it easier to die of it, but such nominal change does not beat it. In order to be naturalized to science, if an existentialist wants to be so naturalized as my contemplation does, then existentialism must contemplate this arbitrary and random social construct power called "law" rationally and seek pragmatic truth to control its Will to Power to kill me and us just as we would small pox or any other natural construct to the extent possible. You may care what gender, sex, or about whatever society nominally calls or names you, but ultimately neither the universe nor society cares. Social constructs are not individual constructs. Individuals die, the society, its social constructs, and the universe in some sense lives on — regardless of whether it is as a godless material continuation; simply as an ideal in the mind of God; or as a Hegelian world spirit.

Part of any existential philosophy of law is rationally to ask and answer whether the law, unlike the universe and society, is somehow a social construct that really cares about the individual or just the society of which it is a social construct? If every social construct is treated as an arbitrary and random creation of individual consciousness, there is no point to making an existential leap to meaning. Again, even a nihilist fight requires a knowing and rational understanding of the opponent in order to make it a good fight — fighting to win that is regardless of a destined eventual loss. If a pretend existentialist prefers the post-modernism view on life, they should do themselves a favor and simply live in the happy timelessness of the moment as do animals until occurs suicide or an arbitrary and random death.

For existentialism to reject nihilism in any sense but aesthetically and thus for it to have a need to go on to contemplate social constructs and to have a philosophy of law that either accepts or rejects nihilism, we must accept and understand existential individual absurdity; but then we need to go on to make a leap of faith into morality, then into social norms, and thus at that point be faced with the Absurdity of social constructs such as "law".

However, even if this leap is not made but pure nihilism is accepted as social reality and the only life consistent with existentialism, even a nihilist should contemplate a philosophy of law to know one's opponent in battle so as to assure a good fight back into nothingness. Law is the unopposed religion of all modern Technological Society but its adherents are all in denial as to it being a religion.

A. *The Existential Leap to Social Constructs*

"From nothing we have risen and from nothing we still rise" (Shanahan, J., Byrne, M., Beattie, C. & Martin, S. 2002. Hollow

Ground" [Lyrics]). Existential religious and secular philosophers such as Soren Kierkegaard and secular ones such as the working class hero Albert Camus have already done excellent work delineating the Absurdity of individual existence in a meaningless universe. Furthermore, while most other existentialist philosophers have been and are satisfied with existentialism as an aesthetical self-contemplation, these two actually went further by trying to set a foundation for existential social norms by contemplating how an absurd existential individual would create a morality and live as a social normative force. However, because their emphasis was on individual existence, neither law nor any similar social construct such as ethics were contemplated as unique problems in their philosophical contemplations nor is law as a social construct seriously contemplated in any existentialist or nihilist philosophy. For Nietszchean nihilism, it argues itself to be the next stage of human development, it gives no value to what happened before nor to what happens next after nihilism — if anything happens. In an existentialist view of reality, law and other social constructs such as ethics only become problems once the individual rejects suicide and makes a leap of faith or a leap to faith into social construct existence. The existentialist concern is with rejection of the suicide part; a rejection that seems for them to negate nihilism but really does not.

Once the absurd individual rejects suicide, does this by necessity negate nihilism? After such rejection, to negate nihilism must an individual next by act of will create a morality, a construct by which to differentiate right and wrong? Then, as a next step, can an individual create a social construct of right and wrong?

Rejection of suicide is not in itself a rejection of nihilism. Living as a completely self-centered amoral individual in which one's Will to Power is an end in itself is probably the most god-like an individual can be and is a rational way of life. If life has no meaning, making oneself its meaning is a completely rational result. Rejection of nihilism requires a further act of will, freely made or predestined, of a morality; even if that morality is simply a nihilist fight against any nihilism lacking morality.

For Kierkegaard, the creation of morality is by old school application of Christian Divine Law accepted as pragmatically true and acting through individual Faith converting "possibility to actuality" (Kierkegaard, S. 1974. Vol 1, p. 314-315). The emphasis is on understanding individual existence and then creating by an act of will individual morality; Faith and God will do the rest. This type of social construct normative creation is exhibited in fiction by Leo Tolstoy. After spending most of his early life as an atheist, he spent years contemplating this conclusion eventually creating his universal, ageless, existential *magnum opus* "War and Peace". He eventually made a leap to Christian Faith and acted on his beliefs by freeing his serfs, writing books to help them learn to read, and giving them land to farm and live on. He never gave a rational reason for his acts nor argued politically or socially about them, his language became the "actuality" of Kierkegaard. These acts were good for him and hopefully for his serfs, and his leap was joined with enough of the Other to act as further incentive for the 1861 emancipation of the serfs in Russia (two years before our own Emancipation Proclamation). However, historically, such individual faith that leaves social construct creation to Faith and God did little and does little for existentialism and did little for the Russian nation state social construct and its law. Russians despite having killed their last official tsar 100 years ago have always been governed and still want to be governed by tsars with the only difference being the tsars no longer call themselves tsars. Russia is no more a free and open society by Western Enlightenment standards now than they were under the tsars. However, Tolstoy's purely individual path of morality is acceptable and is accepted by all modern religious existentialism and is consistent with Kierkegaard.

    Not much can be said about such existential path toward morality and social constructs — be they ethics or law — unless one has faith in a loving God. As much as theologians try to deny it, the concept of Divine Law eventually becomes a matter of divine predestination and provides almost no guidance on how the absurd individual unable or not allowed to make the leap to faith of a Christian loving God is to understand or deal with any social construct including law.

This type of existentialist predestination had and has much appeal to religious patricians and their intelligentsia such as Tolstoy who have the opportunity, time, and resources to contemplate it and the option and power to leap to faith or not to leap. However, as existentialists such as Dostoevsky bring out in their writings, it does not add much to the reality of the plebeian and other lower classes. About the only choice the lower classes and especially the working class have had historically and have now is to make an irrational leap of faith or leap to faith to religious Faith and Hope since they usually have nothing else for which to hope. A drowning man thrown a life preserver, if they want to live, does not really have a choice to leap or not to leap towards it; to live life, they must make the leap.

Secular existentialism also does little for anyone but patricians and their intelligentsia regarding social constructs other than to justify their patrician status. For Camus, his early death left his initial contemplations — such as *The Rebel* and *The Plague* — on a secular existentialist concept of socially constructed norms such as law an open issue. All other secular existentialist philosophers from Heidegger to Sartre ignore social constructs to concentrate on contemplation of individual life and consciousness that usually means self-absorption on their individual needs thus resulting in little more than poetry useless for anything but aesthetically pleasing verbiage — apparently assuming that Wittgenstein's "I am my world" is a metaphysical not just a language reality (Wittgenstein. 2009. Prop. 5.62, p. 64).

For some unknown reason, Camus always feared and rejected nihilism. Perhaps he did not have as much in common with Meursault of his *The Stranger* as his readers assume he had. In *The Plague*, he sees hope "that there is more to admire in men than to despise" (Camus, A. 1991. p. 318) when they join in a social struggle against physical or spiritual annihilation by a plague — that supposedly was an analogy for tyrannies such as fascism or communism. However, in *The Fall* and *The Rebel*, he gives a pessimistic view of human nature by his previously quoted, "[t]he slave begins by demanding justice and ends by wanting to wear a crown". In his <u>Myth of Sisyphus</u>, once Camus' absurd heroes reject suicide and nihilism, he binds them into social existence by values for three variables of individuals:

    1)   Don Juan, the serial seducer who lives a personal and social life of passion to the fullest. "There is no noble love but that which recognizes itself to be both short-lived and exceptional" (Camus. 1955. p. 48).

    2)   The actor, whose life on a social stage "demonstrates to what degree appearing creates being. ... In those three hours [on a stage] he travels the whole course of the dead-end path that the man in the audience takes a lifetime to cover (*Ibid*. p. 52).

    3)   the conqueror, the warrior who forgoes promises of eternity in order to engage in human history, choosing action over contemplation while constantly aware of the Ides of March — that all glory is fading, nothing will last, and no victory is final (*Ibid*. pp. 62-68).

Considering his working class hero life, these three social categories have always puzzled me about Camus and seem to derive from his fear of nihilism or perhaps they were just preliminary contemplation cut short by his early death. The first two are no better than the patrician artist worship of a Schopenhauer or Nietzsche in which the only reason to prefer life to nonexistence is aesthetic creation as an end in itself giving meaning to individual life without giving meaning to life. Considering his working class beginnings, it seems Camus was much corrupted by his later life with the intelligentsia leading to these two categories of social absurd heroes. Modern patrician versions of Narcissus can spend their lives gazing at their reflection consisting of their aesthetic creations and fall in love with them without concern of losing their will to live and slowly dying of thirst and starvation because there are plenty of wage slaves and other plebeians to do the dirty work of feeding and taking care of them, but such is not true of those doing the dirty work. These two social categories are not really social acts or constructs but patrician delusion ignoring humanity's social struggle to survive a universe at best indifferent to our existence but usually antagonistic to our survival.

Camus' conqueror is an absurd hero leaping into social constructs but it is an old school version that has little in common with modern Technological Society conquerors. Old school conquerors such as Alexander the Great and Caesar onto Napoleon, Hitler, Churchill, and such did not reject promises of eternity; being a conqueror was a means to an eternity as a god in the same way that Achilles found immortality in Homeric epics. In many ways they were successful. For example, even the word "tsar" is derived from the Latin word Caesar; I expect this name and the lives of history's other Caesars will be remembered long after billions of other lives have disappeared into the forge of humanity's struggle with the universe. They lived in simpler times. "They were conquerors, and for that you want only brute force — nothing to boast of, when you have it, since your strength is just an accident arising from the weakness of others" (Conrad, J. 2016. p. 9).

Rather, new school Technological Society conquerors are exemplified by the Orwellian O'Brien of *1984*. Our conquerors do not forego promises of eternity but replace eternity with the timeliness of always being in the present: according to the Inner Party O'Brien, "[p]ower is not a means, it's an end" (Orwell. 1977. p. 332). Our modern Inner Party conquerors work behind telescreens; have others or machines do their killing for them; and are hidden by Wizard of Oz creations maintained by their Outer Party house servants varying from Richard Posner to Ta-Nehisi Coates, so it is almost impossible to see them work. One can see Technological Society O'Briens and a significant aspect of the Outer Party and the banality of evil at work by stepping into any session of a federal courtroom fiefdom of a life time tenured federal judge — what happens in the behind-the-Wizard-of-Oz screen inner sanctum of the judges' chambers is still sacrosanct. One can see multiple O'Briens at work in any session of state or United States Supremes and most state or federal appellate courts. So even the absurd hero conqueror of Camus misses becoming a social construct contemplation of modern Technological Society law.

Saying each individual is a conqueror of their life's struggle makes good marketing but misses the mark again because of the emphasis on the "individual".

The unfortunate reality is that the only way a plebeian individual *qua* individual without aid of society can conquer life's struggles is by suicide. Patricians and their intelligentsia can use their trust funds and other surplus capital generated by *hoi polloi* to play at Camus' Don Juanism, at playing the conqueror, and at being or pretending to be an artist so as idly to admire their reflections in their aesthetic work; by doing so, they thus rely on social constructs for their meaningful lives yammering about the meaningless of their lives. But, for the vast majority consisting of plebeian and wage slave humanity, all conquests of the meaningless of life require a community and thus social constructs. Even giving meaning to one's life by living the solitary life of a hermit requires a society to reject and from which to become a hermit; without a society to reject, the life of a hermit would just be another meaningless life. Similarly, to become a nihilist such as Meursault proclaiming "for everything to be consummated, for me to feel less alone, I had only to wish that there be a large crowd of spectators the day of my execution and that they greet me with cries of hate" (Camus. 1954. p. 154), one would still need the crowd. Unfortunately, plebeians need each other to survive and to defeat patricians, this is one reason so much social effort by patricians is spent on assuring plebeians do not unite with each other in their struggles but are divided by racism, classism, sexism, or whatever other -ism patricians through the law create to keep plebeians fighting among themselves.

Thus, irrespective of patrician existentialists pretending to live solitary lives, the common existentialist — once suicide is rejected — will have at least to create a morality for dealing with social constructs such as law even if involvement in social constructs occurs solely as a hermit-like rejection or nihilist fight against them.

As I will contemplate later when contemplating an existential philosophy of language, the new school conqueror hero ignores, just as existentialism as a philosophy itself ignores, the existential reality of the word "individual". This word as with many words expressing "I am" has a metaphysical thing-in-itself meaning of existence but it exists in a world of language in which almost all other words have only pragmatic meaning: their use or usefulness. The "individual" has a metaphysically real meaning of existence but exists in a universe of social construct variables whose meanings are their use and usefulness. For an existentialist philosophy of law, we must have an understanding of this ontology having an "individual" at the center of the fabric of our meaningless universe who is not just an observer or an outsider to it but a part of its meaninglessness and Absurdity. The Orwellian O'Brien of *1984* has a clear ontology for his modern philosophy of law that he calls the Party:

> You believe that reality is something objective, external, existing in its own right. You also believe that the nature of reality is self-evident. When you delude yourself into thinking that you see something, you assume that everyone else sees the same thing as you. But I tell you, Winston, that reality is not external. Reality exists in the human mind, and nowhere else. Not in the individual mind, which can make mistakes, and in any case soon perishes: only in the mind of the Party, which is collective and immortal. Whatever the Party holds to be the truth, is truth. It is impossible to see reality except by looking through the eyes of the Party. That is the fact that you have got to relearn, Winston. It needs an act of self-destruction, an effort of the will. You must humble yourself before you can become sane. (Orwell. 1977. p. 314)

To have an existential philosophy of law, existentialism must either accept or respond to O'Brien, the modern conqueror of our Technological Society.

B. *Our Heart of Darkness: Accept It as a Necessary Part of Existential Reality and the Material Progress of Humanity*

Though existentialist philosophers spend most of their time pontificating about the absurdity, meaninglessness, and despair of life, very few have actually lived lives of absurdity, meaninglessness, and despair. None considered significant by intelligentsia have committed suicide; a few nihilists of the intelligentsia have but not as many as one would think given their preaching of it as a viable option. If one studies their personal lives, for many including almost all French existentialism including present day so-called post-modern existentialism called structuralism, post-structuralism, or whatever, existentialism is simply a means used by European male philosophers to pick up women and to give their lives meaning and money and they are very successful at it. According to the philosopher Robert C. Solomon in Chapter 3 of the philosophy movie *"Waking Life"*, the existentialist philosopher/guru Jean Paul Sartre stated in an interview: "he never really felt a day of despair in his life" (Linklater, R., Dir. (2001). *Waking Life* [Film]). Based on his life of catering to Marxist (Stalinist no less) intelligentsia and his disdain and nausea of "bourgeois" materialistic and capitalist society despite its having allowed him a life of leisure to sit around and complain about the bourgeoisie while creating no useful solutions for his complaints, it is doubtful Sartre ever knew any existential despair. Thus, Sartre had no business giving out advice attributed to him and to existentialism generally in popular culture such as "life begins on the other side of despair" or that "the absurd man will not commit suicide; he wants to live, without relinquishing any of his certainty, without a future, without hope, without illusions … and without resignation". What a jerk. I doubt that either Sartre or any of his followers or associates lived with, without, or even materially experienced anything he advises others to ignore.

    Most existentialists, with a few exceptions such as Kierkegaard and Camus, talk about despair, absurdity, and meaninglessness in the same way a biologist talks about DNA; it is simply a means to a end though it supposedly is life. The practical end for most of European existentialism, at least for the males, is to get laid. For the females, it seems to be a continuation of the basic division defining the difference between the sexes since the Garden of Eden: man is put on earth to suffer, woman is put on earth to enforce that rule. Germans Husserl and Heidegger and similar so-called continental existentialists were obsessed with generating verbiage as an end in itself for aesthetic reasons and are thus more poets than they are philosophers. One of my few agreements with Nietzsche is a definition of poetry that is commonly attributed to him though I cannot find its source: "the art of creating ripples on shallow water to give the appearance it is deep". As to the remainder of existential aesthetics, its beauty is defined by the willingness of patricians to pay money for it and not in any other social construct sense nor in any use or usefulness other than aesthetics as an end in itself — beauty as truth.

The complex and tragic despair and meaningless of human existence that drives an individual to suicide is not felt by reading, writing, and talking about the universe and humanity's inhumanity to humanity nor about the phenomenology of "being and time", "the Other", "being and nothingness" or whatever wordgame tricks exist to make words seem more real than reality. It is easy to hate humanity and the universe or to be indifferent to it as it is to us and yet to continue to live life. Such is especially true of life as a patrician. Such pretend existentialist disdain for reality serves to separate and raise the individual patrician and their aesthetics to something better than reality and *hoi polloi* thus reducing philosophy essentially to group therapy for patricians.

It is not the attributes of the universal "humanity" that gives us the existential absurdity of life, it is looking into the eye of the individual human besides you to see the hate and Heart of Darkness within their soul willing to kill you and the Heart of Darkness within one's self that makes life unbearable — that is why the majority of humanity at any given time including existentialist intelligentsia supposedly contemplating the indifference of the universe avoid both. Those on the political left ignore such existential reality by creating safe places for cosmic justice that ignore the cosmos. Those on the political right ignore it by creating a loving God. In a choice between the Red Pill and the Blue Pill of the Matrix, most of humanity at any given time will choose the Blue Pill, and rightly so. Rightly so, as they and as we should all logically choose. As Pascal's Wager and Decision Theory logically proves, at any given moment in time and space, taking the Blue Pill is the logical and rational choice. Existentialism is the irrational choice of rejecting the choice.

Reading, writing, or crying about genocide, fascism, nazism, or whatever the latest fad evil political -ism may be and dividing historical individuals into heros or villains is a shallow understanding of the absurdity of life, history, and the universe. Only those ignorant of history divide history into the good and the bad, and into heros and villains, male or female, of one race or of no race. Regardless of the majestic greatness of one's heros or the despicableness of one's villains — be it a Churchill, Hitler, Muhammad, Martin Luther King, Nelson Mandela, Gandhi, or whoever — the historical good or evil of individuals and of social constructs is not the substance of reality. Such concepts of good and evil, hero and villain in history are purely results decided as a matter of luck and the roll of circumstantial dice. The winners in life need not ever worry about morality, ethics, or the law, such are concerns only for the losers. Simple creation of historical heroes and villains gives meaning to one's life and creates a simple morality of good and evil that ignores the banality of evil and the haphazardness of both good and evil in daily existence — that is in individual life, the only reality of which an existentialist is certain. If Hitler had died in his youth in the trenches of the Western Front or during one of the first half-dozen assassination attempts upon him, he would be remembered as a courageous recipient of two Iron Crosses who died for his country and for workers' rights — in fact, if he had died during one of those early assassination attempts upon him, he would probably to this day be remembered as a hero and martyr for socialism. In which case, Churchill — if remembered at all — would be remembered as he was known during World War I: as a self-aggrandizing, dishonest, ambitious, political hack psychopath from a rich family whose fortunes he squandered and who was responsible for the Gallipoli Campaign disaster. Muhammad is essentially a 7th Century Hitler who succeeded in creating a 1000 year Reich and thus as victor is a prophet instead of a villain. Dr. King and Mendela were lucky to have racism as their opponent. As exhibited by their sexual conquests of women, patrician personal ambitions, and political shrewdness to take credit for the work of others and to let others do their killing and dirty work for them, they would be just another *1984* O'Brien Will to Power conqueror if they had a more sympathetic opponent. Gandhi was a racist patrician wife-beater who was lucky to have others do is killing for him. Such individuals are not really individuals but social construct values for the old school Camus conqueror bound variable created for marketing purposes by patricians.

The reality of history is that 90% to 95% of individual humans regardless of status in life as poor, rich, slave, free, beggar, worker, and so forth if put in the right circumstances would knowing and intentionally kill every other human being or watch idly as others knowing and intentionally kill every other human being — including eventually those watching. The only difference for the modern patricians of our Technological Society is the law allows them the power to have others do their killing for them. The individuals who make up each of these two classes of bound variables — those who kill and those who do not — arbitrarily and randomly change each moment of life. The heros who make up the 5% or 10% at any given moment who would rather be killed than kill another or watch another be killed will move over randomly and arbitrarily as a coincidence of sometimes insignificant changes in circumstances to the other set made up of killers. Meanwhile, some of the killers will at that same moment transfer over to become heros. The existential reality is that 100% of individuals under the right circumstances would knowing and intentionally kill every other human as a matter of brute and irrational or even rational force.

One of the interesting facts about World War II genocide that is directly relevant to our contemplation of the nature of law is the ratio of guards to prisoners in both legal extermination and legal prisoner of war camps. It only took about a dozen armed guards to march 5000 - 6000 prisoners legally to their death camps. This is true regardless of whether the prisoners are civilians going to extermination or work camps; harden soviet soldiers marching west to German prisoner of war camps; or battle-harden German soldiers after the Battle of Stalingrad marching east to Soviet POW camps. Unfortunately, to my knowledge no one has done any statistical study on these ratios and I base my figures on my reading of World War history books, but my approximate figures based on decades of reading history and particularly World War II history can be confirmed by any World War history book that has any such figures within it.[4] The camps and any extermination process at the camps could only be operated with the help of the prisoners themselves or the entire imprisonment and extermination process would have collapsed. According to the testimony of Rudolf Hoess, Commandant of Auschwitz, the entire concentration camp system consisting of 20,000 camps and the extermination of 6 million was operated by about 45,000 SS and regular military personnel.[5] Consistent with the Natural Law of the universe, the greatly outnumbered guards chose the strongest and the healthiest of the condemned, prisoners, and POW's to assist them in killing the remaining majority.[6] In addition, as has been true of all genocides

---

[4] *See generally*, Browning, C.R. (2017). *Ordinary Men: Reserve Police Battalion 101 and the Final Solution in Poland.* Harper; Bailey, R.H. (1981). *Prisoners of war (World War II).* Time-Life Books.

[5] Hess, R. (1946). *Testimony of Rudolf Hoess, Commandant of Auschwitz*
[Testimony on Monday, April 15, 1946]. http://law2.umkc.edu/faculty/projects/ftrials/nuremberg/hoesstest.html; Holocaust Encyclopedia. *United States Holocaust Memorial Museum.* https://www.ushmm.org/wlc/en/article.php?ModuleId=10005144

[6] *Ibid.*

throughout history — even those occurring before the word "genocide" was created to describe the events — modern genocides occurred with the knowledge of the majority of individuals and society whose law and religion allowed the killers do their killing for them.[7]

Such ratio of minority to majority does not work for anyone or any group acting outside the law — that is for criminals. According to historical and economic empirical measurements, in all modern societies and internationally, violent criminals are always approximately 6% of the population. (Sovell, T. 2008. pp. 20-53). "The career criminal cannot simply be dismissed as irrational, because there is too much evidence from too many countries that he is indeed quite rational" (*Ibid*. pp. 24-25). Despite having resources based on violence, a minority of criminals cannot enforce their normative statements upon society; it takes a monopoly on violence to go beyond the serial killer stage of killing dozens or hundreds to become a patriotic killer of thousands or millions. The existential historical reality is that most intentional genocides (not those caused unintentionally by natural disease) only succeed through a social construct created by a synthesis of the brutality of the greatly outnumbered killers and the weaknesses of the much greater in number killed.

For those natural genocides resulting from disease such as that of the inhabitants of the New World, only one entity: God and his created diseases were necessary. Criminals kill dozens or even thousands but it takes mother nature or a village to kill millions.

At this preliminary state of contemplation, it seems that in all pragmatic, practical, and descriptive senses, the few killers and the

---

[7] *See generally,* Goldhagen, D.J. (1997). *Hitler's Willing Executioners: Ordinary Germans and the Holocaust.* Vintage; Kiernan, Ben. (2009). *Blood and Soil: A World History of Genocide and Extermination from Sparta to Darfur.* Yale University Press.

social construct of hierarchy, duties, and rules by which mob gunmen "lay down the law" may be the first universal value of the bound variable "law" or Law with a capital 'L' to represent the meta-universe of law or set of all laws.

Unlike most existentialist writers and readers, I do not exempt myself from this critique of a Heart of Darkness. In fact, I accept it and for an honest contemplation of any philosophy of anything it is necessary to accept it as a necessary part of existential reality. Our hearts may be dark, but the darkness and nothingness of the universe indifferent at best but usually antagonistic to our existence is much darker. There is without doubt a need for someone or something to control this Heart of Darkness and to channel its power to constructive goals in humanity's struggle against the universe — that is, once we make the existential Will to Power leap that such a goal is meaningful or at least is our or my meaning.

For any honest existential contemplation, a philosopher must accept our Heart of Darkness as a necessary part of existential reality and as a necessary part of the individual's Will to Power over the indifference and antagonism of the universe to individual existence. Historically, patricians granted plebeians the opportunity for material progress only during natural disasters or wars that forced patricians to deal with plebeians as equals for a limited amount to time. This path of opportunity is absurd and causes as much suffering to plebeians at the time as it creates material progress for the future but is an reality of life that must be accepted and dealt with in any philosophy of law contemplation.

Despite the quantity and magnitude of modern genocide and war, the historical fact is that our modern Technological Society is the most peaceful or at least non-violent era in history. The 20th Century gave us so much technological progress materially improving human life that humanity was able to negate by several multiples the 20th Century's genocides and war deaths so that global population saw its greatest increase in known history: rising from about 1.6 billion in 1900 to over 6 billion in 2000.[8] ("World Population", 2022).

The knowledge that 100% of individuals under the right circumstances would knowing and intentionally kill every other human being as a matter of brute force should not serve solely as an existential contemplation by which patricians through aesthetics differentiate themselves from that reality but as a necessary attribute of any social construct contemplation. Patricians who do not commit suicide but instead enjoy their reflections in their aesthetic creations as meaning for their lives do so as a coincidence and not as an exemption to our Heart of Darkness. What existentialist philosophy does not contemplate or does not want to contemplate is the "right circumstances" and the "how" of trying to control reality so we do not kill each other into oblivion. "Accept diversity" is as worthless as "love thy neighbor" in pragmatic reality. Unity of values and ideas creates more peace than any diversity while also creating social stagnation. Love thy neighbor, as even Christianity admits, must begin with loving yourself which is the whole problem since myself includes a Heart of Darkness. If one is still contemplating suicide when viewing a Heart of Darkness, these circumstances and the "how" do not matter. However, once one passes that point and makes a leap to morality, the circumstances and the how including law do matter and existentialism must make a leap of faith to social constructs.

C. *The Reality of Which The Individual Is Conscious*

"We feel that even if all possible scientific questions be answered, the problems of life have still not been touched at all" (Wittgenstein, L. 2009. Prop. 6.52 p. 81). Existentialism has a fairly limited relationship and contemplation of the empirical scientific reality of individual consciousness. Much of this has to with their individual surrender to aesthetic creation as the only meaningful

---

[8] *See generally,* Gat, A. (2006). *War in Human Civilization.* Oxford University Press.

way of life *a la* the likes of Sartre, Beckett, Schopenhauer, Sartre, Heidegger, Husserl, and of course everyone's favorite Nietzsche. They seem only to love science when they claim it has proven there is no God but seem to ignore the fact science has neither given such proof nor can it give such proof given the pragmatic nature of its proofs. But, most importantly, it should not matter whether it gives such proof — just as it should not whether or not there is a God. Saying individual existence is meaningless, indifferent, absurd, and irrational is one thing but to use science as a basis or means to argue the universe is meaningless, indifferent, absurd, and irrational is disingenuous and unfair to the universe, science, and consciousness. Scientists can be as delusional as non-scientists when it comes to purpose in life: "I think I would say that the universe has a purpose, it's not somehow just there by chance ... some people, I think, take the view that the universe is just there and it runs along – it's a bit like it just sort of computes, and we happen somehow by accident to find ourselves in this thing. But I don't think that's a very fruitful or helpful way of looking at the universe, I think that there is something much deeper about it" (Morris, E. 1991. Film Script at Sir Roger Penrose).

At present, it appears science can and does give meaning to reality: mathematics. When non-scientists view reality either in its wide screen version consisting of the night sky or in its small screen version at the microscopic level, we see things in a particular time and space. According to scientists what we really see and what is really there when viewing reality at any given non-intuitive 4-dimensional or multi-dimensional and mathematical space-time is mathematics in various forms: numbers, equations, geometries, algorithms.[9] According to science, the universe and ourselves are made up of either Platonic forms or of Leibnizian monads consisting of mathematical forms not created by our consciousness but

---

[9] *See generally*, Tegmark, M. (2014). *Our Mathematical Universe: My Quest for the Ultimate Nature of Reality*. Deckle Edge.

discovered by it and so is our consciousness. Apparently, as individuals we are all a Schrödinger's cat made up of probability waves with infinite possibilities until the reason-there-is-something-instead-of-nothing looks inside the geometric space-time Wittgenstein Beetle Box containing us to view us and thus turn us into finite mathematical entities. According to some mathematicians, we can get around Kurt Godel's Incompleteness Theorem so as to establish that mathematical formal systems are "out there" as an external reality not just as creations of the human mind as most of language appears to be.[10] Thus the scientific hope or faith for our future is that we will not be left asking why there is something instead of nothing requiring we call the creator of this mathematically beautiful aesthetic creation God, but the reason for something instead of nothing will be the beauty of mathematical axiomatic forms that are their own reason for there being something instead of nothing. According to science, reality may be the ultimate aesthetic creation by the reason- for-there-being-something-instead-of-nothing for us to contemplate; that magical verbiage is acceptable, just do not call it God — or a god.

It appears Leibniz may get the last laugh on Voltaire by modern science and its mathematical language establishing by empirical scientific evidence revealing through mathematical necessity that we do in fact live in the best of all possible worlds because all possible worlds make up our universe.

If we assume existentialists are not elitist artistic slobs or snobs whose lack of creativity assumes only the likes of a Jackson Pollack, Picasso, or Andy Warhol are creative (simply because patricians are willing to pay big money and can pretend to understand their mess), then contemplating a universe made up of the creativity of pure logic and mathematics should give meaning to all our lives when we contemplate it just as such contemplation

---

[10] *See generally*. Hut, P., Alford, M., & Tegmark, M. (2006). On Math, Matter and Mind. *Foundations of Physics*. 36 (6): 765–94 (2006).

gives meaning to the lives of mathematicians, physicists, astrophysicists, cosmologists, and their less able groupies. Aesthetics is good enough for scientists and pretend worshipers of science — but maybe not all real scientists.[11] Must we accept aesthetic wordgames as normative power?

I first realized the power of defining meaning in life based solely on aesthetics and one's reflection defined as aesthetics when as a student at Harvard I went to visit the art and architecture classroom buildings. They are easily found because they are the ugliest buildings on campus. The insides are worse: the original dull white paint of the walls had long ago turned into a dirty, peeling, bruised, dusty white that for some reason no one is ever concerned about repainting colorfully or even in the original white. There is dirt, dust, and trash everywhere because I assume the artists left their maids at home. The broken and haphazard furniture and other interior furnishings match the dirty and cracked walls and ceilings. Many areas smell of dust and mildew. I felt more aesthetic beauty standing watch in the battleship grey engineering spaces of a US Navy submarine surrounded by the physical beauty and harmonious music of machinery than standing in any hallway or room of Harvard's architecture and art classes. The only items in the buildings or classrooms that had any resemblance of beauty was the art in any given student's work area — which is all they cared about. Some of it was really beautiful art. Much and most was not. It did not matter because the individual who make it considered it art. The power of patrician existentialism: the whole world could be a dirty, smelly, dusty, chaotic, falling apart mess but none of that matters as long as the supposed art a few inches in front of the artist's face is pretty. A pragmatic solipsism, is that all existentialism is good for?

Patrician existentialism can only give aesthetic meaning to

---

[11] *See generally,* Holt, J. (2013). *Why Does the World Exist?: An Existential Detective Story.* Liveright. ; Field, H. (1980). *Science Without Numbers*: *A defense of nominalism.* Blackwell.

life using scientific ignorance as an excuse for laziness.

Now what? So what? Now that we supposedly know scientifically what reality is, what do we do with it? Now that we know reality is simply aesthetics, does this answer our contemplations as to what it ought to be? If I am just a collapsed probability wave, so is everyone else. So what ought I do with my life's probabilities and the lives of so-called Others except to contemplate the aesthetics and beauty of the universe until I starve to death, die of thirst, or the universe kills me for some other reason? According to the scientists who study the mathematical beauty of the universe, just as with the patricians who spend their life contemplating their aesthetic creations and want society to expend its resources on these creations, we should be spending more money and energy contemplating and experimenting with everything from atomic bombs and anti-quarks to positrons and quarks. Why? I only have one life, why would I waste the product of my hard work on their religious faith and hope of creating a universe that is a beautiful formal mathematical and logical system — a aesthetically pleasing formal system whose abstract mathematical beauty only a small percentage of humanity is capable of appreciating or, in the case of abstract art, of buying? What difference does their aesthetic creation mean to my life? Forget them. If I am going to live, should I not join Orwell's O'Brien by loving Big Brother and know the clarity and passion of power as an aesthetic beauty in itself and know the timelessness of the moment? Is that not what God is and does? "If we take eternity to mean not infinite temporal duration but timelessness, then eternal life belongs to those who live in the present" (Wittgenstein, L. 2009. Prop. 6.4322, p. 80).

The universe is not meaningless and absurd because science or scientific empirical evidence shows it to be. It is so because it is. Even if science gives it aesthetic mathematical meaning — the only meaning science can give it — it is still meaningless and absurd. In the absence of Kierkegaard's leap to faith, I would consider it my duty to defy it just as I would a god who is no more but a more powerful version of myself. Should not every existentialist and nihilist do so?

"The real question of life after death isn't whether or not it exists, but even if it does what problem this really solves" (Wittgenstein, L. 2009. Prop. 6.4311, p. 80). Answer: none. God's scientific existence is irrelevant to existentialism and to nihilism as philosophy is irrelevant to social constructs such as law. Even if God exists and created the present absurd universe in which only a predestined few will know its meaning, in the absence of Kierkegaard's leap to faith, are not these facts alone enough reason for me to defy God and to accept nihilism? "Why, the whole world of knowledge is not worth that child's prayer to dear, kind God" (Dostoyevsky, F. 1983. p. 303). Should not every existentialist and nihilist reach the same conclusion regardless of what science tells us?

If the answer to these questions is yes, then in defiance of both God and His universe, the existentialist or nihilist once suicide is rejected must make a leap to morality, immorality, or amorality and then to social constructs such as law so at least to understand the opponent and to fight the good fight. It does not really matter which choice is made. Unless the leap is made to being a Orwellian *1984* O'Brien, any choice made will involve opposition to the presently unopposed normative power of the law with its monopoly on violence over individual morality. Any existentialist who makes such leap must have an understanding of this opponent law if the leap is to give meaning to the life of the absurd hero which was the point of making the leap in the first place. In many ways, unopposed secular law is more like Divine Law and Natural Law than is Divine Law and Natural Law. Just as "God is Power" (Orwell, G. 1977. p. 333) whose meaning is simply to exist as an end-in-itself, the law also may be a power whose only meaning is to exist.

IV.   Ultimately, All Truth in Existential Language Will Be Pragmatic Truth

"On pragmatistic principles, if the hypothesis of God works satisfactorily in the widest sense of the word, it is true" (James, W.

1907. pp. 105-116).

As already contemplated, patrician existentialists spend a lot of time whining that all is relative, arbitrary, and random while living nice lives in their arbitrary and random universe lacking any truth but the opinions and beliefs that are aesthetically pleasing to them. I do not believe and no plebeian existential should believe such result to be random and arbitrary. If whining about the meaninglessness of the universe did not give patrician lives meaning and pleasure, most of these patricians would have gone on to communism, fascism, critical legal studies, critical race studies, law and economics or whatever the latest patrician fads among their social group is available to give them justification for telling others what they ought to be doing with their lives. Existential truth is pragmatic: something is true if it works to achieve your will to power. Once an existentialist has given up on suicide and made a leap to morality, no other truth matters either for physical survival or for the survival of the leap to morality.

Otherwise, there is no truth and one can deal with the consequences of this contradiction as language incompleteness as I will contemplate later.

Pragmatic truth is the truth of science. Classical physics is true until it stops working and becomes relativity physics. Relativity physics will be true until whatever comes along to solve its contradictions takes over and so forth.

As one of the founders of philosophical pragmatism William James points out in the quotation above taken from his "Pragmatism and Religion" at *Lecture 8 in Pragmatism: A new name for some old ways of thinking*, pragmatic truth will even work with theology. It will also work with morality as I hope to contemplate at a later date. With or without Godel's Incompleteness Theorem, by logical necessity based on the existential reality that the "I am" comes before the "I think", all rational truth in language will either be incomplete or inconsistent.

If an existentialist wants to make a leap of faith beyond pragmatic truth, such leap is irrelevant to this contemplation but is an issue for existential theology.

Pragmatic truth does not mean completely self-centered amorality, though it could mean such if an existentialist leaps to a completely self-centered amorality, morality, or immorality. Patricians need each other to survive in their struggles against the universe and against plebeians and thus do not hesitate to make the meaning of truth pragmatic when it serves their will to power. Plebeians should be just as willing to accept pragmatic truth as truth in their struggles with each other, with patricians, and with the universe — including in their religious beliefs.

A.   *Existentially, There Are Right Answers: Ugly Ones*

Plebeians therefore also should not hesitate to define truth pragmatically because they also need each other to survive in their struggles against the universe, against patricians, and, according to historical evidence, with each other and the law. Pragmatic truth requires decisions as to what social constructs are "true" or "good" and which are "false" or "bad"; that is which social constructs work to win the struggles against the universe and our Heart of Darkness. Though there are probably an infinite number of possible social constructs for morality, ethics, and law, at any given time and moment, only a finite quantity of them will work in our struggle against the universe, patricians, and our Heart of Darkness to survive.

However, it is important to look at pragmatic truth existentially not idealistically as is done by many proponents of popular versions of pragmatism such as the law and economics crowd. A very enjoyable book by Peter T. Leeson entitled *The Invisible Hook, The Hidden Economics of Pirates*[12] ably describes — after the fact of course as with all economics — how well the freely chosen governance of pirate ships operating outside the law worked without the monopoly on violence required of the law to work. This book points out for example that pirate ships were true

---

[12] Princeton University Press (2009).

functioning democracies long before democracies became a fad among the law and that pirate democracies might have been the motivation for New World democracies. However, despite their few decades of success, the end result was that the law with its non-democratic demand for a monopoly on violence beat and killed off the pirates with most pirates having lead miserable lives just a little better off, if at all better, than the miserable working lives of wage or chattel slaves from which they fled. So, pragmatically and existentially, the lesson is still that if you fight the law, the law will win.

The absurd individual accepts the reality that the few will always govern the many through force and what we now call the aesthetic truth of propaganda. Regardless of this universal law of nature, would you rather be governed by the few while living in poverty through subsistence farming or in middle class suburban living with free time for contemplation of philosophy?

Thus, it is important for plebeians not to allow aesthetic truth to hide pragmatic truth as it does for patricians because they have others to do the dirty work of survival for them. There is much aesthetic truth in life that gives or can give some insight into the nature of our Heart of Darkness but there is also much that serves simply to rationalize away its most evil of acts after the fact. However, such aesthetic truth is by definition aesthetic, it will not be the ugly truth that pragmatism will supply when necessary to solve a problem. Mr. Leeson's book and economics, as does many aesthetic fiction books varying from *Charlotte's Web* to *War and Peace* and on to many pretend and pseudo-sciences varying from astrology to psychology, gives aesthetic knowledge and even some practical knowledge about human nature, but few if any give pragmatic knowledge. Reading *War and Peace* or *All Quiet on the Western Front* may give an aesthetic experience of war but it will not be the pragmatic truth of war. To get the latter knowledge to develop strategic and tactical acts for winning or losing a battle or war or, the best option, to avoid war, one must actually experience random acts of violence or read at a minimum an actual descriptive history of war with all of its ugliness described in numbers and facts not just through individual existential fictions — though unfortunately, none of this will ever answer whether a war "ought" to be fought, won, lost, or avoided. The ugliness of pragmatic truth will be true for any plebeian struggle against patricians.

Making a leap to morality including Christian morality as part of the struggle with the universe is fine for an absurd hero but the intent must be to win the struggle. Christians to whom losing is acceptable is one of the means by which the law has become an unopposed normative power. Just as the law does not accept losing, neither should anyone or anything that is to be its equal in normative power be willing to accept losing.

All present philosophy of law is worthless to those plebeians in the trenches of struggle with law. An existential philosophy of law should not be so worthless. Normative statements of what ought to be to win a normative battle will always be an act of the existential Will to Power. The pragmatic truth of an existential philosophy of law should give a sense of what normative statements will work to solve the problems of a given existential problem once the leap to a morality, immorality, or amorality is made.

So, like it or not, despite the aesthetics of post-modernism and its cowardly delusions denying it, there are not only existential answers, there are "objectively" and existential right, correct, good and true answers to questions. This objective truth applies to questions regarding what individual or social constructs such as morality, ethics, cultures, religions, and laws are true or good while others are false or bad. This truth derives from a very simple question: who won or what is needed to win? If you are one of the losers, your options are either to try harder so as to beat them or to join the winners. The winners are always right until they become the losers. The plebeian existential absurd hero in order to give meaning to life thus can and in fact must contemplate, make judgments, and choose what moralities, social constructs, and cultures deserve to exist and flourish and which do not once this hero leaps to a morality, amorality, or immorality. Patricians need not make this choice and preach multi-cultural diversity because they will always win. The plebeian absurd hero does not have this option: the choice of a pragmatic truth must be made or do not bother to make a leap to morality, amorality, or immorality. Western Civilization including its Judeo-Christian religions have so far by their creation of such constructs as logical formal systems; rationalism as a means to discover, explore, and conquer the universe; the Scientific Revolution; the Industrial Revolution; the Technological Society; and much more have beaten Eastern Civilization and all warrior religions such as Islam. So, for the present time and space, Western Civilization is the right social construct and is true and good; its truth is by definition objectively true. How long this will last is a philosophy of history question beyond the scope of this essay.

V. An Existential Theory of Language
"To imagine a language is to imagine a form of life" (Wittgenstein, L. 2009. ¶19, p. 11)

The substance and essence of existentialism is popularly summed up in the adage "existence before essence". What exactly does this language mean, if anything? As with any modern philosophy, now that I have described the existential problem of law needing to be solved, I must begin the solution, if any, with a philosophy of language.

Philosophy of law contemplates the word "law" as a universal, that is as a word describing what particular things have in common; for a philosophy of law, the problem is what do particular laws or legal systems have in common that would warrant calling all of them "law" or Law with a capital 'L' as a universal or meta-language. As a universal, law can mean a type of thing, a relationship between things, or a quality of a thing. As a meta-language, Law would be what all laws necessarily have in common — which is really what philosophy of law seeks; so, really, as I will contemplate latter, this meta-language distinction is not a substantive in our contemplation. So, at some point in my contemplation, I must decide what it means for a word to be a universal and in what sense the word law is a universal.

The ability to create by abstraction universals as part of our language may be the only difference in substance from human thought and that of animals. "What can be shown, cannot be said" (Wittgenstein. 209. Prop. 4.1212 p. 29). I can point you to a red apple but this is distinct from stating to you that an apple is red. Unless you have or we share previous social experience using the words red and apple and acting on a red things and apple things, pointing to a red apple and saying "red apple" has an almost infinite amount of possible meanings for you and our interaction thus is worthless as the meaning of the words "red" and "apple". The infinite of meanings would be gradually reduced by actions that we take while saying "red apple" until eventually we get to a point where saying "red apple" makes you pick up a red apple. Without universals, all language would only have at best a particular descriptive meaning; one would not be able to talk of a bridge, chair, person, and particular thing without pointing to a particular bridge, chair, person, or other particular thing. Thus, universals cannot be dismissed dogmatically as evil generalities or stereotypes that "ought" to be ignored.[13] This is another example of a normative statement that is pragmatically and thus existentially wrong.

A philosophy of language is not the same as linguistics, as behaviorism hiding itself as cognitive science, nor as any Noah Chomsky-like technique of creating pragmatic solutions and algorithms that allow translation of human language into computer language regardless of whether it calls itself structuralism, innate language skills, synthetic structures, surface structure, syntax structure, deep structure, semantic structure, Chomsky hierarchy, or whatever pragmatic language translation techniques are used to ignore philosophy of language problems to achieve translation from one language to another — including from human language to computer coding language. These techniques do nothing for philosophy of language nor usually do they even involve

---

[13] For purposes completeness, I attache in the **Appendix** an essay describing when generalizations become stereotypes.

consideration of it. Such technique serving to hide ignorance works but is not philosophy. It is similar to scientists creating the word "entropy" to reference the remainder in thermodynamics calculations to get around the fact they have no clue as to why they have a remainder in their thermodynamics equations; it is similar to their creating of the words "dark" matter and dark energy to avoid acknowledging science is ignorant of what makes up 95% of the substance of the universe.

A philosophy of language for an existentialist theory of law cannot be allowed to play such wordgames despite the fact they pragmatically work and thus are pragmatically true; they do not pragmatically work nor are they pragmatically true for the problem at issue: the nature of law. I am seeking to describe what "law" is only if it is possible to describe what it is. If it is not possible to describe it in any pragmatically true sense other than by pointing to a particular law and dealing with its particular problems, then as an existentialist I must accept "whereof one cannot speak, thereof one must be silent" (*Ibid*. Prop. 7, p. 82) and see where that leads.

It must be noted that this mantra of silence is only a requirement for logical contemplation of language; that is, language that accepts as axioms the three classical rules of logic: the law of identity, the law of non-contradiction, and the law of the excluded middle. It does not stop contemplation of language through non-logical means such as fiction, analogy, dialectical reasoning (reasoning that rejects one of the three classical rules of logic), emotion, and anything else that works to get a meaning across. This is why aesthetics is a powerful creator of powerful truth. In fact, the description of language as a form of life is best exemplified not by any academic books based on rational discourse but by the best of fiction or histories in which words create a world of life or a universe of discourse made up entirely of language discourse distinct from the existential universe of our struggles — in the same way numbers may create the universe according to science. When done right, such as the existential *magnum opus War and Peace* by Tolystoy, such a wordgame universe or universe of discourse contains either explicitly or implicitly all the ambiguities of real life and thus allows for the contemplation of reality not only of which we cannot rationally speak but also without suffering the actual physical pain of the reality of which we can speak — something not true of logical language such as scientific language forced to make logical pragmatic truth from painful existential descriptive reality.

This is why in the end though I ridicule their verbiage, modern philosophers of law will always get the last laugh on me. As good fiction and even language cults such as psychology and politics empirically establish, aesthetic creations of verbiage with only nominal meaning and existence seem to be and most likely are much more powerful sources of ultimate truth — whatever that may turn out to be — since it is something of which existentialism (concerned only with pragmatic truth) is not able to speak. Aesthetic sources of power as an end in itself are much more powerful than any rational concept of the pragmatic truth that can be provided by science or even by existentialism. Making $2 + 2 = 5$ is the sign of a god regardless of whether it works or not; actually making through aesthetics $2 + 2 = 5$ when it does not work is even more the sign of a god than when it does. "The pursuit of beauty is much more dangerous nonsense than the pursuit of truth or goodness, because it affords a greater temptation to the ego" (Frye, N. 2000. p. 105).

However, though the patrician existentialism of a Sartre and of the likes of post-modernism and so forth may be satisfied with aesthetic truth, this should not be acceptable for any honest existentialism and its philosophy of law. It is not my goal to create an aesthetic reality that allows for contemplation of that of which we cannot rationally speak so as to avoid the actual physical pain of silence. If the contemplation leads to something of which we cannot speak, we will not speak of it but will still have the pain as our own to remind us of what we are not speaking. Ultimately, the pain must remain and is the substance of existential thought.

In proceeding with this contemplation, I do not want to start by committing the same mistake made by all modern philosophers of law in which the word "law" is contemplated irrespective of the use or usefulness of the word law including using it as a universal and as a particular interchangeably — as a universal in "rule of law" and as a particular law. As I contemplated in *Why Tolerate Law*, philosophers of law constantly commit this logic error of using the same word for different uses and usefulness, assume the meaning stays the same, and ignore that the meaning has changed with such change in use or usefulness. Also, I do not want to repeat their logic error of using different words for the same use and usefulness, assume the meanings have changed because nominally the words are different, and ignore that the meanings must be the same because the words have the same use and usefulness. If the same word has different uses, it will have different meanings. A simple example: "wave" has multiple different meanings varying from use at the beach to use in quantum physics despite it being nominally the same word in all these uses. If different words have the same use, they will have the same meaning. "A rose by any other name would smell as sweet".

  I must not forget the intend of my contemplation. For now, I am contemplating an existential philosophy of law and not an overall existential philosophy of language. The goal of this essay is not to create an existential philosophy of language but an existential philosophy of law. For existentialism, law and any social construct including a philosophy of language has no meaning until it is accepted by the individual through a leap to caring, morality, meaning, or whatever the individual wants to call their Will to Power rejection of suicide. For an individual, existentially, anything goes until this leap is made. Only once made, does law — or any social construct — become a problem whose relationship to my leap I need to understand in some meaningful sense.

  So, before I get into a convoluted contemplation of philosophy of language and the metaphysical nature of universals with its many paradoxes and subtleties, I want to try a simpler way. Since the goal of modern philosophy of law and even of many philosophers of language — as with almost everything else in Technological Society — is to be "naturalized" to scientific language, after contemplating language generally I will first contemplate the meaning of words including universals in scientific language and the meaning of words including universals in the language of law to see how they compare and what we can understand from the comparison. Since I want a philosophy of language that is also naturalized to science, before getting into the complications of developing an all encompassing entire existential philosophy of language, I want to compare the language of law with the language of science to which it wants to be naturalized. This comparison is done so as to see what if anything they have in common and what is different regarding their universals to determine if this is sufficient to develop a philosophy of law.

As part of this attempt at simplicity trying to develop an existential philosophy of law without a complete existential philosophy of language, I am assuming in this contemplation an understanding and acceptance of Wittgenstein's critique concluding there is no such thing as a private language; that is, the concept of a private language understandable by only a single individual is a rationally incoherent concept despite the fact that such a concept is inherent in the popular concepts of language in the so-called social sciences in which language is assumed to be a translation of ideas known only to an individual mind.[14] Regardless of the undisputed existence of an "I am" known only to the "I am", there is no way for these words or any purely existential words such as the additional "I exist therefore I think"; and "I exist therefore I will" to be the meanings of words in any language of which we can speak and thus not in any language that is the philosophy of law. The existential thing-in-itself meaning of such words is undeniable and will have eventually to be contemplated as part of an existential philosophy of language. However, it will have to be contemplated with the understanding that we are contemplating something of which we cannot speak.

For now, it is sufficient to understand that "existence precedes essence" means all essence, including the essence of any language and of a universal.

---

[14] *See,* Wittgenstein, L. (2009). *Philosophical Investigations*, §§243-271.

A. *The Existential Basics of Language and Meaning in Language*

"The limits of my language mean the limits of my world" (Wittgenstein, L. 2009. Prop. 5.6, p. 63). The philosophy of language in its earliest forms goes back to Plato, Aristotle, and the Roman Stoic schools of philosophy. It took up a dominant role in philosophy in the 20th century when through philosophers such as Ludwig Wittgenstein arguments were made that much of philosophy consisted solely of word puzzles that had no real purpose, meaning, or answers. According to this early analytic school of philosophy, the sole purpose of philosophy is to help science and other disciplines dealing with real-world physical problems maintain clear and logical syntax and semantics for their theories and solutions. Purely philosophical inquiries, such as metaphysics, ontology, ethics, morality, philosophy of mind and consciousness, epistemology, theology, aesthetics, and politics, all of these according to the early analytic school are derived from confusion over the syntax and semantics of words and language. Certain subjects of human consciousness simply cannot be talked about. Thus comes the famous expression by Ludwig Wittgenstein, "whereof one cannot speak, thereof one must be silent" (Wittgenstein. 2009. Prop. 7, p. 9), though no one ever is but I will try to be.

The initial intent of the philosophy of language was to understand language and to derive its essential nature. We cannot think logically or illogically without using some form of language. Even for Christian theology, "[i]n the beginning was the Word, and the Word was with God, and the Word was God" (*The Holy Bible Saint Joseph Textbook Edition*. (1963). John 1:1.)

Without language, we simply have action. "What can be shown, cannot be said" (Wittgenstein. 209. Prop. 4.1212 p. 29).

This initial intent was a noble purpose, especially from an existentialist perspective. However, as is often the case in philosophy, initial noble intentions for a clear vision of the forest have gone on to be used by many outside philosophy — such as philosophers of law — to create more trees by which to hide the forest of reality.

But then again, there is the popular adage attributed to Einstein, "Everything must be made as simple as possible. But not simpler."

One reason for this verbiage by philosophers of law about that of which we cannot speak is purely existential and pragmatic: being silent about that of which they cannot speak would make their lives meaningless and also put them out of a job and they might be forced to go out and actually practice law. It is much easier to create academic word puzzles with arbitrarily created rules of recognition, change, and adjudication and to have fun with them then it is to actually practice law just as it is much easier to play Monopoly and MotoGP videogames then it is actually to run a business and to race in MotoGP.

Another reason for the unnecessary verbiage ignoring the limitations of language and assuming it is an unlimited source of meaning is its aesthetic value. As noted previously, the "one must be silent" mantra is only a requirement for logical contemplation of language. It does not affect language as aesthetics. Using words and giving meaning to words through their use and usefulness are two different things. Just as sparsity in words such as in poetry can be used to hide shallow thought, shallowness of thought can just as easily be hidden by verbiage. A philosophy of language is necessary to obtain the necessary balance for keeping matter simple in accordance with an Ockham's Razo pragmatic truth but also as pragmatically necessary to win once an existentialist makes the leap beyond just aesthetic meaning for words to descriptive meanings and pragmatic truth. Verbiage generated solely for satisfying one's Will to Power through the creation of aesthetically pleasing words is for patricians who already have power but does not do much good to plebians opposing that power. In the end, as I have admitted, though I ridicule their verbiage, modern philosophers of law will probably get the last laugh on me because their aesthetic truth is more pleasing than most than the ugliness of reality, however it is the reality of law of which I am trying to understand and explain to the few who may care; my audience, if any, is not made up of "most".

B. *So, Existentially What Are Words?*

We can define a word as a symbol used to communicate. Immediately, there is a problem with this definition and in all definitions. Is the word "word" a symbol used to communicate? Yes. Therefore, I am logically and essentially telling you the following: a symbol used to communicate is a symbol used to communicate. Or, by "word," I mean word. How is this definition in any way meaningful?

What is the meaning of a word? For the purposes of this contemplation limiting itself to the languages of science and law, this question was answered by the philosopher Wittgenstein in ¶43 of his <u>Philosophical Investigations</u>. For a "large class of cases" — though not for all — in which we employ the word "meaning" it can be defined thus: "the meaning of a word is its use in the language." The meaning of a word is not isolated but is a thread in a fabric sewn together with other words rationally used in life's social interactions. The popular phrase is that words, their meanings, and language are social constructs or wordgames. I will be using these words language, social construct, and wordgame interchangeably in parts of this essay.

However, are the meanings of words or any associated social constructs made from arbitrary and random uses or only intentional ones? If this is true of "a large class of cases", what about the remaining cases? To say the meaning of words is their use immediately seems to be incomplete because we immediately run into the problem of existential reality; indeterminacy of translation; and of the Humpty Dumpty problem of intentions:

> "I don't know what you mean by 'glory,' " Alice said.
> Humpty Dumpty smiled contemptuously. "Of course you don't—till I tell you. I meant 'there's a nice knock-down argument for you!' "
> "But 'glory' doesn't mean 'a nice knock-down argument'," Alice objected.
> "When I use a word," Humpty Dumpty said, in rather a

> scornful tone, "it means just what I choose it to mean—neither more nor less."
> "The question is," said Alice, "whether you can make words mean so many different things."
> "The question is," said Humpty Dumpty, "which is to be master—that's all." (Carroll, L. 2009. p. 50)

Which is the master, the word or the speaker? This distinction is also brought out by the indeterminacy of translation thesis of the philosopher Willard Van Orman Quine.[15] When translating a word from one language into another, there is no "meaning" thing-in-itself being moved from one language to another because each word in each language has an infinite number of possible uses; translation can only occur by similarity of individual actions and behaviors when using words and then tying the words and the acts together as a "translation".

The "I am" of existentialism and the intentions of this existential reality of which we cannot speak cannot be defined solely as use because any time the "I am" speaks there is individual Will to Power involved in the speaking. Because we cannot speak about this existential thing-in-itself meaning of my words, the meaning of words is both their use and usefulness and their use and usefulness for dealing with this existential thing-in-itself meaning of which we cannot speak.

Ultimately the meaning of that large class of words consisting of non-existential words is a relationship between the intentions or goals of the speaker and the acts the word causes in sense experience. However, the acts aspect is the only sense

---

[15] Quine, W.O. (2013). Chapter 2: Translation and meaning. *Word and Object* (New ed.). MIT Press. pp. 23–72.; Quine, W.O. (1969). Chapter 2: Ontological relativity. *Ontological relativity and other essays*. Columbia University Press. pp. 26–68.

experience in this relationship. When you try to speak about "intentions", that is about what "I am" wants, we can only speak about the acts associated with the intentions and about the words used for that association, there is no way to actually talk about intentions or the acts themselves as things-in-themselves; again, "what can be shown, cannot be said". The intentions are an existential reality of which we cannot speak except in terms of the acts. Though the existential meanings of existential words are the substance of consciousness that leads to language, logic, and everything else, they are not something that can be described by language and logic in any complete and consistent sense, their speaking will always be incomplete and usually inconsistent. All we can do is associate words with the acts associated by those words, acts that are in turn associated with the word "intent" or its equivalent.

Thus, the meaning of words is not only their use but their usefulness to that use: their pragmatic truth. The existential thing-in-itself meaning of which we cannot speak are the substance of consciousness that leads to language, logic, and everything else. It is these words that make it possible to use language to contemplate language. The meaning of these existential words is existence itself: "I exist"; "I exist therefore I think"; and "I exist therefore I want more than to just exist". They retain these meanings in all possible worlds in which I exist and thus are metaphysical real meanings of which we cannot speak unless we use words whose meaning is only their use. Just as with Godel's Incompleteness Theorem in logic, any speaking about these existential words will always be either incomplete or inconsistent unless we are silent about them as that of which we cannot speak.

This is why objecting to existentialism as contradictory by such arguments that life must have meaning because we are using the word "meaning" to describe life is an unsound argument. Yes, all words must have meaning based on their use and usefulness since words are the only means we have to speak about anything including that of which we cannot speak but such does not mean all words also have an existential meaning. The words 'I am' are a social construct to speak about the thing-in-itself "I am" existing independently of the use of the words 'I am' of which we cannot speak thus these words have an existential meaning of which we cannot speak. The word 'hammer' is used to get someone to pick up this thing with which I was beating on nails and that is its meaning of which we can speak; its existential meaning of which we cannot speak is non-existent except for the fact that an "I am" is using the word. This is why the expression, "if one is a hammer, the whole world is a nail" accurately describes the relationship between words, acts, and intentions. It is nonsense to talk about the meaning of the word 'meaning' in "no meaning in life" in the same way one would talk about the 'meaning' of the word "hammer" or of a hammer because it would be nonsense to talk about the existential meaning of my "I am" existence being the same as the existential meaning of "hammer". My existence precedes all meaning. I know a hammer has meaning in life because I use the word "hammer" to get someone to hammer nails. I know there is no meaning in life in the same way I know I exist; it is not in the way I know the meaning of hammer or that a hammer has meaning in life. Repeating the same word twice is simply repeating the same word twice not talking about that of which we cannot speak.

1. The Problem of Universals in Interpretative Language. A word used as a universal describes what particular things have in common, namely characteristics, qualities, and attributes plus relationships between any of these characteristics, qualities, attributes, or relationships or just between the words used. The classical problem in philosophy is whether these universals describe repeatable or recurrent real entities that are distinct but simply exemplified by a particular thing or are they simply words that are shorthand for a collection of particular entities. For example, suppose there are multiple red, strong, round, chairs next-to-each other in a room. These chairs share the quality of "chairness" with all other chairs in the universe as well as strength, roundness, and redness or the qualities of being strong, round, and red with some other chairs in the universe; and they share the time-space relationship of "next to" for these particular chairs. In other words, they share universals consisting of qualities or characteristics describing types or kinds (chairs), properties (strong, round, red) and time-space relationship (next-to). Are these qualities Platonic forms existing independently of the particulars or just words representing a family resemblance among particular existing individuals?

No one should underestimate the power of universals especially in relation to pragmatic truth. Without universals we essentially live in the moment. No one should underestimate the power of living in the moment. "If we take eternity to mean not infinite temporal duration but timelessness, then eternal life belongs to those who live in the present" (Wittgenstein, L. 2009. Prop. 6.4322, p. 80). Just as with the power of aesthetic truth, a leap to the power of timelessness is more godlike than living in time and space. If one adds a leap to amorality, one would truly become a god.

However, if we limit ourselves to being human instead of becoming the Nietzschean Dionysian gods beloved by patricians, reality forces us to live not in the moment but in what Leibniz described as the relationships between our "I am" and our sense perceptions that creates the universal "space" and the perception of these relationships changing that creates the universal "time" — now named by the new word "space-time". Living as individual humans, universals are unavoidable pragmatic realities especially for pragmatic truth attempting to solve problems in space-time. I will start with the basics of universals to work my way toward an existential meaning for them that we can use to contemplate law as a universal.

If you ask me what red or redness means, I would tell you to get a red apple and a red ruby and see if you actually do it. If you do, then you know the meaning of red, apple, and ruby at least. I then tell you they both are red and then, since you are not color blind, you will agree they both are red and say they both are red and thus we would use "red" as meaning a universal "red". The sharing of this particular "red" is the universal "redness". In one sense, "redness" is a social construct because we only have the concept of redness because our sense experience is not totally color blind. Some but not all apples and rubies share "redness". Regardless, a universal word such as "redness" if it gives a descriptive, predictive, or pragmatic truth about reality has a use and the universal is just as useful and thus just as meaningful and often more meaningful pragmatically than the reality of any word used for an individual apple or particular red apple or, in the sense of predictive value, even of any individual apple.

Regardless of what may or may not be outside of our consciousness, saying that this universal word "redness" is entirely a social construct is logical error because regardless of what I call it and what it may or may not be, there is something common to our consciousness of apples and rubies. No one really knows what this commonality is in the same way no one knows what consciousness is nor what other attributes of reality are there to which our sense experience is blind and thus for which we have no particular or universal words. Science would not be science without universals in various forms of either type, relationship, or properties: hot, cold, color, white, dark, atomic, energy, matter, mass, space-time, and so forth. No one has any problem nor should they with such unobservable universals or generalizations such as photons, quarks, neutrinos, and so forth, some of which exist solely as universals constructed of other universals — consist solely of numbers created by joining together other numbers.

It is error to assume that universals are necessarily abstract and only individuals or particulars are concrete. In our existential struggle with the universe, numbers are as particular and as real as any number of bricks or stones thrown at us, yet numbers and the universals of mathematics are treated as abstractions. It is for this reason that many mathematicians are Platonist believing they discover numbers in the same way one discovers a rock.

In fact, as contemplated earlier, one can argue that according to the descriptive, predictive, and pragmatic wordgame of science, particularly physics, we and our entire reality are made up of universal relationships — consisting of mathematical relationships — between universal properties — again consisting of mathematical properties — creating universal kinds or types. For example, the concept of atomic particles is made up entirely of mathematical relationships between mathematical calculations that make up waves, particles, and four basic forces that exist entirely as numbers. None of these universals exist as observable particulars or individuals, we can only observe their effects upon particulars such as a screen, tube, or some other measuring device. Just as you will never see the "red" or "redness" of an apple without seeing a particular red thing, you will never see subatomic particles, the probability waves of electromagneticism or the gravity and strong and weak forces of an apple without seeing the particular thing consisting of a measuring instrument measuring them.

As with all words, the meaning of universals is both their use and their usefulness. However, the usefulness part is often ignored.

For example, if the modern world is going to treat the meaning of words as purely social constructs depending on use distinct from their usefulness to give pragmatic truth, it should be willing to accept the consequences of both sides of this two-headed coin social construct coin, but it clearly is not[16]: if everything is a social construct then everything is a social construct, that is the meaning of any word can be changed through its social use. If so-called liberal social construct definitions of sex, sexual orientation, and gender involve multiple, uni, none, or whatever sexes and genders they socially construct irrespective of social usefulness, then, there is no rational basis to deny to conservatives the same power or ability to change the social construct meanings of the same words into binary or in the case of sexual orientation into unitary. Once pragmatic usefulness is ignored in meaning, as Humpty Dumpty said, words simply mean what we or even I want them to me and this is an existential wrong answer because pragmatically and existentially this is not want happens: they mean their use and usefulness not just their use.

---

[16] It just pretends to do so for normative reasons that as always have no descriptive meaning.

2.   For an Existential Leap to Morality To Act as a Counterbalance to Law the Meaning of Universals and Words Cannot Be Simply a Matter of Power. If the meaning of words is simply their use then meaning is dependent solely on power: the power to force or deny certain uses of a word regardless of the pragmatic truth or the usefulness of the word. Since law is the present unopposed normative power for social constructs, if the meaning of words is dogmatically accepted as purely their use, then the meaning of words becomes a question of law. For the existentialist who has made a leap to power as an end-in-itself meaning in life, this is not a problem. For any other existential leap, including one to nihilism, this is a problem. It is definitely a problem for any existentialist who wants to fight the good fight against the indifference or outright antagonism of the universe to our existence because the universe does not care how we use words. Our use of words must be useful to beating its indifference.

As previously contemplated, language is laden with theory that often decides what facts we experience, observe, and use. Thus, again, the meaning of words must have two parts if meaning is going to put more than just an question of power: use and usefulness. When we speak, our "I am" unavoidably includes a will to power or an intention for what is spoken. Thus, usefulness in unavoidably a attribute of meaning as is use. Meaning based on use of social construct words such as wave, gender, sex, and so forth may be arbitrary and random but this does not logically require the usefulness to be arbitrary and random. For example, the use of the word "wave" is the same from beach to physics lab but its usefulness is not and thus neither is its meaning. Further example, if the meaning of "gender" is defined solely by use, then gender can be anything it is socially used to mean. However, if the meaning of "gender" is also defined by its usefulness to sexual reproduction in society, it is limited by the empirical reality of sexual reproduction in society. This does not require the meaning of "gender" to be fixed as binary or that it can never become useful for any meaning other than its classic male and female distinctions; if sexual reproduction through technology becomes asexual, then "gender" will lose its usefulness and meaning until and if it finds a new usefulness and new meaning perhaps by adding new gender identities or perhaps not, instead to simply disappear into the history of language as a meaningless word.

I am not saying meaning changes based solely on use — even just nominal use cannot be done aesthetically unless it is done solely for power as an end-in-itself. Anything, even contradictory logic, can be ignored or achieved aesthetically. "Doublethink means the power of holding two contradictory beliefs in one's mind simultaneously, and accepting both of them" (Orwell. 1977. p. 270). Allowing law to force changes in the use of words and to do so without regard to the usefulness of words leads not only to pragmatically false truths but absurd ones that only serve as aesthetic truth supporting power as an end in itself. For example, allowing those with the power to change the use of words to change the use of "gender" while ignoring the usefulness of "gender" to its use is equivalent to ignoring the taboo against siblings parenting children because taboos are social constructs and is equivalent to forbidding the use of "race" in science to instead use the word "population". For example, saying "the population of Jews has a higher frequency of Tay-Sachs disease" is now allowed. However, saying "the race of Jews has a higher frequency of Tay-Sachs disease" is now forbidden as racism. It serves an aesthetic function to use "population" instead of "race" but that is it. Both words have the same use and usefulness and thus the meaning for "race" and "population" in these sentences is the same except for aesthetics.

Empirically, the universe does not care whether we use the word 'race' or the word 'population' to study Tay-Sachs disease, Tay-Sachs disease will kill Jews either way unless science is allowed to study the disease, it progression, and therapy. The only entities that care which word "race" or "population" is used are some speakers of the words with the power to aesthetically alter their use. Again, aesthetics usually trumps reality, but it should not do so for an existential philosophy of law.

This view of language and universals in which usefulness is removed from the contemplation ignores the intertwining of interpretation and description. An existential philosophy of law cannot make this logical error or we will lose all pragmatic truth in our struggle against law and thus negate our Will to Power leap to making this struggle. Meaning involves both use and usefulness to that use.

    3. Interpretative Wordgames. How does modern philosophy of law and its treatment of "law" as a universal fit into this metaphysical mess? It treats it in the same way that much of modern science, non-science, pseudo science, and practically everything else treats the language problem of universals: by ignoring it. Worse, philosophers of law particularly legal positivists start talking about "meta-language". Since language consists of words whose meaning is their social construct use or usefulness, language is part of Quine's fabric of knowledge in which altering one thread affects all threads and the integrity of the entire fabric. Therefore, unintentionally or intentionally in order to avoid this intertwining or perhaps to take advantage of it to create aesthetically pleasing verbiage, legal positivists and other pretend sciences create a language to talk about language calling this new wordgame about language "interpretative" or a meta-language.

    Without doubt, meta-languages and interpretative wordgames are useful in scientific language for such matters as the science of artificial intelligence. When one is trying to create a language that robots can speak that is not really a language since it has no words whose meaning is the existentially conscious "I am", one necessarily needs a human meta-language to speak about what is being created. If someday the robotic language spontaneously becomes self conscious as the religious faith of so many scientists believe it will, there will no longer be a need for human meta-language relevant to robotic language; there will just be language. The concept of meta-language or interpretative wordgames as being a scientific language makes sense in situations where the goal is pragmatic and predictive: to solve a problem by predictive language.

    However, it is at this point that legal positivists and all who treat language and especially universals as "social constructs" whose meaning is their use while ignoring usefulness should be consistent and must live with the reverse side of the social construct coin they love to preach and pontificate about to realists. If meanings that we can talk about rationally are only social constructs of use, it is incoherent to state we can transform the social construct meaning of words and wordgames into a thing-in-itself simply by talking about them in a different wordgame in which the meanings of words will be their use and usefulness in talking about the language we are talking about. This is equivalent to saying that if we use English to talk Latin we will know the meaning of words in Latin. If a judge uses *"mens rea"* in a jury instruction that is otherwise entirely in English, does it have an English meaning or a Latin meaning? What if the judge says instead "mental state", derived from the Latin *mens rea*, does it have an English or Latin meaning? There is no coherent answer to such questions. If there is no thing-in-itself just use in the meanings of words and wordgames, then creating another wordgame to use it as a useful way to talk about words and wordgames as things-in-themselves is a contradiction with no predictive, pragmatic, or other value just nominal meaning and is thus worthless except for disguised aesthetic meaning — a significant meaning in its own right with the advantage that it does not become incoherent by contradiction; however, one should admit that one is just creating aesthetics and aesthetic truth and not predicting or describing reality.

Such contradiction if ignored is a gateway to realism regarding universals. If a social construct use can be transformed into a thing-in-itself that can be described and "interpreted" through a meta-language that is independent and distinct from the meanings in the language of which we are talking about, than what is this thing-in-itself meaning? If it is not a realist thing-in-itself meaning for the language being interpreted then its meaning is simply its use in our meta-language and thus we are back to every meaning being its use that can be arbitrary and randomly changed even though meanings cannot be arbitrarily and randomly changed when usefulness is included in the meaning — again, except for aesthetic truth.

This would not be a problem if the so-called interpretative or meta-language of philosophy of law was predictive. As with the science of artificial intelligence, if philosophy of law could make quantifiable predictions of repeatable, parameter controlled, falsified hypotheses of what law will be using its interpretations or meta-language, than it would be meaningful to come up with as many interpretations and meta-languages as it wants as long as they work. But, it cannot. There is no way rationally to predict from what is to what ought to be — even for the law and economics statistical theory/Bayes' Theorem crowd. This contradiction is present in all legal positivism and is why natural law theorists still have some power in the philosophy of law though they, like religion, are afraid to give it any substance. Legal positivism considers itself a meta-language or interpretative language describing and interpreting scientifically what "law" is but not what it "ought" to be. According to legal positivism, law is a social construct created by social practices, tolerations, decisions, orders, and the sum total of social practices. Yeah, so what? Philosophy of language tells us that all language is a social construct. How does such a conclusion aid in anyway in defining what the universal law is or if there is any such universal? It does not.

Saying the word 'law' or the universal Law represents a social construct dependent solely on use would be helpful in the same way that saying the universal 'game' or "meta-Game" wordgame represents a social construct shorthand for particular games such as chess or checkers. If we were to stop at that conclusion entirely with its necessary implication of arbitrary and random game rules and changes as deemed necessary by the game players as with all other games without arguing further. If it makes no sense to talk of the universal "game" as being distinct from the playing of individual games and their rules such as chess or checkers because they are all simply social constructs, it should be just as senseless to talk about the universal "law" being distinct from the social constructs that are individual laws and how they are executed upon. Since the word "game" as a universal is not the value of a variable bound by necessary attributes but just a free variable to be used arbitrarily and randomly as a social construct, the universal "law" should be simply such a free variable and it too should mean an arbitrary and random social construct. Denying law has any relation to reality beyond the words of any individual law would serve to break law away from the Christian Divine Law and Natural Law concepts of St. Augustine that 'an unjust law is no law at all', but that would be too simple for philosophers of law. For legal positivists to leave "law" at just being another purely social construct shorthand for an uncountable number of daily particular laws in the same way "game" is shorthand for the rules of basketball, baseball, hockey, or cricket and an uncountable number of other rules would be too simple and insulting to their skills because they could easily be replaced by minor league referees or umpires with little or no academic skills but with more actual experience calling the games.

Instead we get aesthetic verbiage rules of recognition, rules of change, and rules of adjudication and the separability thesis that are everywhere, anywhere, and nowhere at the same time with no predictive value as to what any particular law is or will be nor can they rationally have such value because there is no rational way to conclude from what the rules say ought to be to what is or will be or the reverse. Legal positivism is unable to explain how it knows the distinction between rules and laws without knowing what law is in the first place. By saying there is a universal "law" that legal positivism is describing and interpreting independently and distinctly from the daily descriptions and interpretations of particular laws and the execution upon them, it leaves open the possibility of divine law and natural law as being part of the universal "law" or Law, that is that there actually is both Divine and Natural Law. "Ah --- there's the rub!".

For example, in cases such as *Citizens United v. Federal Election Commission*, 558 U.S. 310 (2010) or *Goodridge v. Dept. of Public Health*, 798 N.E.2d 941 (Mass. 2003), in which the decisions total over a hundred pages of verbiage and their interpretative literature make up a law library of further verbiage, the conclusions much more honestly with the application of Ockham's Razor could

have been naturalized to science and written in a few lines:
1. Based on the life experience of the majority, we have concluded corporations are good for this country and therefore have decided they ought to be treated as persons for purposes of the First Amendment. Judgment shall enter forthwith. By the court. — *Citizens United et al*
2. Based on the life experience of the majority, we have concluded homosexuality is moral, medically not a disorder, and that homosexuals ought to be entitled to get married. Judgment shall enter forthwith. By the court. — *Goodridge et al*

The problem with this descriptive and normative simplicity is that it creates a simple interpretative wordgame or universe of discourse about law that is truly democratic allowing for all in society to rationally discuss law and have a say in it as a social construct. However, it achieves this result by giving the appearance of law as simply morality or ethics by violence and threat of violence. This result is something no modern lawgiver wants law to be — or at least not appear to be.

The above one paragraph decisions even if issued by the Supremes would not be considered law but an abrogation of law. They would be considered lawlessness. So, instead we get hundreds of pages of interpretive verbiage and their interpretative literature for *Citizens* and *Goodridge* treating them as normative truth derived from descriptive and normative statements.

Further, such an application of Ockham's Razor is in fact existentially too simple. The use and usefulness of the universals "law" and "game" are distinct universals, as different as the universals "mathematics" and "game". If one takes away the rules of football, one can play some other game including football. It might not be a recognizable game of football, perhaps we would call it soccer, but we would still have the empirical physical activity of a game that we can call football. Kids do this all the time, play games with makeup rules that randomly and arbitrarily change depending on who is winning or losing. Take away the law, one is lawless.

There are no other options. One may have customs, rules, etiquette, and similar particular social constructs for dealing with lawlessness but one would still be lawless.

Legal positivism tries to ignore the two sided coin of meaning being both use and usefulness. Yes, it says, law is a social construct, but it is one defined by rules of recognition, rules of change, and rules of adjudication and the separability thesis. The universal "law" has attributes and values consisting of "rules". Law is created by rules. Where are these rules? Everywhere and no where. They exist everywhere around us in our actions, customs, traditions, and all social constructs yet are in no place in particular. Are morality and law really separate? No, because lawgivers can consider morality when creating law. Actually, lawgivers can consider anything they want when creating law. Thus, must not the word "law" be purely nominal, it is just what those with the power to name law say it is? No, because they can only name law if law gives them the power to do so. As contemplated previously, this is nonsense.

Assume a meta-language or interpretative language defining the universal "law" as meaning the use of a bunch of rules and relationships or interactions among a bunch of rules. This can be done and is the same as defining the universal "game" as a bunch of rules and relationships or interactions among a bunch of rules. If "law" and "game" ultimately have the same social construct meaning, why is the former allowed to kill me whereas the latter is not unless the law says it can kill me? Defining "law" as a bunch of "rules" presupposes knowing the difference between law and rules. Are not the rules of "law" Law with a capital L whereas the rules of a game are simply the rules of a game subject to final binding arbitration by the law? The use of the words law and game may be the same but the usefulness aspects of the meanings of these two words are existentially and ontologically different.

Thus, the attributes or values of the bound variable "law" are unique. That natural law theorists are as meek and worthless as is religion in opposition to the nonsense of legal positivism claiming to be a science exhibits how empirically correct is the existentialist's nihilist view of reality.

4.   Existential Wordgames. It is at this point that existentialism comes in handy and why I initially saw it as an option for replacing religion as an equal normative force to the power of law, the motivation that is the initial and ultimate motive for this contemplation. The goal here is pragmatic truth not aesthetic truth — for aesthetic truth, words are useful for any use as long as they sound pretty. We are concerned with ugly truth.

Ignoring the existential thing-in-itself meanings of which we cannot speak except incompletely and inconsistently, pragmatically we are left with three categories of meanings that can be used to deal with the universal called law: 1) descriptive; 2) normative; 3) interpretative. Descriptive meanings can be subdivided into as many subcategories of meanings as there are intentions of the speaker using them depending on the usefulness to that use (epistemic, hermeneutical, deontological, consequential, nominal, and much more). Even nominal is a descriptive meaning. Through the simple act of putting words in quotation marks or of talking about words simply as words we have a wordgame used to describe words used and useful solely as words with no empirical link to sense experience except for the sense experience of other words.

The only subcategory of descriptive meaning that matters for pragmatic truth is predictive meaning.

Normative meaning states what ought to be and is distinct from descriptive meaning.

Interpretative meaning is used and useful to link the other two meanings or to link meanings within the same category in order to solve a problem. Even for scientific descriptive wordgames, it is impossible to talk descriptively without having some interpretative meaning thrown into the mix.[17] The same is true of normative

---

[17] *See generally,* Hanson, N. R. (2010). *Patterns of Discovery.* Cambridge University Press; Kuhn, T.S. (2012). *The Structure of Scientific*

meanings, it is impossible to talk about what ought to be without having an interpretation of existential reality. Interpretation is always present. For the existentialism who has made a leap to meaning, this interpretation is founded upon the pragmatic truth of the descriptive and normative meanings: do they work?

The only limits for changing social construct meanings would be: 1) their use to the speakers; 2) their usefulness to the speakers; 3) any pragmatic truth relative to their use or usefulness. In the first limit, it is the intent of the speakers that controls how the meanings change. In the second, it is a combination of intent and usefulness. In the last, it is the usefulness that controls meaning. The truth of the metaphysics, epistemology, and philosophy of language of existentialism must be pragmatic otherwise it does not matter to existentialism. The essential purpose of metaphysics is to determine what sorts of things are there. Existentialism knows that whatever things are — regardless of whether it is a particular, universal, abstract, concrete, "trope", or whatever metaphysics comes up with to clarify the meanings of scientific words — they only matter if through a Will to Power I make a leap to morality. Otherwise, whatever is out there is just an irrational collection of arbitrary and random events that I can do with as I please until it kills me or I decide to kill me. Whatever is out there only matters if it helps or hinders my Will to Power and leap to morality.

Reason is only a tool or weapon in this struggle against the universe. Always remember that existentially, it is not "I think therefore I am", but it is "I am therefore I think." If you do not want to be, it does not matter whether a particular or a universal is the means by which the universe finally kills me.

However, there seems to be a substantive distinction between a description of law as a universal law and what we call

---

Revolutions 4th ed. University of Chicago Press; Hey, T., Tansley, S., & Tolle, K., Eds. (2009). *The Fourth Paradigm, Data Intensive Scientific Discovery.* Microsoft Research.

law on a daily basis in statements of legality and illegality. An act is definitely legal under the law if it can be enforced by its monopoly on violence but what if it cannot be so enforced or the Powers do not want to enforce it? Is it coherent to talk about unenforceable law? Yes it is, it is done all the time and is done very meaningfully and pragmatically.

So, just as with the distinction between theoretical science and applied science, a description of the social construct universal law must at a minimum have a duality: both a nominal aspect consisting of normative statements that pursuant to Hume's Law cannot be derived rationally from sense experience "is" statements, and a violence aspect that is most definitely derived from sense experience. It seems there may be an important difference between the universal law, its truth, and acts subject to the execution upon by the law as legal or illegal. These sets of words may be wordgames that may be but are not necessarily logically or even empirically related. Law is ultimately a normative "ought" not logically connected to any "is", but legality and illegality may not have this divide.

So, are we able to give meaning — through use and usefulness — to the universal law that is distinct from any particular "law"?

5. **Ockham's Finger.** There was an interesting disagreement among Medieval philosophers that continued on into being a dispute between philosophers Isaac Newton and Gottfried Leibniz during the development of classical physics: is space empirically real or a matter of relative relationships? For example, if everything in the universe moved over six inches would space change? If it was real, it would. If it is relative, since all the relationships are the same, it would not. Newton argued the former, Leibniz the latter. Modern relativity physics has not resolved the dispute despite popular opinion that it has; though space-time may be relative, it supposedly expanded from the Big Bang but expansion was contained in what?

From an even basic philosophy of language, we now know

this is a dispute over a wordgame or wordpuzzle — meaningless except for enjoying the aesthetics of the puzzle. Language is itself a creation of use and usefulness. To the extent it has existential absolute meanings or realist thing-in-itself meanings, they are that whereof we cannot speak and therefore must be silent. No doubt there are absolute truths out there, such as the "I am", but as soon as we talk about them they become relationships to my use and usefulness of the words used to talk about them.

At this point, even philosophy of language runs into the existential problem expressed metaphysically by the Medieval philosopher William of Ockham commonly called Ockham's Finger that was initially intended to disprove realism. Regardless of whether these universals represent actual entities existing in reality outside of our individual "I am" or are simply words used and useful in the wordgames we use to describe life, even the simplest lifting of my finger changes all of reality regardless of whether it is reality outside my consciousness or simply my language reality. If universals are empirically real, as real as the meaning of any other word, when I lift my finger, I have necessarily changed the universal time-space relationship between my finger and everything else in the universe to the farthest star. If universals are simply nominal meanings of use and useful in my universe of discourse, by using the words lift and finger to describe my particular lifting of my finger, I have added to the use and usefulness of those words and thus added to their meaning.

These conclusions seem incoherent on the surface and therefore often lead to assuming that universals are not real just nominal but that only particulars are real, these conclusions should not do so. Logically, there is nothing wrong with these conclusions that every new use of a word for a new usefulness changes the universe or fabric of language; they are in fact consistent with modern philosophy of language in which the meanings of words are their use or usefulness and modern epistemology concluding that all knowledge is "a man-made fabric which impinges on experience only along the edges" (Quine, W.V.O. 2013. p. 42)

As the use and usefulness of a word changes and therefore

changes its meaning, if continued long enough and as actions associated with the words get into greater detail, the ripple effect through the fabric of language should eventually affect all threads of the language and the soundness of the fabric itself — some ripples will be more noticeable than others while some will go unnoticed.

But wait, what about Hume's Law? There is no rational relationship between descriptive and normative statements, is there a ripple effect between them? Must be or we would still be worshiping Etruscan or Druid gods and their normative statements instead of living in a Christian or post-Christian era. Problem is the relationship of the ripple between descriptive and normative language is part of the irrational of which we cannot speak rationally.

Because language is a social construct of use and usefulness, we should be able to describe the ripples in the meanings that make up language in the same way quantum mechanics describes the waves of probability that make up reality: it makes no intuitive sense but it works. How does a particle with no position and speed in space-time exist also as a wave while also able to jump from one point to another without traversing the space between and exist and react with other such particles simultaneously in two opposite ends of the universe? No one knows, but it works which is all that matters. The use of the words and their usefulness give pragmatic truth. Existentially, if it works, it is true. Any descriptive statements that give us pragmatic truth are as real as reality. Quantum mechanics has aesthetic beauty and it works, a nice combination. Sometimes, the pragmatic truths of existentialism have such beauty, but almost always they are ugly.

The lifting of Ockham's Finger begins by describing the finger, what it did, and where it ended up. We have a finger here, it lifts, it is now not there but here. "This is this. This ain't something else. This is this" (Cimino, M., Dir. 1978. p. 30). Such is descriptive reality.

If we can quantify this descriptive reality through Ockham's Razor into hypotheses that can be tested by parameter controlled, repeatable, falsifiable experiments, we have descriptive statements that have predictive value.

Seems simple enough, however even simple descriptive statements of lifting one's finger if examined simply as words are laden with universals and resulting paradoxes based on aspects of the human body and time and space relationships. As exemplified by Kant's Left Hand Paradox and the continuing metaphysical arguments going back to Zeno's Paradoxes and continuing in modern day physics, calling something a finger instead of part of a finger (*i.e.*, at which point does a finger stop being a finger), not really a finger, a hand, arm, or toe and the concepts of motion and spatial position are all concepts subject to interpretation if one were to limit contemplation solely to the use of the words. Interpretation and description in any wordgame are unavoidably intertwined.

This is why existentially, the meaning of words must be considered to be their use and their usefulness. In the struggle to give meaning to the universe, at some point the existential absurd hero must stop contemplating the use of words and start dealing with their usefulness.

The paradox of Ockham's Finger stops being a paradox when we put the finger to work doing something. At that point, there is no infinite chain of ripples in space or our language wordgame discourse but only the ripple that either washes away the problem being solved or does not.

Though I am trying only to create interpretative theory at this point myself to serve my existential leap to opposing the unopposed violence of the law, because interpretative theory is so intertwined with description and normative meaning, it is helpful to my contemplation to consider a particular normative problem and contemplate its progress from description to normative statement.

Consider the example of an Uber or similar service driver trying to make a living. Under every economic analysis that I have seen, in order to make a decent living as a full-time driver other than barely minimum wage, one must drive at least 60 and often more hours a week and violate the law by not paying any taxes. This is pretty much the same descriptive reality as it was for when I was driving a taxicab in college only worse. At least in my professional driver days, I did not have to provide and maintain my own car and it was all a cash business so it was easier and safer to avoid the taxes and jail time for avoiding taxes. As is universally true of all working class jobs, making a decent living and complying with the law are incongruent goals. The rich do not have this incongruence because there are plenty of legal ways for them to avoid taxes and steal a very comfortable living. So, what ought drivers do regarding legally required tax payments that would destroy the chances for making a decent living? There is no 'ought to be' logically concluded from the descriptive reality. The driver can reach as many interpretations about descriptive reality, such as the odds of not getting caught or the consequences of not getting caught, but since infinity in real life cannot be reached as it can in mathematics, at some point the interpretations will have to stop and in the end the choice of what ought to be done will be an irrational jump regardless of the decision or interpretations made.

    After making the irrational leap to a choice and executing upon it, whatever happens will be used by the Uber driver to further interpret the choice only this time it will be to rationalize the choice either as a good or a bad choice. The rationalized for normative statements is made after the fact. This rationalization will serve as an interpretation of descriptive reality during the next irrational decision-making process for normative statements of what ought to be. If the driver decides to break the law and make a decent living at it, this will factor into his irrational decision-making process next time such an irrational choice must be make. If the driver decides to comply with the law, stay poor, and eventually loses his job anyway and goes on to his next temporary job as seems to be the future of *hoi polloi* in modern economies, this will factor into the decision making process next time. It may be the individual driver will decide to comply with the law at all opportunity, remain poor their whole life, and be content at it. It may be that a grudge will develop and the underemployed driver will take to violence. It may be the driver will comply with the law, hit the lottery, and associate winning the lottery with being a law-abiding citizen. There are as many possibilities for irrational normative decisions as there are individuals making them.

Regardless, the rationalization or rational justification of any normative decision will be and can only be made after the decision.

Thus we see the quantum-mechanics-like rationality of the irrational process by which ripples in the fabric of descriptive language dealing with what "is" in sense experience spreads and expands out to then jump the fabric cap between it and the threads of normative language made of fabric of which we cannot speak. The ripple and its jumping of the gap between description and normative does not go forward in time but backward in time. Once the irrational choice is made and that of which we cannot speak irrationally jumps the cap into descriptive language, rational ripples in descriptive language eventually affect that of which we cannot speak in its next irrational leaps of Will to Power into normative language.

This rationalization process for normative statements is usually hidden by the aesthetics of patrician normative statements. A business or economic model reflects the normative judgments and priorities of its creators. For example, when Uber executives made or make the decisions as to what Uber ought to be, they plug in the financial and investment numbers based on prior business history and other ongoing businesses, and then through algorithms decide how they ought to run their business. Part of their assumptions in this process is complying with the law because one cannot plug illegal acts into the algorithms — at least not knowingly and publicly. It is not that they would not violate the law if they had to do so to survive, it is just for now they do not have to violate any law to survive. This resulting "ought" as with science in this process is not a normative statement of what ought to be but simply an is or descriptive statement of what the calculations will be plus the assumption that the calculations ought to be the basis for any decision: even if it puts drivers in the position of making a choice between operating illegally to make a decent living or to be legal but make less money then a decent living. The patrician irrational normative leaps of their Will to Power are there but hidden in the aesthetics of the algorithms.

This example should not be taken as a criticism of capitalism. Capitalism has proven it works and has been very successful in helping us with our struggle with the universe to survive, just as feudalism, bullionism, and mercantilism were successful before it — until they were not. As long as capitalism works in our struggle to survive and to discover, explore, and conquer the universe it is a good (pragmatically which is all that matters) and it is true (pragmatically which is all that matters) to say it is a good — until it is neither. Most likely, the Uber executives have no dispute with this existential conclusion. If the driver is realistic about life, the driver will most likely also not have a dispute with this conclusion. However, these conclusions do not require that either the driver or the executives conclude that capitalism ought to govern their decisions — especially for the driver. If anything, the opposite is true at least for the driver. For the driver as with all plebes, their normative hopes, if any, are all directed to the future not the present. For them, unlike the executives, capitalism and the law are accepted as a necessary evil more than a good. It is this historical class struggle that caused progression from feudalism to bullionism to mercantilism and to capitalism.

What will succeed capitalism, if anything, is unknown at present. However, it is the plebes' struggle with patricians that will cause this progression not the patricians — they are always fine with things as they are. Struggle is the source of truth and pragmatic progress not kindness, acceptance, and congeniality or whatever delusional social justice or cosmic justice safe place demands are made.

Given that plebeians must violate law and act illegally as part of their existential struggle to survive whereas patricians need not do so, the present unopposed normative power of the law is thus not only a danger to them but to the progression from capitalism to better capitalism or to whatever is next.

Thus the Ockham's Finger for universals in normative language such as law, unlike the descriptive language of science, **works in reverse**. It is not the empirical lifting of the normative finger that ripples through the universe changing the relationship between a particular fact and any associated norm, regardless of whether it be a real or language discourse universe, but it is the ripples of changes in normative relationships and statements in the universe that empirically change the associated fact. At least, this is all of which we can speak.

(This answers a question that appellate attorneys have had for decades, especially those that handle the appeals of their own trials: why do appellate decisions almost never have anything but a coincidental relationship to what actually happened or even to the facts in the trial record? Answer: because the appellate facts have nothing to do with either, they are facts used to rationalize or justify the normative statements that make up the appellate decision.[18])

B. *Existential Scientific Language*

"Let them have their belief, if it gives them joy. Let them also give talks about that. 'We touch the infinite!' And some people say ... 'Ya ya, he says he touches the infinite.' And some people say 'Ya ya! He says he touches the infinite!' But to tell the little children in school, 'Now that is what the truth is,' that is going much too far" (Horgan, J. 2016. p. 1).

Imagine sitting under an apple tree when an apple drops on your head. Being or having the scientific curiosity of an Isaac Newton, you decide to make measurements of the motion of the apple over time. Eventually, when enough measurements are taken with enough objects in sufficiently different times and spaces that are at least repeatable and testable, one can inductively reason from the measurements to the scientific words for momentum "$p=mv$". From a finite amount of observations, scientific language begins by inducing these words and the associated wordgame of classical physics for deductive use in an infinite amount of future possibilities to deduce momentum and then on to force and much more. The

---

[18] For example, *see generally,* Rabin, R.L., Sugarman, S.D. (2003). *Torts Stories*. Foundation Press.

language does not deduce what it ought to be in a perspective or evaluative meaning but in a descriptive and predictive use: what it is or will be.

The creation or discovery or whatever you want to call the derivation from sense experience of the word "$p=mv$" of course was not this simple. As all philosophers of science and all scientists that are philosophically inclined have concluded, observation is theory-laden; that is, observation language and theory language are deeply interwoven and involve interpretative meanings.[19] However, the interpretations are rationally or logically related and, unlike normative language, it flows forward not backward and there is no jumping of logical gaps in the fabric as there is between descriptive language and normative language which flows backward. Isaac Newton or any modern scientist was and is only able to make their empirical observations and inductions to deductive formulae as a result of millennia of development and the contingency of the necessary descriptive and interpretative wordgames. Science often needs intellectual anarchy but always needs luck to succeed [20], though as the adage popularly attributed to Louis Pasteur says: "chance favors only the prepared mind" (or as the Romans classically would say, *fortes fortuna iuvat* — "fortune favors the brave".)

So, as a side issue, we could contemplate whether this word "science" fits into one of those classes of words in which their meaning is not only their use and usefulness in scientific language or wordgames but a metaphysical reality. Because of the necessity of language to create theory to interpret the sense data, it is tempting to say the meaning of at least some scientific words are metaphysically real. Clearly science is not entirely a social construct in a descriptive sense because even in the absence of scientific

---

[19] *See generally,* Note 19, *supra.* Feyerabend, P. (2010). *Against Method.* Verso.

[20] *Ibid.*

language by which to describe empirical sense experience it would still exist as something that we cannot control but which we want to control. One can imagine and there is no logical contradiction or other logic error in imagining a person in a solitary existence on earth with "sufficient intellectual power", with sufficient physical power and control of nature, and who could live long enough, who would: observe a falling apple and then spend millennia collecting data, making inductive inferences, making deductions, and creating the necessary theory to reach the same level of science we now have. An individual logically could do this in theory.

The only problem with this imagined person is that the person would not be able to tell anyone of this scientific knowledge; it would be knowledge of which we cannot speak even if the person happens to meet another person — not because it is existential but because there would not be any scientific language by which to communicate it. No doubt, the person would develop a code for recording individual empirical data and keep track of it but this code would not be a language; there is no such thing as a private language — that is a language understandable by only a single individual as Wittgenstein's private language contemplations establish.[21] In order to communicate this individually created empirical code once meeting another person, this individual who created the science would have to go back to day one and then as a couple or group of persons start struggling with the very first data collection and start creating words that achieve the intended acts from the other person. They can then socially construct a wordgame so that the meanings (use and usefulness) of the words allow for communication of the individually created science. If the other person had an individually created science also, they would have to find words that resolve the struggles between them to achieve intended acts and start creating wordgames.

(However, progression of science is a metaphysical side issue at this point of our contemplation trying to lay a foundation of

---

[21] Wittgenstein, L. 2009. §§243-56.

an existential philosophy of law. Again, if anyone is interested in contemplating this issue and an existentialist philosophy of language that goes behind the language of law, I hopefully will be contemplating an existentialist philosophy of language as my next essay project.)

Relevant to contemplating an existential philosophy of law, it is irrelevant whether the word "science" references a metaphysical reality other that simply the use and usefulness of this word in scientific language. Even though it may be much more, science at a minimum in a historical and contemporary descriptive sense relative to law need be only a social construct consisting of a fabric of language with sense experience intertwined with theory so that pulling one thread or removing one thread affects all other threads and may even disintegrate through a paradigm shift the entire portions of the fabric of its language. [22]

In scientific language, even relatively simple derivations from sense experience such as the formula "$p=mv$" for "momentum" entail many substantial philosophical problems such as: the problem of induction; the nature of cause and effect; is there a difference between correlation of facts and a cause and effect relationship between facts; the rule-following paradox; metaphysical problems regarding whether the substance of this formula is real or nominal; and many more. All of these are important questions, especially to philosophers of science and of language and to scientists in their later years when they begin to contemplate their life's work. However, these philosophical problems are unimportant to scientists at work except for one wordgame technique and one useful word: 1) Ockham's Razor; 2) the use of the word "truth".

For any given set of empirical observations, including for the empirical observations of an apple falling from a tree, there are an infinite number of theoretical mathematical functions that could satisfy any finite set of observations taken. The formula "$p=mv$" is

---

[22] *See* Quine, W.V.O. (2013). *Word and Object.* Martino Publishing.

used and useful for the used and useful "momentum" and thus is accepted as the true scientific description of the observations through use of Ockham's Razor. Whether this application is an ontological technique or just a heuristic technique does not matter to the working scientist putting words to use in empirical observation — it simply is. Without Ockham's Razor, science would be even more complicated than it already is. As a matter of existential reality, faced with a meaningless universe, we create no meaning for it by creating unnecessary complications — except perhaps for the aesthetic meaning as an end in itself beloved by patrician existentialism of which science is not usually concerned. "Progress isn't made by early risers. It's made by lazy men trying to find easier ways to do something" (Heinlein, R.A. 1973. p. 53).

    This leads to the second relevant scientific language issue: scientific "truth".
Regardless of whether or not science does give ultimate necessary truths about the nature of reality, scientific truth by existential reality does and always will give pragmatic truth. The formula "$p=mv$" must work to give descriptive and predictive truth about falling apples and whatever other objects are in the same set of objects as falling apples or it stops being a scientific wordgame. The meaning of "truth" in science is pragmatic, this word is used to describe words or wordgames that work to solve a problem. It is not meaningful to say in science "there is no truth" or "all truth is relative". If someone says this statement, it is simple to refute by asking them to slam their head against a brick wall.

    When they stop working, scientific words stopping being science, at best they are a history of science. Eventually, when sense experience contradicts the formulae "$p=mv$" for momentum within the new interpretative meanings of "space-time" and the wordgame of relativity physics, this formula is considered "true" only if the speed is small relative to the speed of light and is not affected by any sources of space time curvature. Otherwise, at high velocities relative to the speed of light requiring the wordgame of relativity physics, the "true" formula for "momentum" is "$p=mv/\sqrt{1-v^2/c^2}$". (At low velocities v is small making the denominator approximately equal to one and the equation reduces to its classical version of p=mv). As before, this new "true" formula becomes true by application of Ockham's Razor. Should we also change the word "momentum" to reflect two truths? In terms of logical discipline, we should but do not — in the same way the word "wave" should change as it goes from the at-the-beach description to mathematical fiction in physics but does not. As life changes, the meanings of "momentum" and "wave" and the fabric of language in which they occur change as their use and usefulness change but these changes are not always reflected in nominal changes in the words.

This pragmatic meaning of scientific "truth" is also the sense in which scientific "law" is now true in modern Technological Society. Originally, the concept of scientific law was derived from the concept of divine law and natural law that was by necessity absolutely true in all possible worlds created by the Christian God. The word "law" in this sense is still a goal of science — only without the God implication. However, regardless of whether scientific law is possible in this sense, maybe or maybe not, scientific laws are always by logical necessity pragmatically true. They are true as long as they work to solve a problem. When they stop working, they are replaced by whatever new laws come alone to solve the scientific problems at issue. For example, Newton's Law of Universal Gravitation has been superseded by Albert Einstein's Theory of General Relativity, but it continues to be used as an approximation in most applications because it works in applications not dealing with very strong gravitational fields — in which case relativity works and is true. Relativity seems to be on its way to being replaced by some wordgame version of quantum physics. Considering that quantum physics cannot explain what makes up 95% of the universe it deceptively calls "dark" matter and energy, using the past to predict the future, eventually there will be a new wordgame to replace it.

1.   Existential Universals in Science. Rationally creating and using even simple universals such as redness eventually lead to more sophisticated universals such as the "redshift" of physics. Quantifying the path of reasoning from "redness" to the redshift of physics is the substance of science, philosophy of science, and its predictive value. As much as popular culture rejects generalizations often calling them stereotypes, such are the stuff of science by which it makes sense of its sense experience to create predictive wordgames.[23]

Science would not be science without the use of universals describing relationships and qualities shared between universal types; so, anything that wants to be naturalized to science must deal with the concept of universals.

It is impossible to explain any particulars in the wordgame of science without having universals such as numbers at a minimum describing relationships between the particulars — or is it just relationships between the words being used to describe the particulars? The latter seem to be a possibility according to some logicians arguing science is possible without numbers because numbers are not universals but merely nominal, just another collection of words whose meaning is their use or usefulness.[24] Science without numbers? Though it would violate Ockham's Razor and this would explain why no one bothers to try it, it would be funny if it turns out to be descriptively true that science is simply one big set of words with predictive meanings but otherwise everything is just nominally true.

This is why the contemplation of universals in the wordgame of metaphysics remains important contemplation. Though such metaphysical contemplation may never give an answer to whether universals are real or nominal, they help in understanding and clarifying the substance of science and thus in understanding and clarifying the pragmatic laws of science. Without doubt, regardless

---

[23] *See* <u>Appendix</u> on the difference between generalizations and stereotypes.

[24] Field, H. (1980). *Science Without Numbers: A defense of nominalism*. Blackwell.

of whether they are real or nominal, universals with predictive value have pragmatic meaning. When language is loose with their meanings, such as "wave" being used for multiple uses and usefulness and the word "DNA" treated metaphysically as actual reality, it is the job of analytic philosophy to correct it.

In scientific language, no existentialist should have a problem treating universals, even those whose use or usefulness is made up of other universals consisting of mathematical fictions, to be as real as any individual, particular, sense experience. For example, in scientific language, the universal "atom" means an unobservable wave of infinite probabilities that become a particle of finite probabilities governed by the Uncertainty Principle that can move from one point in space to another without traveling the space in between. Atoms are as real as any chair supposedly made up of them. Despite how absurd such mathematical fictions appear, there is no existential problem with treating them to be as real as any rock we trip over. As the contemplation of scientific language shows to be the case, universals describing attributes common or shared by individuals have a meaning as real as any word describing an individual because they are used and are useful to reach pragmatic and predictive truth about a reality. In science, if needed to solve a problem, apple and redness are equally meaningful and real.

C. *Existential Language Of Law*

"Nothing is so difficult as not deceiving oneself" (Wittgenstein, L. 1984 *Culture and Value.* p. 34c). Now, imagine sitting under an apple tree and a law falls on your head. If you can imagine such a sense experience, you must be confusing words with reality. One does not experience law in the same way one does an apple. In fact, if one is by oneself, one would never experience a "law" in the modern sense.

If one has been a hermit for one's whole life, in theory, one could look at the universe and develop concepts of good and evil by which to guide one's relationship to the universe, but this would at best be a morality. Morality is simply a means to differentiate good acts from bad acts in terms of how one ought to act in relation to the universe or how it ought to be in relation to the individual. It is logically possible for a solitary hermit to create predictive and resulting interpretive empirical codes for a science and also to create normative codes for actions in a morality. This hermit would be able to describe an apple falling and interpret any resulting observed data from this sense experience to achieve predictive value as to when, where, and how apples may fall in the future. This hermit could also create normative codes as to whether it is good or bad in an evaluative and prescriptive sense as to whether the universe ought to allow apples to fall on the head of the hermit or whether the hermit should eat them or leave them to nature. Because of our Heart of Darkness, however, the morality of which we cannot speak derives from the hermit's Will to Power but not necessarily from any will to live. For moral codes, the truth is not necessarily pragmatic as would be the truth of the science codes. An individual may decide either freely or as a matter of religious or secular predestination that there is a next life with more power than this one and by act of will create a morality that supports this view. Any acts that solve problems in living this morality are true; but, it would also be true that pure intention to commit an act despite an inability to accomplish it or a failure to accomplish it would also be truly good under this morality as would be the person intending the good. Morality deals with what the universe and the individual ought to be or do, not what it is or will be.

However, for this morality — as with for any science developed by the hermit — there would be no need to convert this morality of which we cannot speak into language because there is no language to speak about it yet nor anyone with which to speak; and, there is no need to convert it to anything else including not to any word of law. For the hermit, all law would appear to be a necessary and an absolute standard of good and evil — or what we call divine or natural law — but to the hermit it would simply be.

Of course, if one was purely self centered and unconcerned with the nature of the universe, this hermit would be amoral and thus would not even develop a morality or any concept of good and evil other than a Will to Power over nature in order to survive its indifference or antagonism to the hermit's survival. In this situation, there would be no morality only a science of which the hermit could not speak and the empirical codes for observable actions in that science.

So, right from the first, we have a difference between science and scientific language and modern law and its language. Law in Technological Society is a wordgame in its entirety, there is nothing in the universe such as divine law or natural law of which we cannot speak outside of the language of law that existentially for an individual could be law. Logically, it would not be nonsense to imagine an individual creating meaning of which we cannot speak for the word eventually called "science" in a solitary life with no scientific language. The word "science" in this case would be something of which we cannot speak until the individual meets other persons and starts creating a wordgame in which "science" is useful for an intended use, but it would be there. Such is not possible for "law". It would be nonsense to imagine and to talk about one solitary individual creating "law" for a one-person universe. <u>For the hermit, the law and the universal "law" or the Law would be the same as the individual's morality, there would be no way for there to be a difference.</u> Not only would the word law be nonsense as a private language but nonsense in any sense other than simply a physical grunt that sounds like 'law' that may arbitrarily or randomly be used as a code for something and anything.

In the absence of the language or wordgame law, there is no law. The metaphysical subject matter of science of which we cannot speak would still exist despite our inability to speak of it. This would not be true of law. Whatever its subject matter may be, it is a reality completely dependent on a social need and ability to speak of it. In a one person universe, there at best is only morality. How could the word "law" and Law with a capital 'L' make any sense other than as a morality to a hermit? It could not. There would be no way for an individual to differentiate between acts that are moral, good, or legal; immoral, bad, or illegal; or any combinations of these involving a distinction or even of words separating morality and legality.

Since existentialism rejects any concept of natural or divine normative law except based on the individual's Will to Power, law must be a wordgame in which universals have a different meaning than in the wordgame of science because law is created entirely by language. As always, the meanings of words change with their use and usefulness; thus universals in law contemplating what ought to be are different from universals in the wordgames of science.

1. So, for the Hermit to Use and Find Law Would It be Enough to Meet One Other Person? At first meeting, assuming they do not try to kill each other upon contact, as with the need to create a science, the first act of a couple created by two hermits meeting each other would be to act with each other so as to develop a language. At some point during this process, whatever codes they were using for their observable actions of individual morality, if either had any, have to become words in this language but only if the need arises by a conflict of moralities and a need to resolve a resolving struggle between the individual morality of each person in this couple. Science by necessity existentially involves a struggle between the individual and something out there that is not the individual: nature is indifferent or antagonistic to the existence of both of the individuals making up this couple thus there is a common struggle with something with which both must deal. This struggle is so omnipresent that it leaves open the door for solipsism; to each hermit trying to survive this first contact with the famed Other, it may be the couple is solely a delusion of the solitary hermit who is still alone.

Morality does not necessarily involve a struggle with the natural world as does science, especially existentially. Because the universe is amoral as existentialism concludes it is, there is no morality outside individual morality with which the individual must struggle. If an individual is amoral, it does matter what natural or divine morality the universe or anyone else has or if there is any.

Moral struggle only occurs when an individual makes an existentialist leap to morality in a meaningless universe or when an individual seeks to discover the morality of the universe. The individual struggle may conflict and thus cause a further level of struggle with those who have not made the leap or do not seek it but are satisfied with being amoral.

Even if Divine or Natural Law in the Christian sense does exist in the universe, this would not change our descriptive analysis so far. If it is out there, some individuals are either predestined to discover it while others are not or some will reject it; there is no such thing as a free will regarding this discovery and what to do with it. Either way, there will be a level of struggle between those who see and use Divine or Natural law as a morality and those who do not. If there exists divine or natural law in terms of pure sense experience without Christian dogma by which to interpret it, existentially in a descriptive sense it exists only as a "might makes right" morality (the might of whatever god is its foundation, religious or otherwise) and thus it is existentially worthless in terms of a non-pragmatic morality but leads solely to scientific and amoral wordgames.

An amoral individual's struggle with the universe and with any other person is always the same and is a scientific one, the needed language for such an amoral person or persons in our couple made up of two former hermits would be a scientific one involving predictive values for survival but no normative values. Thus for the amoral person, solipsism is still a viable reality.

The only possible source for moral struggle that would require the new couple of former hermits to create a language of morality would come from conflict between their personal codes of morality either directly or indirectly through their morality of how the universe ought to be or ought to treat them. In these situations, there is a need for a language of morality in the struggle between individual codes of morality. For example, if one thinks they should eat apples while the other thinks apples should be left to the divine, this struggle would convert their individuality morality of which we cannot speak into a wordgame morality of which we can speak. In this struggle, the individual moralities lose the existential nature of the individual morality: the wordgame will no longer be an individual morality of which we cannot speak as there is no private language by which to speak about it, but a "morality" whose meaning is its use and usefulness in the new language. The couple will be dealing with acts trying to get the other either eating apples or to stop eating them. These acts and the attempts to change the acts will be the use and usefulness of the morality wordgame language created by the couple and thus the meaning of the words in the wordgames.

These words and wordgame can be contemplated and discussed rationally and logically. However, the underlying individual moralities that are the existential reality of these morality wordgames cannot be discussed logically regardless of their still being there as the normative force causing the struggle. They exist as that of which we cannot speak. In the language being created by the couple through the acts, intentions, and sense experience they can experience together, the words "morality", "moral", "immoral", "amoral", "good", and "evil" become useful words in their wordgame but now their meaning would be their use and usefulness in that wordgame. These words in the worldgame once they become a social construct by two people will not have the individual existential meaning of the existential codes of which we cannot speak since they are now words in the language. We would only be able to speak logically of the morality wordgame and logically only about the use and usefulness and thus the meaning of those words in that wordgame.

In this wordgame morality, truth now becomes pragmatic. Any acts that help the individual Will to Power morality achieve power especially over any opposing morality are good. Those that do not, are evil. Before, it would also be true that pure intention to commit an act despite an inability to accomplish it would be good under and through individual morality as would the person intending the good. This is no longer true because it is incoherent or meaningless to talk about "intention" separate from any acts associated with words for "intention" in a social construct. Which struggle takes precedence, if any, and thus which struggle between the couple of hermits defines good and evil is contingent upon which struggle is at any given moment most advantageous or antagonist to the group's survival.

For example, right now any practicing Democrat would be primarily concerned with taking power from any practicing Republican — and *vice a versa*. Thus anything that would achieve this result without threatening the survival of the individual in their existential struggle with the universe or resulting in the individual to lose control of their Will to Power would be moral. However, if Yellowstone National Park erupts to become an active volcano or the Russians land on Cape Cod next week, this moral struggle would quickly be forgotten and anything done by anyone regardless of whether they were Democrat or Republican to maintain the individual's existence against these new threats would be moral including any acts that were considered immoral or amoral in the previous struggle. This would not be true for someone willing to be martyred for their devotion to either party, but this is only because they have created a morality that values "death before dishonor" and we are back to the existentialist option of committing suicide as a means to defeat the meaningless of the universe. This morality does not change the pragmatic meaning of truth for morality but only defines a solution for the problem that cannot be falsified — in this life at least.

It is useful to note that only through the wordgame struggles of morality in which our will directly or indirectly is not the final arbitrator of truth can we rationally avoid solipsism:

> We learn that we are separate beings in the world, distinct from what is other than ourselves, by coming up against obstacles to the fulfillment of our intentions—that is, by running into opposition to the implementation of our will. When certain aspects of our experience fail to submit to our wishes, when they are on the contrary unyielding and even hostile to our interests, it then becomes clear to us that they are not parts of ourselves. We recognize that they are not under our direct and immediate control; instead, it becomes apparent that they are independent of us. That is the origin of our concept of reality, which is essentially a concept of what limits us, of what we cannot alter or control by the

mere movement of our will.

To the extent that we learn in greater detail how we are limited, and what the limits of our limitation are, we come thereby to delineate our own boundaries and thus to discern our own shape. We learn what we can and cannot do, and the sorts of effort we must make in order to accomplish what is actually possible for us. We learn our powers and our vulnerabilities. This not only provides us with an even more emphatic sense of our separateness. It defines for us the specific sort of being that we are.

Thus, our recognition and understanding of our own identity arises out of, and depends integrally on, our appreciation of a reality that is definitively independent of ourselves. In other words, it arises out of and depends on our recognition that there are facts and truths over which we cannot hope to exercise direct or immediate control. If there were no such facts or truths, if the world invariably and unresistingly became whatever we might like or wish it to be, we would be unable to distinguish ourselves from what is other than ourselves and we would have no sense of what in particular we ourselves are. It is only through our recognition of a world of stubbornly independent reality, fact, and truth that we come both to recognize ourselves as beings distinct from others and to articulate the specific nature of our own identities.

How, then, can we fail to take the importance of factuality and of reality seriously? How can we fail to care about truth?

We cannot. (Frankfurt, H. 2013. p. 100-01).

Though Frankfurt fails to define truth pragmatically or in any way, it is important to note that the significance of struggle in any existential morality will also continue into any existentialist philosophy of law.

Is this morality struggle within the couple of former hermits what we call law? Is any resolution of this morality struggle what modern Technological Society calls law? Neither would be law or Law.

This morality struggle itself is simply between two individual moralities. If one person simply voluntarily submits to the other's morality while suppressing their individual morality, there are still two competing versions of right and wrong but only one becomes morality in action. Neither the victor by submission nor the loser would have any reason to refer to this situation by the separate word law by which modern society designates a normative situation distinct from any one person's morality. The situation would easily be reversed by the person who submitted then deciding to reverse their submission and demand dominance in morality. In this type of situation there would be no social construct law distinct from the individual moralities of the two persons involved because at any given moment one person's morality can be replaced by the other person's morality. For example, the one opposed to eating apples gives up and the couple eat apples — until the one opposed to eating apples decides they must stop and the other person submits. There is no law normatively controlling the situation just the individual wills of the persons involved.

What if one of the couple submits because the other is enforcing their morality through the pointing of a gun? Though the submission is no longer voluntary, it does not change the existential normative reality. Neither the victor with the gun nor the loser would have any reason to refer to this situation by the separate word law by which modern society designates a normative situation distinct from any one person's morality. The situation would easily be reversed by the person who submitted getting hold of the gun and deciding to reverse their submission and demand dominance in morality. In this type of situation there would be no social construct law distinct from the individual moralities of the two persons involved just a struggle for possession of a gun. There is no law normatively controlling the situation just the individual wills of the persons involved plus a gun they both want to possess to give more power to their Will to Power.

Another possible resolution of the couple's morality struggle is not a resolution involving dominance and submission of one morality to another but of surrendering or modifying one or both of the moralities. For example, the person opposed to eating apples because it is an evil act decides instead that it is a good act or decides that eating half an apple is a good act. This resolution changes nothing in terms of creating a separate social construct of law. If there is a surrender, there is no longer a struggle of morality and therefore there is really even no morality on the issue of eating apples except in a historical sense. If there is a modification, it then becomes an issue as to whether the other person will also modify their morality to agree with the modification. Depending on whether or not the other person does so, we either have a morality struggle as before or we do not.

At best, this couple can give meaning or begin to give meaning to the word "ethics" as useful. They can have a use for this word "ethics" as referring to what they both "ought" to do but it would not be the same as the modern existential use of the word "ethics" because, as before with the word "law", the meaning of this word would be completely contingent on each individual's morality and their willingness to submit, surrender, or modify that individual morality. It is the existential leap to morality that controls this early version of "ethics", there is no separate leap to a social construct of "ethics".

2.   Would More than a Couple of Persons Lead to Law? What if another person or more join the couple and there is a struggle now between multiple individual moralities of which none can speak, of moralities of which we can speak, and of any resulting submissions, surrenders, or modifications of those moralities? From a purely logical or rational perspective, this situation need not be any different from the situation of the couple except for there being multiple morality struggles between multiple individuals instead of between just two individuals. Eventually, though, when the group of persons gets large enough or the struggles get intense enough that the time and resources spent resolving the morality struggles adversely affect the time and resources spent on the primary existential struggle with the indifference or antagonism of the universe to the group's existence, something will need to done if the group is to survive.

Assuming there are enough individuals in the group that have rejected suicide, it is at this point that a social construct will need to create normative meanings stating what the group ought to do separate from the individual moralities in the group stating what the individual ought to do. This social construct will need to exist as long as it is useful to the group for survival.

How would this normative social construct be created? We know it cannot be a logical creation because there is no way logically to go from what reality is to what it ought to be. From the perspective of logic therefore, the foundational premise or premises to create the necessary normative social construct for the group to survive just as with any initial leaps to morality made by any individuals in the social group would be random and arbitrary or at a minimum as an irrational and illogical process — as something of which we cannot speak. The start of this social construct exists somewhere in the existential reality of the "I am" and "I am therefore I think" that we know exists but of which we cannot logically speak. To this is added, "I want to exist" and "I want more than just to exist" or "I will to power". When these latter Will-to-Power premises are made within the context of a group of persons, they become "I want the group to exist", and we now have the basic premises or axioms for logic to create social constructs to keep the existential meanings of which we cannot speak continue existing. Accepting these premises as existentially true gives the rational mind the minimum of three variables plus negation of any of these variables that it needs to create logic and use it to fight against the universe and its will to kill us and our community and for humanity to engage in the struggle that is life: $x, x \rightarrow y, x \wedge z,$ and their negation. Binding these variables by values is the beginning of all the complexities of logical thought needed to create a social construct of norms.

However, what would be the meaning of "truth" relative to this normative social construct? Would it be existential truth just as are the original existential truths that created them of which we cannot speak? No, because we are speaking about them and the group's members would constantly speak about them; they are social constructs and thus their truth must also be a social construct. The only possible truth for such normative social constructs created for the group to continue to exist would be pragmatic truth: does the group of persons as a matter of sense experience and factual reality survive and continue to survive using the created social constructs. Any social construct normative statement resolving struggle between individual moralities is true and thus good if its use is useful to beat the indifference and antagonism of the universe to the group's existence. Or, once there are enough people to create competing individual moralities or social groups and thus competing ethics, an ethics is true and thus good if its use is useful to beat the indifference or antagonism of another social group and with the universe. Though as with the morality struggles between the hermit couple, which struggle takes precedence, if any does, is contingent upon which struggle is at any given moment most antagonist to the group's survival.

This social construct Will to Power normative language created from the morality struggles within the social group is ethics. Just as there is no logical connection between descriptive reality, whatever it may be, and the normative statements of morality, there is no logical connection between the normative statements of morality and the normative statements of any social construct ethics. Ethics exists to keep order among moralities, amoralities, or immoralities. Morality is limited only by the individual's Will to Power. Ethics is limited only by a social group's communal Will to Power: what can it get away with telling its members they ought to be doing without losing members or destroying itself by other means.

For example, back to the political party example, right now Democrats are primarily concerned with taking power from the Republicans — and *vice a versa*. Thus anything that would achieve this result without getting them into trouble with another social group's Will to Power would be ethical. However, if Yellowstone

National Park decided to become an active volcano or the Russians land on Cape Cod next week, this ethical struggle will quickly be forgotten and anything that maintains their join power and existence as political parties against these new threats to their Will to Power will be ethical including any acts that were considered unethical in the previous struggle. As with morality, this ethics would not be true for a group willing to destroy itself for their ethics, but this is only because they have created an ethics that values "death before dishonor" and we are back to the existentialist committing suicide as a means to defeat the meaningless of the universe. This ethics does not change the pragmatic meaning of truth for ethics but only defines a solution for their problems that cannot be falsified — in this life at least which is the only life that matters to existentialism.

Is this social construct wordgame created to conserve or avoid the time and resources struggling between individual moralities that weakens the ultimate existential struggle with the universe what Technological Society calls law?

Calling it "ethics" would definitely be useful and fit the use of this social construct. Problem is there could be multiple uses for "ethics" dependent on the descriptive reality of the time and resources being spent on the struggle between individual moralities; the time and resources being spent on the primary struggle of the group to beat the universe; and the relation between the two. In modern Technological Society, every group of persons that wants to be taken seriously by Technological Society has a code of "ethics" designed to survive and prosper in that Society irrespective of any sense of morality, immorality, or amorality of anyone in the group. The mafia, the Russian mob, and street gangs have codes of ethics. In my experience practicing law and in my personal experience with the sycophants and cowards that call themselves Overseers of the Bar consistent with the initial plantation language discourse meaning of being "overseers", virtues such as loyalty, empathy, and honesty in practice are much more common among the ethical codes and leaders of mobsters and gangsters than they are among any professional codes of ethics or their leaders — including judges.

Furthermore, any enforcement of codes of ethics is always

limited by law and subject to review by law. So, law cannot simply be another ethics.

    3.   Law as a Universal or Even as a Meta-Language. Resolving these inconsistencies with treating ethics as law, we have reached the use and usefulness and thus the meaning of the word "law" as a universal and even as a meta-language "Law" that is used and useful for all law. Law is a universal normative arbiter for any social construct with multiple ethics. Law is used descriptively as a final normative social construct that encompasses and supercedes all social construct normative language of ultimate value including all individual moralities and all ethics in Technological Society. It makes sense to talk about multiple codes of ethics in a given society and even multiple particular laws, but "respect for the law", "the rule of law", and "the law" and oftern even just "law" refer to Law. Could it be that Law is not a universal but simply shorthand for codes of ethics or for sets of codes of ethics? This cannot be the case because codes of ethics and sets of codes of ethics are subject to normative statements of Law. Law is essentially the dominant ethics of the social construct that creates it.

    From a purely logical or rational perspective, the situation of having social constructs called ethics intended to stop individual morality struggles from reaching the point of endangering the social group's survival involves either voluntary compliance or involuntary compliance with the ethics. Thus eventually when the social group gets large enough and there start occurring struggles among the ethics constructs, these ethics struggles recreate on a larger scale the situation of having multiple morality and ethics struggles taking up time and resources so as to adversely affect the time and resources spent on the primary existential struggle with the indifference or antagonism of the universe to a social group's existence. At this point of ethical struggle complexity, as with struggles among individual moralities, something will need to done if the group is to continue to exist. Assuming there are enough groups with enough individuals in the group that have rejected suicide, it is at this point that the social group will need a social construct of normative language stating what the group or individuals ought do that is separate from the struggling ethical norms. As with the social construct ethics, this final social construct will have true and good norms that are defined pragmatically: they are true and good as long as they can be used and are useful to prevent the group's destruction.

This final social construct will not be just another ethics, it is Law.

VI. The Nature of Law and Its Inherent Need for a Monopoly on Violence

"Laws, like sausages, cease to inspire respect in proportion as we know how they are made".

> — *attributed initially in popular culture to a 19th Century trial attorney John Godfrey Saxe but also attributed to many other politicians, writers, and the like.*

Thus there is one substantive difference between ethics and this further social construct called Law: it will need to be a final arbitrator of the ethical struggles that required its creation, it would have to be an unopposed social construct of norms. Otherwise, it would just eventually recreate at a higher level the ethical struggles this further social construct was intended to stop or avoid so as not to endanger the survival of the group. Though this final social construct will involve both voluntary and involuntary resolution by submission, surrender, or modification of its normative statements by members of the social group, this final social construct will not create a further level of struggle among its normative statements requiring a further social construct to resolve them. The normative statements of this construct will have to be final and thus it would need a monopoly on the means to enforce submission, surrender, or modification so as to end the struggle among normative statements as to what individuals or groups ought to be doing.

Thus we have an existential meaning for a universal Law. The use and usefulness of this final social construct universal fits the use and usefulness and thus is the meaning of the word "law" in our modern Technological Society and in all societies and their social constructs be it the United States, Stalinist Russia, San Marino, North Korea, or whatever social groups with struggling ethics and moralities call themselves:

> Law is the social construct set of all normative wordgames of ultimate value to which all other normative social constructs of ultimate value are subject thus by necessity it has or seeks to have a monopoly on the ultimate power of violence by which to enforce its normative judgments. In modern Technological Society, all struggles either of individual moralities or of ethics are all ultimately subject to judgment and execution upon by law consisting of a judgment and then an exection with a monopoly on violence.

Anything else would be just another ethics adding another level of struggle and complexity to an already complex problem and thus inefficient technologically thus endangering our Technological Society's existential struggle with the indifference and antagonism of the universe. Furthermore, adding such a complexity would violate our existential goal of having modern law be naturalized to science. By Ockham's Razor, the simplest solution is the best as long as it works.

Thus, without need of a complete philosophy of language encompassing all language, for purposes of an existentialist philosophy of law, we have a meaning not only for the word "law" as a universal that is bound by values and attributes but also a meaning for truth in law. The universal Law is a normative wordgame whose norms are enforced by one or more persons or things through a monopoly on violence. Something is a particular law within the universal discourse that is Law most definitely if those one or more persons or things enforcing the norms call something law but it will also be pragmatically Law even if it is not called law: the words maintain or strengthen an ability to act as a final arbiter of all ethics by a monopoly on violence. If not, the words are simply another ethics whose Will to Power is struggling with other social groups' Will to Power but are not law.

As a universal social construct, the universal word "law" or Law with a capital 'L' is used and is useful to reference an ethics with a monopoly on violence.

However, it now appears that my problem with law in Technological Society having a monopoly on violence is not a descriptive problem, it is an existential one: law is ethics with a monopoly on violence. By its very existential nature it must have or seek a monopoly on violence otherwise it is not law. Though simple, this conclusion is not simplistic nor too simple because it radically changes how the absurd hero making a leap to morality should view law, legal obligations, and our existential relationship to Law.

For example, descriptively it is possible for ethics to be egalitarian. For example, the ethics of illegality in pirate ships as described in the aforementioned *The Invisible Hook, The Hidden Economics of Pirates*. It is highly unlikely, but it is possible. In practical reality, there is always at least one person or group of persons in any social group that has more power than the remainder and thus the ethics of the social group will be twisted to maintain and enforce that position of power. The powerless in any ethical group are at least legally free to leave the group and seek in comfort in the ethics of other groups. This is not true of law by its existential nature as the final arbiter of all ethics, it is not legal to leave law but illegal to do so. Thus Law will never be and cannot be egalitarian by its nature as a universal despite how much it may pretend to be; by necessity there will always be a minority controlling its violence. Existentially, the word law as a normative wordgame in a more practical sense is a social construct by those who control the monopoly to enforce what they say we ought to do.

This latter attribute can best be contemplated by using the classical rational tool of primitive state analysis for the use and usefulness of words. I will be using this tool next in this contemplation to clarify the nature of the universal law.

As I proceed further into this contemplation, I will call those making the normative statements of law and controlling its monopoly on violence the Powers-that-be or Powers. There are obvious objections to this abstraction that I will also contemplate later, such as how real are these Powers.

A.   *Morality, Ethics, and the Law*

One should not conclude from this contemplation there is no morality in the law, rather one needs to be existential about what morality and ethics are. The Powers-that-be controlling the law and making the judgment calls as to what they can get away with on executing on any particular law are humans with a Will to Power. How they want to exercise their power and upon what or whom is subject to their leap to morality, even if it is a leap to an amorality or immorality. Their leap matters but is the only leap that matters because existentially: morality, immorality, amorality are all the same to the benign indifference of the universe.

As an exemplification of this abstraction at work empirically, look at Law in a way that sees through to the Heart of Darkness by contemplating the often used political philosophy analogy of imagining humans in the state of nature or humanity's primitive state defined as: the hypothetical conditions of what the lives of people were like before societies came into existence. However, do not conduct this contemplation as it has usually been done by patrician philosophers varying from Plato to Robert Nozick in which the result of the contemplation is pretty much predetermined by upper class philosophy. Do this contemplation existentially assuming that plebeians and *hoi polloi* are as real as patricians and their intelligentsia. See our state of nature in its purely working sense by starting with an individual Heart of Darkness and adding individuals one by one to a real world of struggle for survival in a universe that at best is indifferent to our existence but usually is actively trying to kill us.

1. A Primitive State Analysis. So, there you are, trying to survive with nature trying to kill you. What law and legal system do you have? Pretty much nothing other than the rule that whatever works for you to survive or to give meaning to your life ought to be done until it stops working.

Now add another person, someone who is overall either more powerful in their ability to survive life or less powerful in their ability to survive the struggle for life. In empirical reality, there is no such thing as equality — there is always inequality on all empirical abilities or at least on some or one. Now what legal system do you have? Assuming the more powerful is not a total psychopath, pretty much nothing changes except for those instances when there is not enough of something for both of you to share equally. What is the law at that point? Unless the more powerful person is some type of altruistic Christian martyr type that by definition would mean that person is not the most powerful person in terms of their ability to survive in life, the new morality is: whatever works for survival or to give meaning to the life of the most powerful person in the couple until it stops working for them or the weaker becomes the most powerful.

Now a third person joins our dynamic duo in the state of nature. At this point matters start to get tricky. While only a couple of persons, the most powerful person could in theory and in practice keep full control of the weaker person in the two-person state of nature by tying the weaker up at night and once releasing the Other during the day never letting the Other out of sight. However, this gets harder to do when the more powerful has two weaker persons to control. In bad times, the stronger can still keep the weaker tied up at night and never let either of the weaker out of sight during the day but this gets harder to accomplish. If the weaker conspire, they could figure out a way to give the stronger the proverbial and most likely physical stab in the back when necessary for survival. The situation is still might-makes-right. However, the might could now be established by the weaker majority combining together to beat what normally would be the stronger minority in the absence of a conspiracy by the weaker. At this point, the powerful with their superior will-to-power survival instincts naturally come up with the concept of ethics as a means to remain the powerful: *i.e.*, the weaker should not conspire to stab me in the back because this is unethical at this point.

Since there is a possibility of multiple conspiracies by

multiple weaker persons against the more powerful and thus of multiple ethics, the most powerful will make the ethics that is most beneficial to the most powerful the dominant ethics controlling all other ethics: thus law is born. The concepts of law and ethics for social purposes are essentially the same with the former simply being the latter plus a monopoly on violence to enforce whatever the ethics may be.

In order to convince the weaker of the need to give up their potential for joining and killing the powerful, the aesthetics of language discourse starts: law is for your own good to protect the weaker from the powerful — conveniently ignoring the fact that the powerful given the opportunity would stab the weaker in the back and kill them regardless of the illegality of such an act.

As we add more individuals to this state of nature to make bigger and more complex societies, this minority/majority problem gets worse and the law becomes a much easier and a more efficient solution to this problem once it is given a monopoly on violence while also becoming more convoluted with verbiage both to foster the necessary myths for social construction of law and ethics and to act as a smokescreen hiding their falsity. There will always be a minority of Powers-that-be — or the "High" as Orwell calls them in his *1984* — who have through fate, destiny, luck, or whatever you what to call God's hate of the poor a superior might-makes-right Will-to-Power meaning in life. There will always be a majority of the powerless or less powerful — or "Middle" and "Low" from *1984* — who could make meaningless the High's Will to Power if they organized, conspired, or combined enough of their Will to Power to overpower the will to power of the High. Why God so hates the poor so much that he would create such a necessary existential three-part division of humanity's Will to Power when it is in social construct form is a contemplation beyond this essay.

Just as with my prior capitalism example, do not take this primitive state analysis as a criticism of capitalism or of any politics or economics. This is descriptive; it is the use and usefulness of the words morality, ethics, and law through the interpretative existential meaning of my Heart of Darkness shared by all individuals. I can no more logically criticize this reality that I can criticize my existence or the existence of the moon and sun. I can criticize the existence of the universe which leads me to existentialism in the first place, but once we reject suicide, our Will to Power is entitled to exist and beat the indifference and outright antagonism of the universe to our existence. We owe nothing to the universe for our existence.

Remember the World War II ratio between guards and the condemned contemplated earlier. Once a monopoly of violence is established, given humanity's Heart of Darkness, it takes very little superiority in the ability to control violence to establish a small group of High controlling both the existential and normative reality of a much larger majority of Middle and Low. As almost all philosophers of history have concluded, there is one universal historical descriptive fact that created and defines all historical movement other than the struggle with the universe: class struggle. Again, I can no more logically criticize this reality that I can criticize my existence or the existence of the moon and sun. I can criticize the existence of the universe which leads me to existentialism in the first place, but once we reject suicide, our Will to Power is entitled to exist and beat the indifference and outright antagonism of the universe to our existence.

The universal law and its aesthetic creations such as "the rule of law" come into existence at that point of social creation or progression from the state of nature in which multiple ethics are created by social construct. Law is the ultimate ethics controlling all other ethics with its actual or demanded monopoly on violence controlled by its Powers. In their exercise of their judgment calls as to what they will get away with on execution, it is only their morality and ethics that matter and only their morality and ethics that limit that execution. So, there are morality and ethics in the law and in the execution of all particular laws: the morality and ethics of the Powers. The minority powerful are concerned about being overpowered through shear force of numbers by the majority having less power or who are powerless.

Such is the favoring of the needs of the minority Powers is their universal social construct meaning of law: to control the struggle among ethics and moralities to assure the survival of the group who created the social construct law as the final arbitrator of its ethics. The Powers must keep and must want to keep their Power or they are no longer Powers. The law is created to abrogate "might makes right", but not in the sense of abrogating "might makes right"; it abrogates the might-makes-right of the powerless and of those with less power who are in the majority in order to protect the might-makes-right of the powerful. law is created to protect the powerless from the powerful but not in the sense of protecting the powerless from the powerful; law is created to prevent the power of the majority powerless through unity from overpowering the power of the minority powerful.

B. Universals in Law Kill

I now have an existential meaning for "law" so that it becomes Law, but what is the empirical reality of such a universal in a nonscientific language such as Law: is the universal law as real as any particular law just as mathematics seems to be as real if not more real than any particular number? Universals are everywhere in the language of Law and "law" is used as a universal in law just as it is used in science but with different uses and usefulness. As concluded earlier, the meaning of law in science and in Law cannot be and therefore are not the same simply because we use the same word "law". The use and usefulness of universals are so different between the two languages that they cannot be said to have the same meaning. We are in a similar situation as the use of the word "wave" in the language discourse of being-at-the-beach and in quantum physics though much worse in terms of difference in meaning. "Wave" is nominally the same word but the meaning has changed radically, so radically that it should be a different word such as wave-beach and wave-physics if we were as precise with our language as analytical philosophy wants us to be. The essential difference between scientific language and the language of law is that the former is talking about something outside of language whereas the latter is completely a social construct whose only link to sense experience is the sense experience of other words. Thus, the meaning of universals in the language of law must be radically different from their meaning in science.

Scientific "law" is descriptive of empirical reality because it has predictive and pragmatic truth. Scientific "law" at a minimum consists of hypotheses subject to Ockham's Razor that lead to quantifiable predictions that can be tested and falsified in repeatable parameter controlled experiments. In science with its pragmatic truth and predictive meanings, even the most abstract of universals is used and useful if it is descriptively threaded to empirical sense experience by its predictive value and pragmatic truth creating "a man-made fabric which impinges on experience only along the edges". (Quine, W.V.O. 2013. p. 42). Pragmatically, the redness of apples is just as real as the apple until it becomes another color. At which point the new color becomes just as real as the apple. As the experience changes, the law of science may change as needed to maintain their predictive and pragmatic meanings.

This is not the descriptive reality of the nonscientific universal "law" we are contemplating. The universal word law in its nonscientific normative sense is a universal used and useful to describe ethics with a monopoly on violence. This law has no threading to pragmatic or predictive meaning. It exists only in a universe of words stating what ought to be. The word law as a universal exists only in its own universe of language discourse distinct from the universe of struggles of which we are conscious except for the fact that we are conscious of the struggle and through our Will to Power want the universe or the struggle to be different: it ought to be what the powers of the law say it ought to be regardless of what it is. For an existential philosophy of law, law is a word describing an ethics that by the logical necessity of its nature has or needs a monopoly on violence over all other norms. It stands alone. Regardless of whether there are millions of other moralities or ethics out there and regardless of whether they are moral, immoral, or amoral, law will be law as long as it is the only ethics with a monopoly on violence. The law of North Korea, Stalinist Russia, the United States, and the Republic of San Marino share in the universal that is law, the word in the "rule of law". The universal law is shared by all particular laws including completely different, particular, concrete laws. Such is the meta or existential set that makes up Law. So, is Law just a nominal truth?

These initial appearances are deceptive. The Law is not just nominal because it does have one very important threading to sense experience that exists independently of any particular law: it kills. Just as no one kills or dies for the ontological proof of the existence of God, no one kills or dies for the scientific universals of matter, energy, or whatever nor does anyone kill for any particular law. People die and kill for the law of the "rule of law". The extent to which they will die or kill for law varies from San Marino to Stalinist Russia, but ultimately, by its monopoly on violence, law demands and its goal is to make its Powers the only ones who can kill and who decide who is to be killed — other than God. The universal law needs a community of at least three people to exist as a meaningful word, but once it does so its meaning is more than just nominal, it is aesthetic to the point of killing and dying for its aesthetics.

The Law is not just a word representing particular laws such as those of North Korea, Stalinist Russia, the United States, and the Republic of San Marino because it needs none of them in order to be law. Ideally, it just needs one Power-that-be and one particular law: decide what ought to be and enforce it by a monopoly on violence. Law is its own universal and particular if need be. Particular laws differ only in the empirical reality of execution: what acts can the Powers get away with through their monopoly on violence. The difference between the law of North Korea, Stalinist Russia, the United States, and the Republic of San Marino is only in the particular execution of the universal law or of a particular law. Unlike science in which existentially universals and particulars are equal if they have predictive value and pragmatic truth, the universal discourse of Law with its many uses and usefulness for other universals despite having no descriptive value other than just nominal and aesthetic have more power than any individual law though it is individual laws that through execution upon the nominal aesthetics of Law gives Law the only descriptive reality it has.

Law and laws existentially exist in the universe of normative language in the same way that mathematics and numbers exist in scientific language: laws and numbers are as particular and as real as any bricks or stones thrown at us, yet law and mathematics are abstract universals. Just as mathematics become particular and real by their use and usefulness in science to give pragmatic truth, the same is true of law and laws except that because law and laws are dealing with normative statements, the only descriptive "is" of their pragmatic truth is their execution: can the Powers get away with violent execution upon their normative statements?

C. *Ockham's Finger in Reverse: Legality and Illegality and Their Unopposed Power of Violence upon Execution*

Now that I have reached a meaning for law as a universal, is the truth for this meaning anything but nominal and aesthetic? As I have concluded previously regarding universals in normative language, the ripple effect of changes in the meanings of words and their impingement upon experience at the edge rationally works in reverse: it is changes in normative meanings that reason uses to change experience and not the usual scientific way of experience rationally changing meanings. Because the universal law has normative meaning, this reverse rationalization of experience must be true of Law.

Since Law is purely a social construct of normative words with no rational threading to any existential reality out there distinct from the words of law, at first glance it appears we need not consider the possibility of the universal law and Law being a real entity distinct from the nominal word law. Law as a universal appears simply to be a wordgame with its only connection to sense experience being other words, except for one problem: execution. Because of the monopoly on violence this wordgame has, its words have a significant descriptive thread to sense experience: it may kill us. This raises the thought mentioned in my Prologue: if the word "law" means both a descriptive and normative wordgames that cannot be logically linked, how can a philosophy of law describe them in one wordgame called Law?

In one sense, such contemplation is behind our needs in this existential contemplation to which scientific truth, regardless of what it may be, is irrelevant. As an existentialist, I do not really care what the world is because it is nothing. What matters is what I want it to be if I want it to be anything. Since I know the Law is a normative wordgame whose only connection to reality is through the execution upon law, my only concern should be to avoid any law that leads to acts I do not want executed or to control any law that leads to acts of execution.

Existentially, the individual is always rationally free to reject what ought to be and do the opposite. So, we are stuck with both a universal law that is just nominal and aesthetic and the execution of any law that makes law descriptive.

Before getting into further abstraction on this unexpected conclusion, it would be helpful to contemplate some particular empirical and historical problems with law and laws that have bothered and confused me for years and for which these conclusions serve existentially to clarify and resolve so that there can be a counterbalance to the unopposed normative power of Law, which after all is the purpose for this contemplation. Some of these problems are very simple but hide complexity, others are complex but hide simplicity.

For example, for the entire twenty-five years I was practicing law and for all the entire history of this particular law as far as I know up until November 2016, the particular *M.G.L.c. 90C §2* was part of Massachusetts "no-fix" law on traffic citations. It and all interpretive case law required strict compliance with its procedures enforceable by a traffic court's monopoly on violence. The intent of the law as written in multiple statutory and case law was to provide a strict procedure for issuing traffic tickets to avoid fixing tickets by those that knew police officers, court clerks, and others who could fix a ticket in one of the lowest levels of our judiciary system: traffic court. It is not perfect; tickets can still be fixed by those with the clout or connections to do so by having the ticket lost somewhere in the process, but at least the strict process makes it harder to do so because there will definitely be someone to blame if procedure is not followed and a ticket dismissed. This "no-fix" law contained the following simple undisputed often so-called "easy case" of law for the issuance of a traffic ticket that is as undisputable a law as one could ever find: "[s]uch citation shall be signed by said police officer and by the violator, and whenever a citation is given to the violator in person that fact shall be so certified by the police officer." *M.G.L.c. 90C §2* (before November 2016). Simple enough. This provides a simple procedure that avoids all sorts of factual disputes: both the police and violator ought to sign the ticket. This normative statement descriptively is a particular law and thus I can put it in quotes as I have. If need be, it can be converted to a declarative form and used by a lawyer or non-lawyer as a statement of law in deductive logic to argue for predictive "ought" conclusions of legality and illegality in the same way a scientist may use the statement p=mv for arguing how to put a rocket on the moon.

The particular law "[s]uch citation shall be signed by said police officer and by the violator" is the apple to the appleness and redness that is the law — it is the number to the mathematics that is the law.

However, what happens in descriptive reality? In the thousands of citations issued each year no police officer in the state of Massachusetts complied with the simple statement "[s]uch citation shall be signed ... by the violator" nor were any violators required to sign it. Bringing the issue up in court as part of a traffic hearing for dismissal based on technical violation of the no-fix requirements would always result in one or the other of two judicial decisions: "officer safety, denied" or simply "denied". So, though without doubt it is the law that "[s]uch citation shall be signed ... by the violator" and the nominal form of this rule existing in all other states is empirically followed to my knowledge, from this descriptive quotation of what the law is, it does not logically follow by necessity or empirically either what will occur or what ought to occur when these words are spoken. It has no predictive value just as the universal law has no predictive value.

Why was this particular "no-fix" law never enforced or complied with? Was there really a safety issue? Was the law not enforced so as to allow traffic courts to fix tickets by dismissing them for lack of the required violator signature when they wanted to do so — unfortunately, I never had the clout to use the missing violator signature as a means to fix the ticket (or any other means to fix the ticket). Was it not enforced because it was unnecessary: since the violator showed up in court, they must have gotten the ticket. Was it not enforced because there was no lack of notice so the signature requirement was not needed. There are many more possibilities. Was not the purpose of the "no-fix" law and its strict but simple procedural requirements to avoid all this questioning?

The law and this particular law as with any particular law has beautiful nominal and aesthetic meaning as verbiage especially when combined with other particular laws to create such universals as "motor vehicle law", "the rule of law", "Due Process", and so forth, but any Power as a matter of both logical necessity or empirical sense experience can reject it or comply with its "ought" requirements and with all the ought statements in the universals as they wish — for a reason, for any reason, or for no reason.

Though it states what ought to be done, neither logically, empirically, nor pragmatically does what ought to be done lead to what will be done logically, predictively, or pragmatically. The argument can be made that it ought to be done pragmatically because it works to control ticket fixing but the Powers are free logically, empirically, or pragmatically to make the conclusion that it ought not be done for some other reason or for no reason, so we are right back to the universal law having no logical, empirical, or pragmatic value. Despite knowing the meaning of the law descriptively as words, any normative meanings of the law are distinct and do not necessarily follow from these descriptions of what law is. Thus, it is perfectly legal for traffic citations not to be signed by the violator despite law stating they are to be signed by the violator and it is not illegal to issue citations that are not signed by the violator but legal to do so.

Nominally, the descriptive meaning of this law or of any law or rule of law, by law, or through law has predictive value but only nominally not empirically because, unlike science, there is no reality distinct from the normative meanings, and they have no logical relationship between the nominal descriptive meanings and any argument for predictive normative meaning that can be made from those nominal meanings. So, one can argue from the words "[s]uch citation shall be signed by said police officer and by the violator" to the words "such citations must or ought to be signed by the violator" with these words creating aesthetically pleasing argument, but that is it. One cannot use the words to create scientific language. Whatever predictive argument that can be made based on pragmatic concerns can be rejected based on normative concerns or based on no concerns.

This is why the funniest and most existentially accurate scene in the movie *My Cousin Vinny*[25] is the scene where the trial attorney Vincent LaGuardia "Vinny" Gambini played by Joe Pesci after stumbling on law through the whole movie finally gets his stuff together and learns the "law"; that is, some of the aesthetic nominals that make up the universal law. Toward the end of the trial, he concludes that a particular law does not allow a surprise expert witness to be used against a Defendant in a criminal trial based on such nominal aesthetics of the law such as Due Process, procedural due process, fairness, justice, rules of criminal procedure, and so forth. So, he makes a legal objection using this law to the admission on the last day of trial of a surprise expert witness to be used against his client Defendant in a criminal (murder) trial. The result is the judge looks at him and states: "that is a lucid, intelligent, well thought out objection. Overruled."

Why did or would a judge overrule such objection? You never know nor will know. Perhaps simply for no reason. All normative conclusions are irrational. Often perhaps even the judge does not know why one normative decision is made instead of another. The existential irrational normative decision is based on the existential private morality of the Power making it of which we

---

[25] Lynn, Jonathan. (1992). *My Cousin Vinny*. 20th Century Fox.

cannot speak. Once the judge starts talking about the decision and trying to explain it, it will be described not in existential meanings but in the meanings derived from use and usefulness and thus will involve pretending that normative decisions were rationally derived from descriptive ones such as: fairness required the prosecution be given an exception in this case.

Fairness did not require anything, what the judge considered to be fair as part of the judge's Will to Power over life required certain acts be done. Since the judge as a Power could enforce the judge's normative requirements upon the social group involved in the trial, the judge did and will do so as long as these norms can be executed upon by violence.

Please note that only a novice, ignorant, or delusional attorney would protest that the objection was made to preserve the record for appeal at which point the legality or illegality of the overruled objection will actually become known as law. Having the irrational normative decisions of one judge's morality reviewed by the irrational normative decisions of a group of judges' ethics is different in degree but not as a universal in the language discourse of normative language. As any experienced trial or appellate attorney who is honest enough to admit it will tell you (a vanishing and almost distinct animal[26]), in appeals especially appeals of serious matters such as murder cases, the appellate decision is based on whether the appellate court has an undisclosed belief that a party may be innocent or deserves a requested relief not on what objections were or were not made. Objections can be easily ignored or created on appeal if "justice requires" — which means as the appellate judges require. Not only is the irrational existential morality of an individual judge having such belief something of which we cannot speak as a matter of logic, but the reality as a matter of the ethics of the social group called appellate judges is something of which we cannot speak so instead they and we pretend

---

[26] *See generally*, Diviacchi, V., Ed. (2021). *The Law Illusion.* Creative Space Publishing.

the decision is rationally related to the facts of the case. As any experienced trial or appellate attorney who is honest enough to admit it will tell you, the facts on appeal usually have little or no relationship to the facts at trial or as they actually may have occurred.[27]

In November of 2016, *M.G.L.c. 90C, §2* was revised to encompass electronic signing by police and the requirement for violator signing was deleted. So, we will never known why the pragmatic goal of "officer safety" in Massachusetts — unlike every other state — allowed police legally to ignore the signing requirements of the no-fix law. The reason is irrelevant; there are an infinite number of reasons for there to have been no rule-following of the rule distinct from how the rule is actually followed — regardless of how one views the Rule-Following Paradox of Wittgenstein or even if one considers it a paradox.

The point is that no matter how much emphasis is placed on a normative statement, the Will to Power and Heart of Darkness of existential reality logically allows the normative statement to be ignored. It is delusional to say that a judge not following law is really not law nor making law. The execution upon a law is the only empirical reality or connection of any law to law as a universal. One can argue that a law did not allow Pontius Pilate as a matter of descriptive fact to order the Crucifixion. This would make a nice academic aesthetic argument that itself would have no meaning other than aesthetics. There was execution upon Pilate's decision therefore the crucifixion was legal and law and still is law regardless of whether or not it was wrong, immoral, evil, or whatever dispute one may have with that execution.

The rationality of any law and in Law goes in reverse from execution to facts, from normative statements to descriptive empirical statements. Murder is murder not because of the facts but

---

[27] For example, *See generally,* Rabin, R.L., Sugarman, S.D. (2003) *Torts Stories.* Foundation Press; *infra* at Part VIII.

because the execution of law as a murder conviction makes the facts murder. This is why a killer of dozens or hundreds is a serial killer but the killer of millions is a patriot and this is the Power of the Law.

For the moment, we will not get into the practical day-to-day irrational existential reality that allows even such simple normative statements as "shall be signed" to be ignored. This is a contemplation of a philosophy of law not a practical guide to law. As such, I must concentrate on a logical analysis of the meaning of the word "law" and be as analytical as possible given the existential universe of discourse of this essay. In the practical reality of the law, the ignoring of simple normative statements such as "shall be signed" can be descriptively explained in many ways: in practical reality, no one really knows or cares what law or any law is, but few if any would admit to this existential Heart of Darkness reality. Such contemplation on the practical reality of law should eventually occur once we decide on a philosophy of law.

The divide between law and decisions of legality and illegality gets subtle and hidden in more complicated empirical events but the forest can still be seen through the trees. For example, again we can go back to the cases of *Citizens United v. Federal Election Commission*, 558 U.S. 310 (2010) or *Goodridge v. Dept. of Public Health*, 798 N.E.2d 941 (Mass. 2003), in which the decisions total more than a hundred pages of verbiage and their interpretative literature make up a law library of law verbiage. As contemplated previously, the conclusions much more honestly could have been naturalized to science and written in a few lines:

1. Based on the life experience of the majority, we have concluded corporations are good for this country and therefore have decided they ought to be treated as persons for purposes of the First Amendment. Judgment shall enter forthwith. By the court.— *Citizens United et al*
2. Based on the life experience of the majority, we have concluded homosexuality is moral, medically not a disorder, and that homosexuals ought to be entitled to

get married. Judgment shall enter forthwith. By the court. — *Goodridge et al*

As contemplated previously, if the Powers-That-Be had written such honest decisions, there would have resulted truly democratic moral and ethical discourse throughout society and the government; there would have been demands for disclosure, discussion, and examination of the life experiences and personal morality and the beliefs in the majority's life experience that served as the basis for their normative conclusions; and there could have been honest and open discussion as to the normative soundness of their decisions. Unfortunately, what also could have occurred is the worse that could happen to law would occur: since this law and the law for now still relies on third parties to execute its judgment, there would be doubt as to whether execution upon the law would occur and thus law would lose its monopoly on violence. If the majority had written their decisions in the above straightforward and honest matter, would the judgments have been executed upon? That is, if the Defendants were in contempt of the order, would Law's monopoly on violence succeed in forcing compliance with the judgment or would the majority Powers-that-be risk losing their monopoly on violence?

In terms of descriptive reality, if the *Citizens* and *Goodridge* decisions had been written in the honest Ockham's Razor words of the above, most likely there would be lawless chaos and law would have failed in its social construct meaning in life: to be a final arbitrator of the ethical struggles that required its creation. It would no longer be law but just another ethics. No one wants that; no Power-that-be; no one in their Inner or Outer Parties; and no one whose existential leap to morality consists of a leap to the aesthetics of verbiage as law wants it.

So, instead the powers in *Citizens* and *Goodridge* wrote more than a hundred pages beautifully hiding the existential reality that they were using hidden irrational beliefs and their personal leap to morality to create and enforce normative conclusions on all of society through their monopoly on violence. By writing such hundreds of pages of beautiful verbiage having no descriptive value just nominal and aesthetic value, the Powers were able to execute upon *Citizens* and *Goodridge*. Again, existentialists must not underestimate the power of such artistry; it marks the difference between life and death for many individuals and for entire societies. Whether the Powers-that-be who wrote the aesthetic intellectual beauty of *Citizens* and *Goodridge* actually knew what they were doing or did it instinctively from their Will to Power will never be known. This question is similar to asking whether any individual Christian really believes in God or are they just pretending. Since there is no private language that would give us an insight into their reality of which we cannot speak, we will never know.

There are actually and literary libraries of law review articles written by law professors about *Citizens* and *Goodridge* and all other case law that no one reads and no one cares about except for other law professors. The situation is analogous to painters painting and sharing paintings only with each other and deciding by consensus what formulaic combination of paint, material, brush strokes, brushes, images, and such is to be used in order to consider a painting "good" for purposes of calling and ranking each other and thus their students as artists. Law is a self-contained, self-replicating aesthetic wordgame analogous to playing any game such as chess, checkers, Monopoly, or Dungeon and Dragons only the losers suffer real empirical loss; the powers have an actual power of life and death through the beauty of their aesthetics and the worshipers of their aesthetics game.

Law is self-contained except for one attribute: in the end, the aesthetic truth of the law can and does kill — physically, financially, personally, and more — through decisions of legality and illegality empirically enforced by execution.

Another famous historic yet simple but not too simple example of the power and distinction between the universal law and of particular laws is the Crucifixion where the Power-That-Be Pontius Pilate states descriptively of the accused before him, "I find in him no fault at all". Yet, he legally executes the miserable soul before him saying *quid est veritas*.[28] The descriptive reality of what is going on has nothing to do with the normative reality of law. The aesthetic beauty of the Roman law allowed for the execution decision to go either way. The Power Pilate decided to go for the crucifixion and he got away with it regardless of what descriptive reality was or was not. Because he got away with it and many more by his monopoly on violence, it was legal and the acts of the condemned illegal.

Do not get delusional and starting talking as if there is a reality behind the words of Pontius Pilate and the execution upon them: saying such things as what Pontius Pilate did was unjust and not fair. Remember, law is simply an ethics with a monopoly on violence. It exists as a social construct to maintain order among struggling social construct ethics lacking such a monopoly on violence. Ethics itself is a social construct existing to maintain order among individual moralities in the social group. Just as there is no rational connection between ethics and any morality other than just the need to have power over any morality, there is no connection between law and ethics other than to have power over all ethics that do not have a monopoly on violence and to keep any other ethics from getting a monopoly on violence. If Pontilus Pilate was able to execute upon a particular law, then what he did as a Power-that-be controlling the monopoly on violence of the law was legal, ethical, and moral regardless of whether or not it was moral, immoral, or amoral by any other morality. What Pilate did was pragmatically true because it maintained the survival of the Roman social construct Will to Power as exhibited by their great victory at the Siege of Massada and the Roman Empire continuing for another 1500 years. It was replaced in the West by the Holy Roman Empire much earlier. However, both the continuation of the Empire in the East and its replacement in the West resulted from the pragmatic

---

[28] John 18:38. *The Holy Bible Saint Joseph Textbook Edition*. (1963). Catholic Book Publishing Co.

truth of the events of the Crucifixion and the morality struggles and social construct struggles and associated history it started and created. Whether what Pilate did was just or fair is a meaningful question only to an existentialist who has made a leap to morality and what to do with the answer would be the follow-up question an existentialist should ask as part of their individual existential morality. There is no question that the Crucifixion was legal and the rationalization for its legality occurred after the decision was made by Pilate to wash his hands and to allow it.

The aesthetic truth of the meaning of the universe of Law is real and as real as mathematics in science but its reality is purely normative and nominal and its truth aesthetic so unlike mathematics in science it has no predictive value. The Law is as real and as real as any particular law because it is the aesthetic truth of Law that allows particular laws to kill. The only descriptive truth in Law however consists of the execution upon particular laws, these acts are the nominal equivalent to numbers in science. It is through execution that the pragmatic value of Law is created through legality and illegal acts.

D. *Law, Its Truth, and Its Legality Are Distinct Wordgames that* *May Be but Are Not Necessarily Logically Related*

As with science, there is often an inconsistency between theory and practice. The difference being that with science the theory and practice both involve empirical sense experience outside scientific language. For law, there is nothing outside its language except irrational normative intentions of which we cannot speak and its execution upon those intentions. There is no logical or even rational relationship between what is and what ought to be. Thus, regardless of how accurately we describe what the law or any particular law is and what is nominally true under law, there is no way to conclude or to make any descriptive predictions of what will be the execution upon any law — that is what acts are legal or illegal empirically. Legality and illegality will only be true pragmatically: can a law be executed upon by its monopoly on violence or what is it the Powers can get away with executing. Whether it can be executed upon is the judgment call made by the Powers. Since they are human with a Heart of Darkness, one factor and perhaps the only factor in that judgment call for purposes of legality and illegality is whether execution maintains or strengthens the law's monopoly.

What any particular law existentially "is" at any given moment is usually simple enough to determine especially in a modern Technological Society in which all particular laws of even trivial significance are usually in written form; just ask anyone involved in executing its monopoly on violence what law is. What is legal — or illegal for that matter — is a different matter and is much more convoluted. It gets much more convoluted when dealing with more complicated matters than traffic citations.

It is tempting here to object to the pragmatic meaning of truth for legality by arguing it is not whether "the act maintains or strengthens the law's monopoly on violence" but rather whether the law maintains or strengthens the intent of its creation: the existential continuance of the social group or groups whose social construct the law is intended as a means for arbitrating their struggles for power (their ethics) among themselves. This may have been a sound objection in prior history when law was faced with a normative force opposing it as an equal power to its monopoly on violence such as Christianity. However, in Technological Society, this type of objection ignores the existential Will to Power reality that started and continues the whole irrational process of creating normative language starting with morality onto ethics and then to law and the existential Heart of Darkness of the individuals involved — especially of the individuals involved in enforcement of the monopoly on violence. Ultimately, all normative statements of good and evil derive from individual Will to Power. In any social construct given a monopoly on violence, the pragmatic truth required to maintain the monopoly and the associated nominal truths of the norms enforced by that monopoly become one and the same pragmatically just as morality and divine or natural law would be one and the same for a hermit in a one person universe.

Just as a hermit would have no need to question morality except in relation to its success or failure in achieving individual Will to Power over the universe, a social construct with a monopoly on violence would have no need to question its norms except in relation to its success or failure in achieving and maintaining its monopoly on violence.

Even if an existentialist makes a leap to morality concluding something ought to be in order to give meaning to our lives and the universe, we can reject what ought to be and do something else for the same reason. The leap into morality is irrational; there is no meaning in life or in the universe and there is no logical way to go from what "is" to the perspective or evaluative what "ought" to be of morality as Hume's Law established centuries ago. The same is true for ethics that is a social construct by social groups to survive individual morality struggles and thus for law that is essentially an ethics with a monopoly on violence.

There is no rational way for those involved in maintaining and enforcing the monopoly on violence to create normative statements of what morality, ethics, or the social construct of law ought to be from what the Law is. At best they can describe what it is nominally at any given moment. The only universal attribute of the law at all times and places is its monopoly on violence. Thus, this is the only universal and descriptive attribute that those enforcing the monopoly on violence will universally enforce — all else is subject to irrational change as part of the struggles that make Law a necessary social construct for survival in the struggle by humanity or any human society against the universe. Throwing our Heart of Darkness into this mess, without doubt, the attribute of a monopoly on violence will be the only descriptive fact universally enforced as legal and thus this is the only attribute that will be omnipresent in all decisions of legality or illegality.

E. Indeterminacy in the Language of Law Does not Existentially Derive from Indeterminacy of Language but from Individual and Social Construct Will to Power

"It's a beautiful thing, the destruction of words" (Orwell. 1977. p. 65-66). It is tempting at this point to start implying and contemplating the serious philosophical issues of the indeterminacy of language and Wittgenstein's Rule Following Paradox and fake philosophy of law issues like "hard cases" and "weak cases" in law. This would be error because the difference in the meanings and in the aesthetic truth of the law and the pragmatic truth of legality and illegality is not based solely on use but on the usefulness of this word; that is, it is controlled by the individual Will to Power of the Power-that-be using it. What is meant by a word such as "vehicle" in a law may be indeterminate, however whether or not it is indeterminate as a word is not decisive in any decision of legality or illegality. If a word, regardless of how determinate it may be, has a meaning inconsistent with the Will to Power intentions of the Powers of which we cannot speak, they will not follow the rule or will create a rule around it — if they can get away with doing so by their monopoly on violence and without endangering that monopoly.

Without doubt, indeterminacy of language results in rule following problems but the problems are exaggerated by the Powers and their philosophers of law. Indeterminancy of language was not a problem in *Roe v. Wade, Citizens United,* and *Goodridge* or even in my traffic citation example. The language was very determinate and clear, the judges simply did not agree with the determination and clarity. The judge majority in *Roe v. Wade, Citizens United,* and *Goodridge* and the vast majority of appellate cases were and are very determinate about what they were and are doing but used indeterminate wordgames as the means to hide their determinacy. Abortion was legalized, corporations were made persons, and marriage was redefined not because the indeterminate nature of the law at issue but because a majority of the judges reading the language wanted very specific determinate results, concluded these results "ought" to be, and then reverse rationalized the result by aesthetically pleasing language of what "is".

There was nothing indeterminate about the rationalization either: they knew what they were doing; they knew the meanings of the words; they knowingly and intentionally did it; and they expected to be able to execute upon what they did by violence if need be. Otherwise, they would not have done it. By saying they knew the meanings of the words and knowing and intentionally used them as they wanted to use, I am saying they knew the usefulness of the words to the use they were making of them. This is the reality of even the simplest of factual court cases and legal issues that is revealed in any simple descriptive history of jurisprudence for those that have little experience in actual legal work.[29]

There is probably more language indeterminancy in the practical descriptive day-to-day experience of the lowest of plebeian courts such as traffic courts than there is in the esteemed ranks of the Supremes. At least in the lower courts just as in local politics, the Powers must look in the eye of the individual whose life, family, fortune, and future they are destroying. In the Supremes, all they look at is the aesthetics of the universals of Law. They need not even come down from on high after the legal battle is fought below and when the dust and smoke of the battle clear to shoot the wounded, they simply have others do their killing for them.

The rule "[s]uch citation shall be signed ... by the violator" is about as simple a normative rule as one will find in law. In terms of "form of life", the acts that give meaning to this rule are clear to anyone with basic proficiency in the American language. All indeterminacy of language issues and the Rule Following Paradox apply to this simple rule to create ambiguity if one is looking to create ambiguity. It is a finite rule based on finite possibilities; reality is made up of infinite possibilities. What is meant by citation? What is meant by violator? What is meant by signing? Is signing *de jure* based on the judge's view of the facts equivalent to signing *de facto*? On and on, if one wanted. At some point, as with Ockham's Finger, the possible infinite chain of rule-following paradoxes need to stop and you need to move your finger. At that

---

[29] For example, *see generally*, Rabin, R.L., Sugarman, S.D. (2003). *Torts Stories*. Foundation Press.; *infra* at Part VII.

point, the law and its truth is not made "hard" or "weak" by language but by problems the Powers-that-be speaking the rule have with its usefulness when followed. If it is inconsistent with their Will to Power intentions of which we cannot speak, they will not follow the rule. As shown by Kripkenstein versions of the Rule Following Paradox of Wittgenstein, such problems can even occur or be created through logic with the simplest of rules and algorithms of addition.[30] (So it appears that Orwell's O'Brien of *1984* did have a logical basis for arguing that 2 + 2 = 5.)

If one can logically create such truth problem in science and mathematics that logically deal with a separate reality then in their own language — at least for science if not mathematics — there is no way to remove normative rule-following paradoxes with even the simplest or so-called "weakest" of law problems that have no reality outside its own language.

Just as one cannot go from what "is" to what "ought" to be, one cannot go from what "ought" to be to what "ought" to be if one does not want it to be. The reverse rationality only occurs if it is consistent with the Will to Power of those rationalizing. This is the nature of normative statements, they state what ought to occur but have no predictive meaning except nominally. Anyone, especially a Power-that-be with a monopoly on violence, can always decide they do not want what ought-to-be to be. Unlike scientific predictive statements nominally hiding as normative statements, in pure normative language there is no reality separate from the normative language. Again, in scientific language, if one predictively calculates what *"p=mv"* ought to be and then decides not to use the answer when intending to send a rocket to the moon, your intention may fail and will be pragmatically false. If one normatively states what *"p=mv"* ought to be and then one ignores it when descriptively attempting to send a rocket to the moon because one normatively concludes it is evil for "p" to be a certain value or for

---

[30] Kripke, S. (1982). *Wittgenstein on Rules and Private Language*. Harvard University Press.

rockets to go to the moon, the result is still true normatively despite the rocket not making it to the moon. The truth of a normative statement has nothing to do with anything outside of the normative language — including its irrational foundation premises.

This conclusion answers one practical question that I and most attorneys that have done significant appellate work based on their own trials have: why do the facts stated in appellate decision have little if any relationship to the factual events as they actually happened? They have no such relationship because appellate facts are rationalizations of irrational normative decisions intended to hide the irrationality of the normative decision. Appellate decisions act essentially as independent abstract opinions on fictional facts. The facts stated in appellate or in any judicial decision are not descriptive but only meaningful in relation to the rationalization of the irrational normative decision made by the Power. The underlying facts are essentially irrelevant until the decision is made and facts are chosen as necessary to rationalize the irrational decision.

VII. Unnecessary Verbiage and Objections

"Don't for heaven's sake, be afraid of talking nonsense! But you must pay attention to your nonsense" (Wittgenstein, L. 1984. p. 56e)

The existential meaning of law as a universal appears relatively simple. It is because of this simplicity that it will be rejected by the Powers-that-be in addition to rejection based on their self-interest need to hide their power. As contemplated later however, it is the simplicity of this existentialist philosophy of law that will give it pragmatic truth for use and that is useful for existentialism or nihilism to act in opposition to the unopposed monopoly on violence of Western Law.

The self-interested need to hide a self-interest Will to Power is universal in all morality, ethics, and thus Law. Luckily, existentialism has none of these so we do not need to hide it and ought not to hide it when we make a leap to morality such as by deciding we should not hide it when we make a leap to morality. It is part of our Heart of Darkness. It will always be there as a source of opposition to any philosophical contemplation rejecting as a matter of metaphysics not just aesthetics but any meaning for life. Do not forget the intent of this contemplation: I have not assumed law to be a good in life and am not concerned with justifying law and its power as is true of almost all modern philosophy of law. My intent is to discover what law is in relation to the existential truth that life is a meaningless endeavor yet an individual has made an existential leap to giving it meaning.

Despite claiming a desire to be naturalized to science, the Powers-that-be of the law avoid Ockham's Razor as one avoids the plague. This is especially an accurate description in the modern big firm business of law dependent on the billable hour method for a large part of its profits that in turn pays for the academic universe of discourse that is modern philosophy of law protected from plebeian reality by its patrician safe places.

An objection based on simplicity to my meaning for law and legality as worthless argues that such a simple existential definition of law as a universal and as a particular is too general to be of any worth. This type of objection is outright fallacious nonsense. Any universal by its very nature is and should be simple and general; its use and usefulness is its ability to encompass a large reality of other meanings in our struggles with the complexity of the indifference and antagonism of the universe. Despite having achieved a concept of law as a universal, a concept of legality, and of their distinct truths, these simple conclusions involve an infinite amount of technical pragmatic problems needing to be solved on a daily basis. This should not be discouraging nor should we immediately jump to the intelligentsia conclusion that this existential meaning is too simple or general to be useful and thus start creating rules of recognition, rules of change, and rules of adjudication and other such nonsense.

Bertrand Russell described mathematics, "as the only subject in which we never know what we are talking about or whether what we are saying is true" (Russell, B. 1901. p. 1). Even if existentialism finds itself in the same position as mathematics regarding the philosophy of law, this would be a significant and material improvement upon its present delusional state.

Also, as contemplated earlier and as I will contemplate later, one must not underestimate the importance of a purely nominal aesthetic meaning for truth in law that is otherwise meaningless because this nominal meaning also provides aesthetic meaning and with the associated power of aesthetics. As I have written before, a word may lose its meaning but not its power; in fact, in many ways both in law and in religion, language becomes more powerful as it becomes more meaningless in any sense but aesthetics. For words or wordgames with no predictive value such as law, aesthetic value is as good a value as any other value. Nothing is more aesthetically pleasuring to the rational mind than listening to words that sound nice. For example, if asked to define a messcook's duties aboard a submarine, the following two definitions are of equal meaning just nominally different:
1. aqua-thermal treatment of ceramics, aluminum, and steel under a constrained environment;
2. washing dishes and utensils in warm water under the supervision of his chief.

For sure, there is a nominal difference in meaning but which is more aesthetically pleasing? Meaning derives both from use and usefulness. Just as Nietzsche supposedly according to a popular adage defined poetry as "the art of creating ripples in swallow water to give the impression they are deep", the universal "law" defined by modern philosophy of law with its nominal aesthetic value for truth can be described as the art of creating religious meaning for secular normative statements even if its truth serves no use or usefulness but such aesthetics.

In the days when secular law was competing with the Divine and Natural Law of Christianity for normative power, nominal aesthetically pleasing words were a great marketing tool in the same way such words are in all marketing and advertising. Now that the law has no normative opposition, it still needs to maintain some version of aesthetic truth. Since it lacks any version of empirical or pragmatic truth other than maintaining its own power through violence, the power of its nominal aesthetic truth should not be underestimated as a means in use and useful to the Powers to justify that violence.

Before getting into more detailed contemplation of legality, its pragmatic truth, and the pragmatic problems presented by the duality attributes of law, there are objections that should be covered because this existential meaning of law is similar though still materially different to the legal positivist definition of law by legal philosopher John Austin that legal philosophy has spent over a century trying to ignore, avoid, and get around through numerous objections. Most likely, if anyone is reading this, these same objections will be presented to my existentialist definition of law. It will help our contemplation to understand the difference between the existentialist definition of law and Austin's legal positivist definition and the objections to it. Modern philosophy of law considered the premises of its creator or innovator John Austin to be too simple, regardless of their practicality, and as lowering the majesty of the law by making it equal to that of a gunman's threat. This practicality and lowering has the risk of lowering the power of law in relation to religion, its only opposition, and of lowering the practice and the teaching of law to a craft or trade. Given the Heart of Darkness shared by lawyers and law professors with the rest of humanity, this was unacceptable. So, there came along H.L.A. Hart and legal positivism to market law as a science.

At a minimum, such comparison will further highlight the descriptive difference between the wordgame of law and the wordgame of science to which law wants to be naturalized. Scientists love Ockham's Razor and relatively simple formulae that allow them to concentrate on the infinite amount of technical pragmatic problems needing to be solved to achieve predictive value and meaning for their words. Law professors and most lawyers, especially those making money on an hourly fee basis, hate both the Razor and simplicity in thought, word, and action but do not admit their hate of the Razor. Instead, they go to great extremes either unintentionally or intentionally to hide it.

A.   *Legal-Positivism*

"Law, by definition, cannot obey the same rules as nature" (Camus. 2020. p. 58). John Austin essentially started the modern fad of trying to make law a science, or, as philosophers of law now call their fad, of naturalizing law to science. To do this, he argued it was necessary to purge law of all morality and to define legality in strictly empirical terms. Austin argued law is a social construct consisting of commands issued by a sovereign to members of an independent political society enforced by sanctions and having two attributes: (1) law and morality are separate and (2) all human-made laws can be traced back to human lawmakers. Existentially, we now know there is no such thing as meaning in "strictly empirical terms". All empirical description is theory laden. For the wordgame law, the theory begins with irrational leaps of faith to morality with struggles among moralities resulting in irrational leaps to social constructs called ethics with struggles among ethics finally resolved by irrational leaps to law — essentially an ethics with a monopoly on violence. In an existential sense, law is purged of morality and ethics but only of morality and ethics with which it disagrees. Law is itself the ultimate solitary ethics that conquers all normative wordgames below it — until its monopoly on violence is conquered by one or more moralities or ethics it is unable to control by violence which then become the new law in town.

Adding the word "sovereign" to our existentialist meaning of law is descriptively, normatively, predictively, and pragmatically worthless — the only meanings that matter so far --- because it is included in the meaning of "monopoly". The same is true of the word "command" because all commands are normative statements but not all normative statements are commands. A normative statement states what we ought to do. A command is limited to what we "must do" or "should do". This may appear to be only a nominal difference in law because an ought statement that can be enforced by a monopoly on violence acts as a command in pragmatic reality, however this description is not accurate. Even in the military we were instructed that in theory at least we had the legal option and even the legal duty to disobey illegal commands — we ought to disobey illegal commands. Thus ought statements are not the same but encompass commands.

According to legal positivism, the key concepts of law, sovereign, command, sanction, and duty are definable by empirically verifiable social facts. This is nonsense. They are definable only by law; in the absence of a social construct of normative statements with a monopoly on violence to define a legal sovereign, command, sanction, and duty, there is no way to empirically define any of these terms because regardless of the empirical facts there is lacking the necessary theory by which they can be defined.

1. Morality and Ethics are the Fuel of the Fuel Cell Container that is Law. Austin and logical positivism hides its existential delusions about morality by arguing a pretend complete division between morality and law according to which no moral judgment is necessary to determine what the law is; they argue morality is only a concern for what the law ought to be. They claim no particular morality but this is false or otherwise they would not be concerned with the meaning of social constructs. To be concerned with what law is requires having already made a leap to morality. One does not discover law as one does science by tripping over it, one must look for law. Austin himself for example was a utilitarian who argued laws should promote the greatest happiness of society.

Scientific language is a fabric of intertwined weaves of sense experience and theory. Though legal positivists are correct that law is not an intertwined weave of morality, ethics, and law, it is incorrect to state morality and law are distinct and separate. Law is the social construct container of a society's moral and ethics struggles. While morality and ethics engage in their struggles with each other and the meaninglessness of the universe, the law is the container that by violence compresses and contains these struggles within it. Morality and ethics compressed and struggling within the container of the law, because they lack the law's monopoly power on violence, existentially affect the container that is law only by leaks and weaknesses in the law's monopoly on violence. The only other means for morality or ethics to affect law would be by a normative force from outside the container. What law "ought to be" is a meaningful question only for the Powers-that-be controlling the force that is the container, and they have already decided what the law ought to be: what it is. The morality of the Powers is the only morality that ultimately has any meaning in the law but this is still a morality. One can no more remove morality, ethics, and their struggles from the container that is law than one can remove fuel from a fuel cell.

Existentially, when a Power-that-be — those whose normative conclusions control law's monopoly on violence — view the law stating "[s]uch citation shall be signed ... by the violator" and conclude it is legal not to sign the citation or conclude it is illegal but decide to do nothing about it, the individual Power-that-be is making a moral decision as well as a legal decision and one of law. It is a moral decision of what acts ought to be, of what is good or bad. If this decision involved a struggle with other moral decisions by other Powers on the same law and legality or illegality, the judge is also making an ethics decision. Finally, the decision is one of law and legality or illegality because the moral and ethical decisions can be enforced by a monopoly on violence. These are all decisions within the same fuel cell container of law. The only difference is in their meaning for the word truth. The truth of morality and ethics may have irrational norms and truths of which we cannot speak. The truth of law is nominal and aesthetic. The truth of legality and illegality will be pragmatic: can the Powers-that-be execute by violence the decision if they want to do so or will the decision protect, enhance, or endanger that monopoly on violence?

For existentialism, there is no question of what law "ought to be"; the question is what morality ought to be. The existential question, the only one that matters for the absurd individual making a leap to morality, is what ought to be good or evil. Once that leap is made, if it is made, law is simply an obstacle for making what "ought to be" be.

Again, I must not forget the intent of this contemplation. Life and the universe have no meaning or purpose, it just is. I give it meaning or purpose by a leap to morality. I am only concerned with a philosophy of law to have an understanding of its relationship to my morality. The relationship is simple and is as follows: it does not care about my morality. The law only cares about maintaining its monopoly on violence. Its truth of good and evil is decided by whether or not it can execute upon this monopoly.

For the law, the Will to Power is an end in itself and provides meaning and truth for its wordgame. It is the nature of law to require and to have a monopoly on violence in order to control the struggles between moralities and ethics. The truth of law is purely pragmatic: does it work to maintain law. If it does not, the only option for law is to strengthen its attempts to create a monopoly on violence. It does not exist to promote diversity but to negate it. Diversity means struggle. For the morality and ethics of which we cannot speak logically and therefore have no wordgames, that of which we cannot speak logically is its truth. This morality and ethics of which we cannot speak is not the morality and ethics of either the morality, ethics, or law of which we are speaking.

For the wordgames of morality and ethics through which we try to speak about the truth of which we cannot speak, what is truly good or evil is also pragmatic. What is good or evil is dependent on what works to solve the individual or group struggle so that the individual or social group can survive their struggle with the universe.

For law, it resolves all moral and ethical struggles through the pragmatic truth of keeping its monopoly on violence. It is not descriptively accurate to state that no moral judgment is necessary to determine what the law is but only in determining what the law ought be. Moral and ethical judgments consisting of the morality and ethics of the Powers controlling the monopoly have already decided what the law ought to be: what the law is.

2.   Objections. In addition to the objection that my existentialist meaning of law is too simple to be useful, the objections made to Austin's logical positivism will probably also be made to my existentialist meaning of law. They fall into the following categories: (1) violence or the threat of violence do not give rise to legal obligation, otherwise there would be no essential difference between a gunman's threat ("your money or your life") and law; 2) most legal systems include rules that do not punish but empower persons or just specify ways that legal rules may be identified or changed; 3) in many modern legal systems, it is difficult to identify a "sovereign" in Austin's sense or a Power-that-be in my sense; 4) defining legal duties in terms of obligation created by violence does not explain why laws remain in force despite changes in the persons or entities using the violence. These objections are considered valid in modern philosophy of law only because there is presumption that law is a "good" despite pretend arguments that they are not incorporating morality into their philosophy of law. Again, to get into philosophy of law and contemplate what law is, one must have already made the leap to morality. Most patricians and modern philosophers of law either make this leap naturally as some type of predestination or make it intentionally but hide their leap in order to hide their status as Powers-that-be or their morality seeking to become Powers-that-be.

a) Mob Island. In the absence of Divine Law or Natural Law that existentialism knows does not exist, there is no essential difference between a gunman's threat and law except that for the threat to be law, it must occur within the context of a mob or social construct of more than a couple of persons: either a group of gunmen or one gunman that is making threats within a group of persons. If a criminal mob or gunman in one social group escaped to an island inhabited by another social group and took it over with a monopoly on violence, then this mob or gunman becomes the Powers-that-be of mob island with the mob's rules, oaths, codes of conduct, contract rules, pragmatic obligations of care, rules of inheritance, family rules of care, and rules for maintenance and distribution of wealth becoming its procedural law, criminal law, contract law, tort law, estate law, probate law, and so forth.

All Powers-that-be will not admit to such reality of mob

island because they do not want to admit it. Also, most inhabitants of mob island will not admit to this because the vast majority of humanity (89% in the United States according to Gallup[31]) believe in God and therefore believe in some form of natural or divine law as the source of secular law. Therefore their belief will be that the law of mob island must involve such form of divine or natural justice not just pragmatic truth. However, as contemplated in *Why Tolerate Law,* once the monopoly on violence successfully defeats religion as a normative force on the island as it has in Technological Society, religion becomes simply another morality or ethics tolerated by this monopoly on violence that need not be tolerated or can be outright eliminated any time any law wants.

This religious belief in a normative force in the universe consisting of a divine or natural law is no different from the multiple of moralities and ethics compressed by force into the social construct fuel cell container that is Law. As with all the other compressed moralities and ethics, the only means by which religious belief is able to affect or become any law is through cracks, leaks, or weaknesses in the container or with the aid of outside force. Since these inside or outside forces will not be part of the Powers-that-be whose normative values are intended solely to maintain the monopoly on violence, all these effects both internal and external will be illegal. Only if and when they succeed and thus become part of the Powers-that-be, will these effects now become legal, law, and the Law cycle begins anew.

b) Ephemerally Non-Violent Laws. Though criminal law is the most obvious example of the universal attributes of law at work, most legal systems also include rules that do not punish but empower persons and also ways that law may be

---

[31] Newport, Frank. (2016). "Most Americans Still Believe in God." *Gallup Polls.* http://www.gallup.com/poll/193271/americans-believe-god.aspx

identified or changed. The difference between criminal law and all other laws is one of degree not substance or essence. Ultimately, the only difference between rules that empower or are procedural from laws that empower or are procedural is that the legal ones and laws can be enforced by a monopoly on violence. The enforcement of all rules ultimately depends on law and Law enforces itself. Philosophers of law see this ephemeral objection as a valid objection because most never practiced law or if they did they practiced it as representatives of the rich and powerful for whom there never was nor is a need to rob and steal because there exists a multiple of legal rules and laws allowing them to rob and steal — only it is not called robbery and theft. As with appellate judges, most philosophers of law like to watch from on high the legal battle fought below, and when the dust and smoke of the battle clear, they come down out of the hills and shoot the wounded.

    *c) **Who are the Powers-that-be?*** Asking this question and objecting to my meaning for the universal law based on an inability to identify the sovereign or Powers-that-be reveals a misunderstanding of the nature of philosophy generally, analytical and existential philosophy in particular, of words generally, and of what universals are — either in terms of realism or nominally as simply a word. Using "... a substantive makes us look for a thing that corresponds to it" (Wittgenstein. 2009. p. 106), but this is not how wordgames work. The meaning of words are their use and usefulness. Though there are distinct differences in the use and usefulness of universals in normative language and in scientific language, ultimately as stated before, the meaning of any word is a relationship between the intentions of the speaker and the acts associated with that word. We cannot speak about the intentions except through the acts associated with them though we existentially know they are there. Whether the acts are free or determined is irrelevant to this contemplation.

    The intentions are an existential reality of which we cannot speak, they are the substance of consciousness that leads to language, logic, and everything else. However, the acts aspect are visible sense experience. I cannot specially identify the "Powers-that-be" in the same way I cannot specially identify redness except by acting upon something red nor can a scientist identify photons except by watching data on a particular instrument, such does not make either word meaningless. Either word is useful for the acts and events associated with them when spoken. I have no idea what another person is thinking when I say "red", but I know when I say "red" they usually, not always, but usually go to an object whose color I reference by the word "red". No scientist has ever seen nor will they see a "photon", but they have seen what experiments are conducted and what data appears on experimental equipment when that word is used:

> Although I'm often guilty of it myself, I think it's a little misleading for physicists to keep harping on about 'wave-like' and 'particle-like' behavior," he wrote. "We have a great mathematical theory which tells us what photons…actually do. And then we have the human tendency to draw analogies and say 'hmm, in this case that looks like what I expect from a water wave' and 'but in this case that looks like what I expect from a billiard ball.' But photons are neither water waves nor billiard balls. ...
>
> ... If two ripples cross in a pool, and I reach a cupped hand in and pull out a handful of water to ask you 'which ripple are these water molecules from?' there is no answer.
>
> There is no answer because it's not a well-posed question, not because there is any deep mystery to the physics of water waves. ...
>
> In the end, quantum mechanics is the same. When you ask careful, experimentally testable questions, there is no paradox. ...
>
> What it teaches us is that we haven't yet figured out how to think about quantum mechanics right – not that there is any

problem with the theory itself or how we use it to make predictions. (Stein, B., Steinberg, A. 2015. p. 1)

As with a scientist searching for a mathematical wordgame with sufficient descriptive meaning and its subset predictive meaning to give pragmatic truth, I am searching for a philosophy of law wordgame that will give sufficient descriptive meaning to give pragmatic truth to my leap to morality in an existential reality devoid of morality. The word 'law' as a universal is a normative wordgame by one or more persons or things acting through a monopoly on violence. By logical necessity, this wordgame entails "one or more persons or things acting through a monopoly on violence", these are the "Powers-that-be".

A better question would be, can I identify specific Powers-that-be at specific moments or at any specific moment? Yes, I can. I can identify plenty of those from the President and the Supremes to the police officers and prosecutors who randomly and arbitrarily decide who they will arrest and prosecute and who they will not. Most important, I can identify one who is not a Power-that-be: myself. Neither the law nor any law cares about any leap to morality I have made and most likely that I will ever make. I am inconsequential to the law and have no say in or control of the normative wordgame they enforce by a monopoly on violence. The aesthetics of democracy pretending to give me a voting choice between Mutt or Jeff and Beavis or Butthead is not better than the aesthetics of poetry giving shallow waters the appearance of depth. It is logically possible that everyone but me in the world is a Power-that-be but such reality would not change anything.

Since we are dealing with an existential reality, if my "I am" is the only individual left out of the law wordgame and its Powers, this is enough to give my philosophy of law existential value.

However, I doubt I am alone in being left out of the Law's Powers-that-be; in fact, I believe there are billions of us in the modern world. I must not forget the ratio of guards to prisoners in World War II legal killings and genocide. In a law-abiding society, it only takes a handful of individuals with a monopoly on violence not only to normatively tell people what to do but descriptively to create a form of life wordgame controlling their actions even onto death. These Powers-that-be are as Orwell described the Party of his *1984*:

> As compared with their opposite numbers in past ages, the new aristocracy is less avaricious, less tempted by luxury, hungrier for pure power, and, above all, more conscious of what they were doing and more intent on crushing opposition. This last difference was cardinal. By comparison with that existing today, all the tyrannies of the past were half-hearted and inefficient. The ruling groups were always infected to some extent by liberal ideas, and were content to leave loose ends everywhere, to regard only the overt act, and to be uninterested in what their subjects were thinking.
> ..
> In principle, membership [in the Party] is not hereditary. The child of Inner Party parents is in theory not born into the Inner Party. ... . Nor is there any racial discrimination, or any marked domination of one province by another. Jews, Negroes, South Americans of pure Indian blood are to be found in the highest ranks of the Party, and the administrators of any area are always drawn from the inhabitants of that area. ... Its rulers are not held together by blood-ties but by adherence to a common doctrine. It is true that our society is stratified, and very rigidly stratified, on what at first sight appear to be hereditary lines. There is far less to-and-fro movement between the different groups than happened under capitalism or even in the pre-industrial age. Between the two branches of the Party there is a certain amount of interchange, but only so much as will ensure that weaklings are excluded from the Inner Party and that ambitious members of the Outer Party are made harmless by allowing them to rise. Proletarians, in practice, are not allowed to graduate into the Party. The most gifted among them, who might possibly become nuclei of discontent, are simply marked down by the Thought Police and eliminated.

But this state of affairs is not necessarily permanent, nor is it a matter of principle. The Party is not a class in the old sense of the word. It does not aim at transmitting power to its own children, as such; and if there were no other way of keeping the ablest people at the top, it would be perfectly prepared to recruit an entire new generation from the ranks of the proletariat. In the crucial years, the fact that the Party was not a hereditary body did a great deal to neutralize opposition. The older kind of Socialist, who had been trained to fight against something called 'class privilege' assumed that what is not hereditary cannot be permanent. He did not see that the continuity of an oligarchy need not be physical, nor did he pause to reflect that hereditary aristocracies have always been short-lived, whereas adoptive organizations such as the Catholic Church have sometimes lasted for hundreds or thousands of years. The essence of oligarchical rule is not father-to-son inheritance, but the persistence of a certain world-view and a certain way of life, imposed by the dead upon the living. A ruling group is a ruling group so long as it can nominate its successors. The Party is not concerned with perpetuating its blood but with perpetuating itself. Who wields power is not important, provided that the hierarchical structure remains always the same. (Orwell, G. 1977. pp. 264-65).

d) *The status of legal duties are not dependent on the monopoly on violence, the monopoly is the legal duty.* The objection that defining legal obligation in terms of an obligation created by violence or by the threat of violence by a Power does not explain how legal obligations stay in force despite changes in these Powers-that-be assumes that legal obligation is different from the violence or threat of violence of which law holds a monopoly. There is no difference in obligation nominally nor based on any sense experience with law. This objection again derives from the hidden leap of faith made by modern philosophers of law to law as a good, despite and perhaps as a substitute for rejecting divine and natural law, in which they either are or want to be Powers-that-be themselves. They therefore assume, either intentionally or unintentionally, that whatever law is that it has a separate "legal" obligation that is distinct from any other type of obligation. This is nonsense. For the existentialist individual who is not a Power-that-be, the legal obligation is the same as the obligation one has to a mob of gunmen with a gun pointed at one's head.

If the monopoly on violence disappears, the obligation to comply with the normative statements that were enforced by that monopoly disappear — there is no "legal" obligation distinct from the gun to the head. The difficulty is deciding empirically when the monopoly has disappeared. Such decision involves obvious risks that are behind the scope of this essay at present. An obvious example of the unsoundness of this objection empirically is our American Revolution and even the Nuremberg Trials. If the minority criminals under British law we call Founding Fathers had lost, many would have been hanged and be just footnotes in the history of the British Empire. Since they won, they became the law and went on to enforce many of the same British laws against which they revolted. During the Revolution, it would have been nonsense to talk about legal obligation to British law for the rebels just as it would have been nonsense to talk about legal obligation to American law by the loyalists. The Nuremberg Trials tried the losers, not the winners — as will always be the case except when some individual needs to be sacrificed by the winners in order to win or maintain a win.

B. *The Hart–Fuller debate*

"A serious and good philosophical work could be written consisting entirely of jokes" (Dribble, H. *quoting* Wittgenstein, L. 2004. p. 87). Yes it could. Unfortunately, they are rare. Instead what we usually get is stuff such as the Hart–Fuller debate. Hart took the positivist view in arguing that morality and law were separate. Lon L. Fuller's reply argued for morality as the source of law's binding power.

As contemplated previously, Fuller's reply is an obvious attempt to hijack Christian morality into law without the Christianity and can be easily ignored by existentialism. Such natural law theory is cowardly and not even aesthetically pleasing. If one wants to be a Christian, one should make the existential leap to being a Christian or, if not, shut up about morality.

Hart is the better artist at the aesthetic truth of the universal that is law. As always, he argued a separation between the law as it is and the law as it should be. Legal rights and moral rights are not related, beyond mere coincidence he argues. Hart argued the method of deciding cases through logic or deduction is not necessarily wrong nor right just as it is not necessarily wrong or right to decide cases according to social or moral aims, but that ultimately all cases are decided by the meaning of the words not by any natural or moral beliefs. He then goes on to the usual distinction between "hard" or "core" cases and "weak" or "penumbra" cases. The former involves facts that a law is intended to cover. For example, a statute that bans "vehicles" from a park is supposedly obviously intended to cover cars. The latter weak cases involve facts not considered by a law or not included in the intentions of the statute writers, such as a skateboard in the example of "vehicles". According to Hart, a judge interpreting such laws does not look to morality for a decision and for creation of a legal obligation to comply with the decision but to the meaning of words in the statute and to social and even perhaps moral norms pursuant to social constructed rules allowing for moral considerations. Ultimately, according to Hart, the decision and the legal obligation created are not based on morality but solely upon the meaning of words and socially constructed rules that may or may not be moral.

As aesthetics will tell you of any work of art, it is the reader and viewer who gives meaning to the art, not the artist. "[A] work of art has no meaning at all that can be abstracted from it ..." (Fogle, R.H. 1958. p. 110). A law does not and cannot give normative meaning, the reader of the law gives it normative meaning. Hart exemplifies the patrician Outer Party *consigliere* whose aesthetic work serves to convert the mob of Mob Island into the Inner Party by creating the illusion that the mob is doing something other than protecting its power. Words in the universal of the law mean what the Powers say they mean as part of an aesthetic nominal creation of truth that has no link to empirical reality except through reverse rationalization of a decision to execute upon those words. The Powers do not make law and decisions of legality and illegality based on the meanings of words, they make decisions of legality and illegality and the law in order to give meanings to words in the law. In the particulars of legality and illegality decisions, ultimately the only truth that matters for any execution that is reverse rationalized into the law is pragmatic: does it strengthen or maintain the monopoly on violence of the law so that it can serve its use and usefulness to be the final arbiter of all ethics thus of all morality in the society of which it is a social construct.

VIII. The Power of Nominal Aesthetic Meaning for Truth

"Beauty is unbearable, drives us to despair, offering us for a minute the glimpse of an eternity that we should like to stretch out over the whole of time" (Camus, A. 1965. p. 6.).

The meaning of law is a duality in the same way "wave" means many things in different wordgames linked together by the social construct fabric of language. Legality and illegality in law are not universals but a nominal shorthand or set of words used and useful to name the millions of ways on a daily basis the Powers-that-be controlling the monopoly on violence enforce or execute upon the law. The law as a universal is a provider of aesthetical truth that is most obvious in such words and wordgames as "rule of law"; "rule by law"; Due Process of law; and the "fairness and justice in law" used and useful as the ultimate arbiter of ethics in the society of which it is a social construct doing so by a monopoly on violence. It is an error to think that any of this aesthetic truth has any rational relationship to empirical reality. Think of it as a mob of gunmen with a gun pointed at your head: does anything they say mean anything other than what you must do to avoid getting shot? No. When they say you are entitled to "equal protection" along with all the others to whom they have a gun pointed at that head, does that stop them from treating everyone unequally if they wanted? No.

When viewing the aesthetic beauty of the law, it is tempting to start believing it has empirical reality: it really does care about factual "equal protection"; it really does care and have factual fairness; it really does care about due process; it really does care about the parties before it; so on and so forth. If you want any of these, go get a loving family, friends, or social construct that is capable of empathy as part of its leap to morality and ethics. The law cares for no one or no thing nor acts in anyway other than to maintain itself and its monopoly on violence to act as the final arbiter of all ethical struggles of the social construct that creates it. Threaten any of these and the individual is expendable.

Even if a Power wanted to care about an individual and through a personal morality acted for an individual at the risk of losing either the power of violence or its status as final arbiter of all ethical struggles, such a caring and act would not be a legal act within the law but an illegal act outside of law.

This universal wordgame of law as long as its meaning is used and useful as a universal in a normative form of life has the ability to create and to constantly renew and adapt the aesthetic intellectual beauty of the law to empirical threats opposing its monopoly on violence, or more generally, an artistic ability to create aesthetic truth entirely made up of words to maintain its monopoly on violence.

For the Powers-that-be artists of the law, they not only have the beauty and power of aesthetic truth to create and control but they have a monopoly on violence to enforce their creations upon others. For the Powers of the law, if they want, $2 + 2$ equals 5 or equals whatever the Powers want it to equal. To think like God, to be a god, is to be a Power-that-be in which one's thoughts have a monopoly on violence to create a world in their image. It is analogous to the sense of power and beauty that comes from playing God because they are gods.

I was first struck with this beauty as a 1L at Harvard law School on my first visit to Langdell Library. It has the same quiet serenity of a church but is full of books. Instead of stained glass, paintings, and statues, I was awestruck at all the books full of words. I had just finished studying philosophy and mathematics as an undergraduate and could not wait to see what these law book words said, meant, and could say or mean within the context of real practical world forms of life instead of the abstraction of philosophy and mathematics. Based on my previous life experience, I had a suspicion they said nothing but still had the hope they might say something. Looking back at it, I find it hard to believe I was so naive and stupid. Despite my life experience with the practical reality of humanity's Heart of Darkness, I had made a leap of faith to a morality believing a rational struggle with the banality of evil was possible through the force of intellectual beauty, not just by the beauty of rational argument but by the resulting beauty of the dialectics of rational argument. It is easy enough to take the words "[s]uch citation shall be signed ... by the violator", put it into declarative form, and make a rational argument out of it. Even many of the taxi drivers I drove with during college could do that when trying to beat a traffic ticket. Langdell had thousands of words in hundreds of pages in dozens of book even on such a simple issue as traffic citations. There were entire sub-libraries of books and words on words such as "due process" and "equal protection" that created wordgames for each word whose players struggled with each other resulting in separate wordgames entitled constitutional law, civil rights law, conflict of laws, and much more. There was not nor is there any limit to the amount of wordgames an artist of law could create. I could not wait to jump into them rationally to create honest and consistent normative truth and meaning to give meaning to an indifferent universe.

    To me, Harvard law School appeared to be Mt. Olympus only with hundreds of gods instead of just the twelve Olympians, and I was the mortal Bellerophon trying to avoid any gadflies that might blind and cripple me and send me back to earth. Despite having lived 4 ½ years on a submarine, Harvard was the biggest culture shock of my life. Growing up, law meant the police. They were little different from criminals — many times they were the same. Both police and criminals were something to be avoided as neither would bring any good into one's life. The only source of law while growing up was Christian Divine and Natural law taught by the nuns and priests in school trying to save our souls. This law contradicted with the reality of saving my physical existence while out of school thus leading to my first existentialist thoughts. Divine and Natural law may save my soul but it was little good in saving my life. Then came military service. Though at first its warrior ethics created a meaning for life that conquered even fear of death, it eventually became clear it did so by making both my life and death insignificant for the greater good; unfortunately, the greater good was what was good for the careers of the career non-com's and commissioned officers and not for any entities called God and country. Thus by my entry into HLS, I was a firm existentialist trying to make some leap of faith into some social construct that would at least keep me working and busy in life if not make it meaningful.

At first, in order not to be corrupted by my studies in philosophy and Christian dogma about divine and natural law that was my only source of hope as a child, I even accepted Judge Oliver Wendell Holmes' advice: "if you want to know the law and nothing else, you must look at it as a bad man, who cares only for the material consequences which such knowledge enables him to predict, not as a good one, who finds his reasons for conduct, whether inside the law or outside of it, in the vaguer sanctions of conscience" (Holmes, O.W. 1897. p. 458).

However, rather quickly, within a few years of working as a practicing solo trial attorney in the trenches of the American legal system, I quickly learned Judge Holmes despite being a cynic had greatly glorified the law and its practice and that my initial instinct that all the books in Langdell said nothing was correct. It is not a "bad man" in the law that cares only for the material consequences of its knowledge consisting of controlling and maintaining a monopoly on violence but this is the law's definition of a good and ethical patrician attorney — the only type of attorney that matters. Any other type of attorney is a freakish *Billy Budd* who, instead of being impressed into the HMS Bellipotent that is the law and its Powers-that-be officers from his old ship *The Rights of Man*, had volunteered to come aboard and therefore deserves any hanging of him as a show of force.[32]

Not that I am objecting to this reality. Such objection would be the same as objecting to the sun being hot. The aesthetic nature of truth in the universal that is law and its monopoly on violence are necessary equal coexisting attributes of the universal that is law — they are two sides of the same coin. Without both, there is no law. This nominal and aesthetic value for truth is applicable to all law regardless of its complexity and regardless of whether it is statutory, regulatory, case law, or whatever — it is a universal attribute of the universal that is law. As contemplated previously, one can easily see the power of such aesthetic truth at work existentially by both so-called conservative Powers and so-called liberal Powers in cases such as the "conservative" *Citizens United v. Federal Election Commission*, 558 U.S. 310 (2010) and the "liberal" *Goodridge v. Dept. of Public Health*, 798 N.E.2d 941 (Mass. 2003). There are no liberal and conservative Powers, there are just the Powers-that-be creating aesthetic truth in their image and then deciding legality and illegality based on a judgment call as to what they can get away with executing upon. Their conclusions in these two cases as with any lawgiver spitting out law based on irrational beliefs, opinions, and conclusions could have been honestly naturalized to science and written in a few lines. Honest naturalization to science is the last thing any Power wants.

An even simpler revelation of the power of aesthetic truth is the statement in *M.G.L.c. 90C §2* of "[s]uch citation shall be signed ... by the violator" that without doubt is true law and true under the law — the Powers-that-be say it is law. Standing by itself and as part of the entire "no-fix" traffic citation law that is *G.L.c.90C* and its thousands of pages of interpretative case law, this statement is

---

[32] Melville, Herman. 2017. *Billy Budd, Sailor*. Dover.

aesthetically beautiful as a logical creation of the intellect. The empirical reality that no one complies with this nominally beautiful statement is irrelevant to its truth or falsehood as law. If they wanted, at any time the Powers-that-be could have started enforcing or executing upon this law but only if they wanted. There is no necessary requirement either empirically or logically for such enforcement or execution. If they do enforce it, it will be as part of their monopoly on violence.

The power of aesthetic truth as meaning in life is well known among the patricians of our Technological Society and is a well formed concept through the philosophies of such patrician greats as Arthur Schopenhauer and Friedrich Nietzsche. The beautifully worded libraries of law intentionally or unintentionally hiding the predetermined irrational normative goals of the Powers' acts of will that go on to decide the legality of facts that have little if any relationship to empirical reality are manifestations of the Nietzschean Master Morality that in turn are fodder for the Powers and their Outer Party to generate even more formulaic but beautiful law verbiage — the truth of all of which is purely nominal and aesthetic. American legal realism has known this to be the case for > 100 years:

> The life of the law has not been logic; it has been experience. The felt necessities of the time, the prevalent moral and political theories, intuitions of public policy, avowed or unconscious, and even the prejudices which judges share with their fellow-men, have had a good deal more to do than syllogism in determining the rules by which men should be governed. The law embodies the story of a nation's development through many centuries, and it cannot be dealt with as if it contained only the axioms and corollaries of a book of mathematics. ...
>
> ...
>
> ... [W]hile the terminology of morals is still retained, and while the law does still and always, in a certain sense, measure legal liability by moral standards, it nevertheless, by the very necessity of its nature, is continually transmuting

> those moral standards into external or objective ones, from which the actual guilt of the party concerned is wholly eliminated. ... The first requirement of a sound body of law is, that it should correspond with the actual feelings and demands of the community, whether right or wrong. If people would gratify the passion of revenge outside of the law, if the law did not help them, the law has no choice but to satisfy the craving itself, and thus avoid the greater evil of private retribution. .... (Holmes, O.W. (1991). pp. 5, 37-38)

Though he did not take his conclusions to their existential conclusion, over a hundred years ago, Judge Holmes set forth this view that the only source of law was a decision enforced by the state. Judges decide cases on the facts as they saw them and then wrote opinions afterward that presented a rationale for their decision often based on an "inarticulate major premise."

Holmes' conclusions by an actual judge considered honorable by the American system of injustice have been reached independently of him and repeated continuously in the hundred years since <u>The Common law</u> by the American Realism school of jurisprudence — but again without making the necessary existentialist conclusions as to what law is and what its truth is. Historically, in the last hundred years, the Powers-that-be have been great artists, so great that they have negated the only other opposing artistic technique: religion. Why has not modern legal philosophy contemplated and used the reality of jurisprudence as clearly explicated by the likes of Holmes and may other judicial realists to the necessary existential conclusion that law and truth under the law is simply a nominal and aesthetic creation? This would save the enormous amount of time, energy, and resources spend on disputing, arguing, writing, storing, and all of the other social energy spent on case law and law libraries. We could eliminate all of that and simply set up a system by which judges issue decisions in the same way that legislators do and in the same way King Solomon issued the first known written decision consisting of his famous resolution of a custody dispute: decide cases through an intuitive sense of justice as well as he or she see thinks best, all things considered. This is what they do anyway, why not be honest about it? Why must the Powers hide their Master Morality? Are *hoi polloi* really so gullible?

The answer is they are not that gullible but in the absence of any option to oppose the law and its violence especially in the absence of any opposing aesthetically beautiful normative truth that was once provided by Christianity, the law must be accepted in the same way that anyone who wants to live will accept the rumblings of a mob with a gun pointed at that head.

This may serve to explain why modern Western law and Technology Society wants to make plebeians into unisex, homogeneous, culturally stagnant, one color, paper-cutouts of each other living solitary lives of temporary jobs without family, community, or other social support except for the handouts they get from Big Brother. As George Orwell wrote in *1984*, in order for the Powers to keep their powers, it is not enough for *hoi polloi* simply to accept Big Brother, they must love Big Brother; "[y]ou hate him. Good. Then the time has come for you to take the last step. You must love Big Brother. It is not enough to obey him: you must love him" (Orwell. 1977. p. 355). Through law and its Powers, our Technological Society is bringing to life O'Brien and his Room 101, but it is not a room with a rat cage but a sterile, pleasantly decorated, warm, friendly room with a surround sound of legality and illegality negating conscious, complex tragedy in the classical sense: replacing it with fear, hatred, and the joy or pain of either winning or losing but without dignity of emotion nor deep or complex sorrow and thought while at the same time denying the truth that 2 + 2 by definition makes four.

One must give the devil his due in order to existentially understand him. Much of this past, present, and future success of law has to do with the historical fact that the Powers now have a monopoly on violence that includes control of the technological techniques available in a Technological Society and thus control all artistic techniques — except perhaps for the pure individual will of solitary absurd individuals whose power is insignificant in relation to the violence controlled by the law. We must constantly keep in mind Orwell's description of how modern Technological Society is distinct from its predecessors:

> By comparison with that existing today, all the tyrannies of the past were half-hearted and inefficient. The ruling groups were always infected to some extent by liberal ideas, and were content to leave loose ends everywhere, to regard only the overt act, and to be uninterested in what their subjects were thinking. (*Ibid*. p. 259).

The Powers of the law were always interested in what its plebeians and slaves were thinking, however they could not do anything about thought. With varying modern technological techniques varying from simple advertizing to modern cults such as psychology and onto pseudo sciences such as psychiatry and "cognitive science", all of which are behaviorism in disguise, though the Powers of the law still are not able to know our thoughts, they can control them.

As contemplated previously, many philosophers and theologians varying from Plato to T.S. Eliot who are beyond the scope of this essay, a society lacking a successful religious tradition emphasizing spiritual concerns to counterbalance the worldly ambitions of secular government will degenerate into tyranny, social and cultural dysfunction, and fragmentation. Unknowing or knowingly, to avoid losing their power to any new mob trying to take over the neighborhood, the Powers of the law create, maintain, and constantly transform law into an aesthetically intellectually beautiful secular religion with its libraries of verbiage as its cathedrals. The existential question existentialists and nihilists must ask, even if only to understand their opponent, is whether the secular religion of law is a counterbalance to secular tyranny, dysfunction, and fragmentation?

IX. Omnipotent Moral Busybodies, *Hoi Polloi*, and Nihilism

"Of all tyrannies, a tyranny sincerely exercised for the good of its victims may be the most oppressive. It would be better to live under robber barons than under omnipotent moral busybodies. The robber baron's cruelty may sometimes sleep, his cupidity may at some point be satiated; but those who torment us for our own good will torment us without end for they do so with the approval of their own conscience." (Lewis, C.S. 1972. p. 298).

I must again remind myself of the questions and goals of this contemplation of the existentialist nature of law. One of these questions and goals is asking whether law as an unopposed normative wordgame is a hindrance or an asset to allowing, fostering, and motivating Technological Society to discover, explore, and conquer the universe. No one takes the risks of discovery, exploration, and conquest of the existential indifference and antagonism of the universe based on rationality; rationality leads one only to be a pundit, critic, or comedian sitting in the stands watching the gladiators fight. Is law or will it be an adequate substitute for Christian dogma as a source of normative motivation in a meaningless universe? Nietzschean aesthetic meaning for life and the law is and will continue to be a great normative wordgame for the Powers, patricians, and their Will to Power. Unlike their predecessors prior to modern Technological Society varying from Gilgamish to Napoleon, they need not risk anything to maintain their normative power and patrician status. They only need to control the risk-taking of others through controlling execution upon their law. Soon, they will need no one but themselves to execute their judgments. As drones and other so-called artificial intelligence become available for direct control over execution of the law, the Powers will be able to eliminate the plebeian middlemen usually required to execute their violence. A lifetime spent admiring themselves and their work in the mirror and executing upon it is a meaningful life for the Powers.

The artists of the law will never be the ones in the arena struggling to discover, explore, and conquer the universe. They will sit in the stands criticizing the techniques of those in the arena waiting for the moment when their irrational decisions will decide who in the struggle lives and who dies. Will the aesthetic beauty of the law be enough to make the struggle in the arena more than just one of struggling for power as an end in itself thus negating the leap to morality that is supposed to be the pragmatic motivating force of the struggle? I do not see how it can, either rationally or pragmatically, because such motivation will endanger the only descriptive reality about which the law cares: its monopoly on violence.

A wordgame of normative statements of ultimate value, regardless of how beautiful it is, is still a wordgame of normative statements of ultimate value in which descriptive words and reality are meaningless. What "is" does not matter to the law, what ought to be is the question of concern in the aesthetic beauty of Law — as with morality and ethics. For the law, the only pragmatic "is" that matters is maintaining its monopoly on violence through judgment calls on execution that decide legality and illegality. The reality of the indifference and antagonism of the universe to our existence is a descriptive not a normative wordgame. We can only beat the indifference of the universe to our existence by pragmatic truths in which the pragmatic goal is beating the universe as it is and not as it ought to be. As with any battle, the goal of our struggle with the universe should be victory — regardless of whether it is an existential struggle that we cannot ever win or a leap of faith to believing in a real final victory. In this battle, the only law or the natural or divine law is "[t]his is the law. The purpose of fighting is to win. There is no possible victory in defense. The sword is more important than the shield, and skill is more important than either. The final weapon is the brain, all else is supplemental" (Steinbeck, J. 2008. p. 1007).

Christianity tried to convert this pragmatic natural and divine law into its normative wordgame of Natural and Divine law with a descriptive reality about which it pragmatically cares consisting not of its power on this earth but the supposed power of a loving God; but in the end, it has surrendered its wordgame to the law that cares only about its power on earth. The law is not limited by such delusional weaknesses as the Beatitudes and thus need not concern itself will giving normative beauty to *hoi polloi*.

For existentialism or nihilism to replace Christianity as a counterbalance to the law to control its tyranny, we must concern ourselves with a leap to a powerful normative aesthetic beauty outside the law to act as a counterbalance. As we see from the World War II prisoner marches, even without technology it only takes a small minority with a legal monopoly on violence to legally march a majority to their deaths thus negating the leap to morality of those marching and of those enforcing the march. With post World War II technology and science, I am not concerned with physical death but destruction of the will to fight humanity's joint enemy: the universe.

Our Heart of Darkness is a necessity to fight in this battle but how do we control it so humanity is not destroyed as part of the fight?

At present there is no existential option other than nihilism as an opposing normative force with the power to take on the law. The power of the aesthetic nominal intellectual beauty of the law is so dominant and has such a monopoly on violence to enforce itself that there is simply no other intellectual force capable or available to "take up our quarrel with the foe"[33] other than nihilism.

---

[33] World War I poem *In Flanders Field* by one of its dead John McCrae:

> In Flanders fields the poppies blow
> Between the crosses, row on row,
>   That mark our place; and in the sky
>   The larks, still bravely singing, fly
> Scarce heard amid the guns below.
>
> We are the Dead. Short days ago
> We lived, felt dawn, saw sunset glow,
>   Loved and were loved, and now we lie,
>   In Flanders fields.
>
> Take up our quarrel with the foe:
> To you from failing hands we throw

I am not referencing here to the patrician pretend nihilism of a Nietzsche, a Bakunin, or of continental philosophy serving only to make "the party on the left is now the party on the right"[34]. The former wants to save the slaves from their Slave Morality by a Master Morality replacing one God with multi-gods or Dionysian demigods and thus is no threat to the law that wants the same. The latter wants nihilism to be a new Moses leading his people from the czar of one God to a promised land of a new Hegelian "eternal spirit" or "world spirit" czar in which the motto is "the rational alone is real" which completely ignores the Technological Society reality in which the rationality of language has little if any relation to reality yet is more real than reality. This is also not a threat to the law because it worships the same eternal spirit of "the rational" — though it is founded and dependent completely on the irrational but rationally does all it can to hide such foundation and dependency. The nihilism of postmodernism, anti-foundationalism, relativism, or whatever are the recent pick-up lines of continental philosophers is no different from the existential pick-up lines of Sartre or Beauvoir with their only difference from the aesthetics of the law is that their aesthetics at least has other than just a nominal truth: it works as a pragmatic pick up line. Forget these posers.

    I am referencing the nihilism of which plebeians, slaves, outcastes, and others of the patrician detested *hoi polloi* have lived with and have used to survive their millennia of struggle against the Powers-that-be. The nihilism of the ancient pillagers of pyramids contemptuous of human gods and their worldly and outer worldly possessions; of the engineers and human pile drivers who built

---

> The torch; be yours to hold it high.
> If ye break faith with us who die
> We shall not sleep, though poppies grow
> In Flanders fields.

[34] Lyrics from the song "Won't Get Fooled Again" by Pete Townsend of *The Who* (1971).

Venice; of the barbarians and legionnaires who fought at the Battle of Adrianople; of the forever to be unknown inventors of the plough; of the crews that sailed with Sir Francis Drake; of those on both sides who defended Stalingrad to their death; of those riders with whom I canyon-raced in the Angeles National Forest; and of the millions out there now fighting to survive life on a $1 a day who have the courage of the rear guard at the Battle of Thermopylae but never get a credit for it. This is the existential nihilism of the "I am therefore I think" and "I want more than just to exist" of which we cannot speak.

A. *If Your Nihilism is Something You Can Talk and Write About, It is not nihilism*

"United we'll fail, divided we'll fall". (Nicholls, M., Kean, M., Malia, L., Fish, J., & Sykes, O. 2013. p. 1). To the extent the Powers can fear or hate anything these days, the Powers and the law fear and hate nihilism instinctively but have no clue what it is and most importantly take it for granted as purely an insignificant destructive force it can easily control without need of studying it or respecting it thus violating the oldest of popular adages for those in power who want to stay in power. "There is no greater danger than underestimating your opponent". The law and its Powers want law more than they want life itself; for them, law is life. They are incapable of conceiving lawlessness as an alternative intellectual power. Even my writing this contemplation will not raise a red flag. Having beaten religion, the law considers nihilism and nihilists too insignificant to notice.

Additionally, religion also fears and hates nihilism instinctively though it also has no clue what it is. The artists of both Western and Eastern religion wordgames have written libraries of protest against nihilism, have been beatified for doing so, and consider it to be an abomination before God — Who is probably the original and ultimate nihilist. Religion however, unlike law, does not take nihilism for granted as purely a destructive force it can easily control. In fact, through religious artists of verbiage such as

Fr. Seraphim (Eugene) Rose who eventually wind up hiding in the woods, religion constantly warns that if nihilism proves victorious as Rose expects it will be — that is why he decided to hide in the woods — our world will become "a cold, inhuman world" where "nothingness, incoherence, and absurdity" will triumph. (Rose, S. 2001. p. 47). Fine, whatever, this is of no matter since while religion was out there whining about nihilism, it has been beaten and negated by law as a normative power in the world anyway. Nihilists need no longer be concerned with fighting religious social constructs as they have already surrendered their fight to the law. Our only opponent is the law.

This is the beauty of nihilism, all of the old school and new school Powers-that-be of the Old World, New World, and of Technological Society fear it, but neither science nor *hoi polloi* fear it. The one truth with which we need be concerned is the pragmatic truth of how individual nihilists will survive its struggle as an opponent to the violence of Law.

1. "My Dear Fellows, This Is Our Punishment for Associating with *Hoi Polloi*" (Lord, D. 1935. "Hoi Polloi" [Film]). For the vast majority of forever unknown souls that have struggled and fought the universe and the Powers for survival and will continue to do so unless killed off by the aesthetic creations of the Powers-that-be seeking to be one with some Hegelian "the rational" while at the same time denigrating the "rational" for aesthetic reasons, the real intelligent design of the universe is more analogous to a cardgame in which the Fates deal, call the game, know the players, and set the antes, raises, and bets. Not only do the Fates know the players and the cards, but the Fates made the players as they are, made the deck and cards and thus the probabilities are what they are because the Fates made them so. The winners and losers of this cardgame are decided by the luck of the draw, the probabilities of the given deck, game, and hands, and each player's ability to read the probabilities and the other players. No one can say their fate is good or evil, it simply is.

Hoi polloi have had to accept the randomness and

arbitrariness of this wordgame universe for their leap to morality for as long as there have been *hoi polloi*. In order to survive, as they most definitely have survived, they had no choice but to leap to morality especially the communal morality provided by religion and still have no choice but to do so. They accept the universe as it is including its randomness and arbitrary nature. They deal with it as it is for their Will to Power morality not aesthetically but pragmatically: if what "ought to be" works to give them a chance of winning the cardgame, then it is true. Patricians have laughed at this simplicity for millennia and always will.

For example, there have been a few published instances in which either a jury or a judge decided a case by a coin toss.[35] Without doubt it has happened a multitude of many other times without it being caught or reported. The judges or juries in these cases were censored and the jury verdict vacated for no real reason other than aesthetics. If a judge, just as with Buridan's Ass, cannot make a choice between two options seen as equal, flipping a coin to decide is a much more honest resolution than randomly picking one and then after-the-fact fabricating reasons to justify the random choice. The problem with this honesty derives from a need to maintain the aesthetic and nominal beauty of the law. This is a need the Powers have, not *hoi polloi*. Similarly, if a jury of twelve people is in the position of Buridan's Ass when having to decide between manslaughter or murder as occurred in the reported case[36], the facts in relation to the fabricated arbitrary and random distinction of the

---

[35] Blair, W.G. (1982). "Flip of Coin Decides Jail Term in a Manhattan Criminal Case", *New York Times* (2 February 1982); Associated Press. (2000). "Jury Flips Coin to Decide Murder Case". *AP* (26 April 2000); Associated Press. "Judge Removed for Deciding Case with Coin Toss", *AP* (13 January 2015).

[36] *Ibid*. Blair, W.G. (1982) p. 1.

law between "murder" and "manslaughter" must have been so close as to be meaningless. Thus a coin toss was as good a resolution as whatever verdict was eventually randomly and arbitrarily decided upon by another jury or judge in which the coin toss was hidden behind verbiage. It did not bother the community of twelve that made the coin toss decision, given the supposed secrecy of jury deliberations, it should have not bothered the one Power-that-be judge that vacated the verdict. It bothered the judge solely because the coin toss put a blemish on the aesthetics of the law. It is the judge and other Powers that want a universe in which "the rational alone is real". *Hoi polloi* can and have survived with the irrationality of the universe and will continue to do so if allowed.

Hoi polloi can survive and deal with nihilism. It is the law and the Powers who do not want to associate with *hoi polloi* who cannot deal with it and consider anyone that does to be stooges. The Powers need and want an ethics based on delusion and denial. This is why, until something better appears, nihilism is the sole counterbalance and source for a Will to Power to fight the violence of the law.

All modern, post-modern, or whatever the present patrician existentialist writers of our Technological Society call themselves reach the edge of the abyss, look down, and then back off. They not only fear suicide but also nihilism, which they fear as eventually leading to both individual suicide and suicide for humanity. This fear shows them not to be true nihilists. Becoming a god by suicide, with or without homicide, is not honest nihilism because it seeks to create a god by being a god. Those who can do it, do it. Making nothing out of something is the closest an individual human can be to becoming a god. A nihilist understands the temptation but also understands it is a temptation to be a god, especially if you can take someone else with you. However, trying to be gods as patricians try to be gods is giving into God. Honest nihilism rejects the cardgame of the universe but does not reject the truth of the game. The moment a nihilist or any person states there is no truth, they have just contradicted themselves and proven there is truth. An honest nihilist admits such truth and deals with the remaining problem of the meaning of this truthful lack of truth: that all is nonsense including truth. A nihilist, an honest one, does not waste time on the bravado of denying truth.

Some men just want to watch the world burn — this is the popular view of a nihilism even by existentialists and most artists and is the popular view held by the Powers and its law. Another view is that of the self-destructive loner or outsider, alienated from society, waiting for the day he can pour gasoline all over his body and light it up. This conception of the nihilist is probably accurate for example for the many artists who pretend to be nihilists or even for the Russian school of nihilism who need to replace a physical czar with a spiritual or metaphysical one which is one of the reasons Russian culture is such a mess. Patricians view nihilism through the eyes of fellow patricians such a Nietzsche and even a Schopenhauer as cowards who hug the Turin Horse and then go back to their safe place to weep while their women take care of them. No, be the horse and its rider: go back to work and forget the hug.

These patricians are not honest nihilists. God is a random arbitrary power and the ultimate nihilist. Becoming or wanting to become a Power is only copying God and admitting defeat. These pretend nihilists are really hedonists who enjoy playing God. They deny both truth and meaning and thus are tools for the Powers-that-be who accept aesthetic truth to create meaning for their lives and then force it through normative truth upon everyone else as God chose them to do. Honest nihilism and honest nihilists see God as He is, accepts that She is the Dealer in the cardgame universe, that They stack the deck for and against some, but then as nihilists still play the game with the hand that is dealt as Acceptance God and of the Godless universe created by whatever is the reason for their being something instead of nothing.

The honest nihilist fights to give order, reason, and meaning to a random, arbitrary, and meaningless universe that neither wants nor needs meaning — knowing that the war eventually will be lost despite winning many battles. There is no dialectic struggle of rationality called history. History is the struggle between the irrationality of the universe and the irrationality of humanity.

Victory is an option only for the religious, including for the secular religious who worship law, science, or whatever the latest fad demigod may be. An honest nihilist does not hide behind cowardly delusions such as atheism, agnosticism, humanism, or any other attempt to hide the nature of reality; nor does not the honest nihilist become solely a spectator and critic of the cardgame such as a Bill Maher, Jon Stewart, Ta-Nehisi Coates, or any of the thousands of other pundits in modern Technological Society media who get rich sitting in the stands and critiquing the gladiators as they fight and commenting on their strategy, tactics, or technique, from the comfort of their seats.

    A nihilist, an honest one, should be in the arena engaging in the physical and mental struggle creating not aesthetic but pragmatic truth used and useful for discovering, exploring, and conquering the universe that has been the leap to morality of millennia of honored and dishonored dead. This existential nihilism of *hoi polloi* or of the "herd" as the Powers privately call them is one of those meanings of which we cannot speak and that, at least for now, is a blemish on the aesthetic truths of law thus they underestimate its power. Unfortunately, the closest that anyone has come to speaking of it consists of a patrician's hyperbole:

> It is not the critic who counts, not the man who points out how the strong man stumbles, or where the doer of deeds could have done them better. The credit belongs to the man who is actually in the arena, whose face is marred by dust, and sweat, and blood, who strives valiantly, who errs, who comes short again and again, because there is no effort without error and shortcoming. But who does actually strive to do the deeds, who knows great enthusiasms, the great devotions, who spends himself in a worthy cause. Who at the best knows in the end the triumph of high achievement, and who at the worst, if he fails, at least fails while daring greatly. So that his place shall never be with those cold and timid souls who know neither victory nor defeat. (Roosevelt, T. 1910. p. 1)

2. Science and The Cuckoo Clock. Science in Technological Society is free from its old school Christian foundation need to prove the existence and rationality of God; it has achieved the freedom of being amoral. This is its weakness that presents a danger to us in the same way the amorality of the universe endangers us, but it is also its strength in our struggle against the amorality of the universe. In order to understand, accept, and deal with this amorality we must first accept this descriptive fact.

Science and scientists once motivated by an existential or even nihilist leap to their Will to Power intent to discover, explore, and conquer the universe are not bothered by social struggle. They are no more in fear of nihilism than they fear tyranny. Science is willing to work for tyranny as long as the tyranny allows science to work; it would be just as willing to work for nihilism. In fact social struggle in competition is their most productive environment. From Athens to the 20th Century, it is struggle and the physical problems of survival that have been the fuel of science not the safe places sought by social construct demands for cosmic justice. The law with its myopic view of reality that cannot see beyond its present need for power views the 20th Century and sees only a World War divided into versions I and II; it then pretends to honor the dead by pitying them and using the pity as an excuse to cement further its power through a monopoly on violence. It fails to notice that despite the quantity and magnitude of modern genocide and war, the historical fact is that the 20th Century and our modern Technological Society are the most peaceful or at least non-violent era in history. It has allowed for the elimination of killer diseases and for a control of the serial killer that is Mother Nature in ways unimaginable in prior centuries so that global population saw its greatest increase in known history, rising from about 1.6 billion in 1900 to over 6 billion in 2000.[37] "After all it's not that awful. You know what the fellow

---

[37] *See generally*, Azar Gat. 2006. War in Human Civilization.

said – in Italy, for thirty years under the Borgias, they had warfare, terror, murder and bloodshed, but they produced Michelangelo, Leonardo da Vinci and the Renaissance. In Switzerland, they had brotherly love, they had five hundred years of democracy and peace – and what did that produce? The cuckoo clock" (Reed, C. 1950). The historical fact that Germany actually invented the cuckoo clock and that Switzerland at the time of the Borgias provided some of the most feared mercenary armies of the time does not change the power of this allegory to speak about that of which we cannot speak: "[w]hen the legend becomes fact, print the legend". (Ford, J. 1962).

"[M]oral character and ethics matter more than science" (Basboll, T. 2017. p. 1). With these words by University of Illinois associate professor Kate Clancy as the call to arms, the University of Illinois dis-invited James Watson, a Nobel laureate who in 1953 co-invented the double-helix structure of DNA with Francis Crick and Rosalind Franklin, from speaking at the University of Illinois. Do they really matter more? Why? Her explanation for her statement of morality trumping science was simply: "[w]ho does the science matters as much or more because it influences the kind of work done, and who else gets to do it in the future" (Jaschik, S. 2017. p. 1). The "who" of course is herself and those of whom she approves; she would make a good lawyer and law judge with this mentality but not a very good scientist who are supposed to be concerned with predicting results not with who is predicting them. Her attitude is an exemplification of all of the bad -ism's of which professors such as Clancy always complain. This type of scientific mentality would exclude from science the vast majority of scientists throughout history and in the present from doing science including the likes of Isaac Newton and Albert Einstein — the former would be dismissed as a religious nut, the latter as a sexist.

Morality is simply an expression of an individual's Will to Power. Its truth is pragmatic, whatever works to give meaning to the individual's Will to Power is good, what does not is evil.
Ethics is the social construct equivalent of morality. Its truth is also pragmatic. Anything that maintains or increases the power of the

group of persons who constructed the ethics is good, anything that challenges or diminishes is bad. Science does not care by which morality or ethics it is employed. Morality and ethics define science as good or evil in the same way they define everything as good or evil: does it hinder or help their Will to Power or the power of an opposing morality or ethics? What is important and most relevant to our contemplation of an existential philosophy of law is that all modern morality and ethics admits subservience to the law as the ultimate ethics with a monopoly on violence.

Unlike morality and ethics, because science sees me as a moral and ethical equal before it, equally worthless that is, it is the only social construct willing to work for me as well as for anyone else as long as I allow it freedom to work its pragmatic and predictive truths. It is much like money, it does not care who owns it. It is science that is more important to me and ought to be more important to any existential morality and ethics than morals and ethics, but not as an end in itself but with the goal to discover, explore, and conquer the universe.

The mercenary nature of science is neither good or evil, it just is. For the existentialist who has made a leap to morality with the intent to have science not be conscripted to only one morality or ethics such is presently its situation with th law, the moral goal is to assure it is a free agent or at worse a volunteer for any morality or ethics and thus it has the freedom to do its predictive problem solving unconstrained by omnipotent moral busybodies. Science is not bothered with philosophy not even the outcaste of philosophy called nihilism. Again, it is only the law and the Powers that are bothered by it, and thus even with respect to science and the freedom of scientists to do their work, nihilism is still our only option against law and its tyranny.

3. Fear of Lawlessness Should not Hinder Nihilism in Western Civilization. Call it luck, fate, destiny, divine, or whatever, but the undisputed historical fact is that Western Civilization has not only survived lawlessness without significant social and cultural collapse but usually has undergone significant material improvement during lawless periods. Why is unknown. It may be because we had Christianity as a normative language to oppose the normative language of law. Most likely, it is a combination of facts that has something to do with our inherent cultural preference for an irrational love of freedom and of rational thought as a means to discover, explore, and conquer the universe instilled in us by the Ancients and by Judeo-Christian culture. Historically, tyranny usually is the only source of social and cultural state order in Eastern, African, and other non-Western civilizations which is not true of Western history.

The reason is irrelevant now that Judeo-Christian normative power as a equal opponent to the law is dead, and thus our luck may run out with this existential philosophy of law advocating nihilism in response to the otherwise unavoidable future of anarchy and then *1984* tyranny. However, if we are going to be naturalized to science and use the past to predict the future then it is a risk we should be willing to take. Such risk is the essence of an existential leap to morality that is the whole purpose of contemplating philosophy of law. Humanity is the same qualitatively throughout known history and everywhere but at least in Western Civilization its Heart of Darkness resulted in material progress to the point of creating science and thus allowing 6 billion to live in relative peace on earth without diseases and hardships that were common place during times when the world population was only a small fraction of this amount.

Regardless, there is no other choice. What if anything will come after nihilism is an open question. We know what will come after democracy in which law is the unopposed normative power with a monopoly on violence: tyranny.

The Powers of the law promote and heighten fear of lawlessness as marketing to maintain and promote their power monopoly ignoring the reality that there is no more peaceful and law and order society than a maximum security prison. The Powers' control of communications and marketing technique allows them to get away with this marketing and promotion despite the fact that though they market and promote law as a solution for all sorts of self-entitled evils ranging from ageism to genocide to sexism to slavery, all these -ism's got their power because they were legal.

Lawlessness in not itself something to be feared in modern Technological Society. The law always has been on the wrong side of history. Almost none of the freedoms we cherish as Americans — varying from free speech to private property rights — are the child of law or its Powers-that-be. As Mr. Leeson's previously mentioned book *The Invisible Hook* points out, illegal enterprises such as piracy were far ahead of legal enterprises in abolishing both chattel and wage slavery and creating working democracies and employee owed businesses.[38]

Historically, lawlessness is usually the only means by which *hoi polloi* can affect in any meaningful way history. It only took approximately 15,000 Vandals to conquer successfully Imperial Roman North Africa with a population of about 3 million[39] including the City of Hippo causing the patrician St. Augustine to warn of a coming apocalypse. The reality most likely is that few of the 3 million noticed a difference between Roman law and Vandal law: all the tax collectors and local politicians remained the same and their lives went on as before. The apocalypse occurred for the Powers at the top — including St. Augustine — who lost their monopoly on violence to enforce their norms to a new set of Powers. The plebeians were unconcerned just as they were with the fall of the Roman Republic. The same is true for the entire falsely promoted Dark Ages of the law when the Roman Empire fell. The Visigoths who finally ended the Roman Empire conquered Rome and the Italian Peninsula of 10 million people with a land area of 800 hundred thousand square kilometers through use of a 20,000 to

---

[38] *See* Leeson, P. (2009). pp. 176-193.

[39] Wolfgram, H. (1993). *The Roman Empire and its Germanic Peoples*. U. of CA. Press. p. 193

30,000 strong military force.⁴⁰ Again, it is doubtful whether any of the 10 million noticed a difference in their lives between Roman law and the Visigothic supposed barbarism of its rule of law except for the Powers who simply moved to the East.⁴¹

As exemplified by the cuckoo clock allegory, ultimately the progress of history has shown the fall of Western Rome did more good than harm. It deserved to fall. At its fall:

> ... the ancient sources are full of complaints about the miserable living conditions of the lower classes and the enormous disparity in wealth between the rich and the poor. In a situation where three Italian senators of the fifth century had a yearly income equal to the entire budget of the West Roman Empire, the *res publica* as the affair of all citizens had become an illusion and, within the sphere of influence of these senators, had been replaced by their personal rule ... [H]istorians and sociologists ... [have] charged ancient civilization with serious systemic flaws and were and are of the opinion that 'a continuation of the *Imperium Romanum* would have impeded the development of mankind, so that Rome had to fall for the sake of progress'.⁴²

Nihilists as well as existentialists and modern humanity must not put themselves in the attitude and position of the slaves of the roman patrician Saint Melaine, a member of the ancient well-established patrician Roman Valerii Family who owned property and between 50,000 to 100,000 slaves on real estate holdings scattered from Britannia to Southern Italy and onto Roman North Africa. When she converted to Christianity in about 400, she freed her 8000 slaves, but many of the liberated slaves were unhappy with

---

⁴⁰ *Ibid.*

⁴¹ *Ibid.*

⁴² *Ibid.* p. 192.

their freedom and volunteered to be slaves with her brother from whom they expected employment and protection.[43] The Powers offer law and order, the absurd hero must decide whether this is enough.

X. Nihilism, Legality, and Illegality

"Lawyers spend their professional careers shoveling smoke" (Knappman ,Edward W. 1973. p. 100 [attributed to Oliver Wendell Holmes]).

As concluded previously, something is legal if the Powers believe the something maintains or strengthens their monopoly on violence by actually being enforced or executed upon by its monopoly on violence. For the universe of Law, what law as a social construct ought to be is what those with the monopoly to enforce it say it ought to be. Thus it is possible without contradiction for there to be a difference between what the law says we ought to do and what acts it enforces upon us as two different truths.

Nihilism is an equal opponent to the aesthetic and nominal that is law, the big question is whether it is an equal opponent to its omnipresent exercise of its monopoly on violence to enforce its aesthetics as pragmatices — that is its power to declare acts legal and illegal and to exercise violence to execute upon its often contradictory declarations. What any particular law existentially "is" at any given moment is usually simple enough to determine especially in a modern Technological Society in which all particular laws of even trivial significance are almost always in written form; just ask anyone involved in executing its monopoly on violence what law is. What is legal — or illegal for that matter — is a different matter and is much more convoluted because each determination of legality and illegality with its concern for getting away with execution on each determination occurs millions of times a day in courts and government administrative offices worldwide.

---

[43] *See* n. 39 at pp. 57-58.

Determinations of legality and illegality get much more convoluted when dealing with more complicated matters than traffic citations.

Given that nihilism in its plebeian form with its existential power is an equal opponent to the aesthetics and nominal truth of law, the remaining question is whether it is an equal power to the legality and illegality of law. Because the universal Law that is the social construct of all law consists of both 1) a social construct of nominal aesthetics consisting of normative statements that no one can logically derive from sense experience and 2) a violence aspect that is most definitely made up of sense experience at its execution, it is important to maintain and understand that the words and wordgames of Law, its truth, and the two headed coin of legality and illegality are distinct wordgames that may be but are not necessarily logically related. The former two might at best can be considered descriptive by their telling us what the Powers consider law to be but this descriptive value is always necessarily nominal and aesthetic — any other meaning derives from the Powers Will to Power execution upon the aesthetics, but the execution is always pragmatic — *i.e.*, a law explicitly may say something must be "signed" but it my be consistent with this rule that something be "not signed"; the classical logical principle of contradiction along with those of identity and the excluded middle do not apply to legality and illegality just as they do not apply to the pragmatics of science or of any other pragmatics.

Legality and illegality describe the law in action exercising its monopoly on power. Something is legal if the Powers — be they legislators, judges, or whoever — can execute its Will to Power to enforce it; it is illegal if the law cannot. The words "legal" and "illegal" are not universals but nominally describe the millions of events each day by which individual Powers balance and judge what law — their universal within Law consisting of aesthetically pleasing normative statements — they can get away with enforcing through their monopoly on violence.

As contemplated previously in this essay, though the universal law, with or without an opposing normative force such as religion, has a purely nominal and aesthetic value or meaning for its truth, the power of such truth should not be underestimated by existentialism nor by nihilism. Despite knowing the meaning of the law descriptively, any normative meanings of the law enforced by the Powers as legality or illegality millions of times daily are each distinct and do not necessarily follow from the descriptions, aesthetics, and nominal meanings contained in the universe law. Thus, for example, for the entire time period it was law that citations be signed by a violator it was legal for citations not to be signed by the violator. Nominally, the descriptive meanings have a predictive value but only nominally because, unlike science, there is no reality distinct from the normative meanings, and they have no logical relationship to the descriptive meanings that could be the basis for predictive value. For Law, there is nothing outside its language except irrational normative intentions of which we cannot speak. There is no logical or even rational relationship between what is and what ought to be. Thus, regardless of how aesthetically we describe what the law is and what is nominally true under law, in Law there is no way to conclude from the law what acts are legal or illegal.

Legality and illegality may perhaps have a use and a usefulness as universals themselves distinct from the universal law but only pragmatically: do the acts work to maintain the law's monopoly on violence? If an act does so act, it can be described as universally "legal". If it does not, the universal "illegal" will have meaning for describing it.

A nihilist struggle or even just an existential leap of morality against the Powers and Law or any particular law is a high stakes gamble that must be taken on and fought with full knowledge of what is involved, the nature of the opposition, and of the proper strategy and tactics to use. The price for guessing wrong on what is legal or illegal is high: personal ruin, financial ruin, family ruin, the ruin of entire businesses and enterprises, imprisonment, and death. In many cases, death is the least punitive option. Mark Twain's quotation regarding the popular news media can be adapted and paraphrased to describe the judiciary:

> Do not fear the enemy, for your enemy can only take your life. It is far better that you fear the courts and the

legislature, for they will steal your honor. The awful power of the law is created in America by a horde of ignorant, self-complacent simpletons who failed at ditching and shoemaking and fetched up the law on their way to the poorhouse.

In the finest tradition of Pontius Pilate, the Powers both in the Inner Party and those in the Outer Party will without hesitation crucify anyone who is a danger to their monopoly on violence, and thus we must be well aware of the following empirical reality and requirements for a successful nihilist opposition to law.

A. The Number One Rule for Existential Nihilism to be a Counterbalance to Law: Look Through the Aesthetics to See the Existential Ugliness of Unopposed Power

"How small a thought it takes to fill someone's whole life" (Wittgenstein. 1984. p. 50e). In the pragmatic struggle against the law, as I have emphasized, it is important to give the devil his due and to remember Camus' warning to us: "a slave begins by demanding justice and ends by wanting to wear a crown. He must dominate in his turn" (Camus, 1991, p. 25).

Despite the aesthetic truth of Law, the ugly truth is that it cares for no one and no particular legality or illegality but law. It must do so. Its entire use and usefulness is to be the final arbiter of all ethical struggles in order to help the Will to Power of whatever social construct created it. In order to continue with this use and usefulness it must have a monopoly on violence or the struggles below it that it is supposed to arbitrate will continue.

Aesthetics is truth and the meaning of life for the Powers of the modern world. Go to any law library and look around at the tons of verbiage that says nothing and means nothing other than aesthetic power. The existential fact that they enforce that truth empirically upon the powerless through a monopoly on violence is not a concern for them and usually does not even cross their mind. The Pontius Pilates of modern Technological Society will just as willingly wash their hands of the innocent they knowingly condemn to death simply for being a threat to their power only with two differences: 1) they live a lifetime of having others do their killing for them; 2) they do not admit to washing their hands of the truth. This makes them even more dangerous.

Despite the aesthetic beauty of Law and law, the existential truth is that it cares for no one but its power. It is a normative system in which power is an end in itself and must be — otherwise it will lose its power and have no use nor usefulness.

1. No One Really Knows or Cares about Legality or Illegality Except in Relation to Their Will to Power. All decisions of legality and illegality start from and end with normative statements that are irrationally derived from empirical statements thrown in between to hide the irrationally of the normative statements. Even if one irrationally made a leap to faith believing a law to be a rational construct from start to finish in which normative statements could be rationally derived from empirical statements, it would be empirically impossible to do. Estimates of the number of state laws alone passed in typical year are at about 40,000 a year[44]. If added into the figure are federal and local laws plus federal, state, and local regulations and administrative rules, bylaws, and all that other rules nonsense all of which can be enforced as law by the law, no one knows has or can in their lifetime have all the threads that make up the complete aesthetic fabric of the law. I know from my practice experience that is confirmed by many publications that the average person commits three felonies a day without even knowing

---

[44] *National Conference of State Legislatures Press Release.* December 27, 2011. https://www.ncsl.org/press-room/new-laws-ring-in-the-new-year.aspx

it.[45] Though we are the most law governed society in history we are also the most legally corrupt because everyone on daily basis breaks multiple laws. One of the powers of the Powers is to decide whom to go after and to choose which laws to enforce or not to enforce. A creative Power can always find some crime of which to convict any one of us if they look hard enough. No lawyer knows and no judge knows the law, they pretend they do. It is empirically impossible to keep track of the law nor any significant portion of the particular laws that are the execution reality of its aesthetics and to rationally contemplate and resolve all of them into one's normative contemplations and conclusions. Even if one created an algorithm to keep track of them, such algorithm as with all algorithms would simply be a rule for creating a pattern based on assumptions and finite observations. Whether any given problem fits into that pattern or whether any given answer is resolved by that pattern instead of an infinite number of other patterns will always be unknown because, unlike science, there is no way to test them by parameter controlled, repeatable experiments, that would pragmatically falsify any predictions made.

    Worse, the day-to-day practical reality of legality and illegality is that clients, lawyers, and judges do not care what the law is. The clients and lawyers just want to win their case and define justice as winning their case. The judges want to keep their government jobs creating a world in their image until dragged away as corpses — even senility does not stop them from wanting to act as gods. In addition every law has multiple exceptions that themselves have exceptions on to infinity. Every decision of legality or illegality by empirical necessity — even if we ignore the

---

[45] Silvergate, H. (2011). *Three Felonies A Day: How the Feds Target the Innocent.* Encounter Books; Roberts, P.C., (2008). *The Tyranny of Good Intentions: How Prosecutors and Law Enforcement Are Trampling the Constitution in the Name of Justice.* Broadway Books.

existential necessity of the attributes of Law as simply an aesthetic nominal universe — is based on only a tiny fraction of the known aesthetic creation of the law and thus is primarily made through ignorance.

Every now and then, small groups of Powers admit to such irrationality such as the American Legal Realism school of jurisprudence, but they make sure no substantive changes to legality and illegality occur as a result of their admissions. Except for the "Idiosyncracy Wing" of this School, all Powers in this School even maintained a dishonest distinction between hard cases and weak cases of predictability and limited their critiques to appellate decisions that make up at this point in time probably <1% of decisions of legality and illegality. It is this American philosophy of law School's argument that the law is what can be predicted to be the judge's decision. It is trying to be predictive in order to be a science. The problem with this attempt is that none of its writings is ever predictive. Realism takes a few past appellate decisions and breaks them up into "hard" cases that it claims supposedly would have been hard to predict and into "easy" cases that supposedly would have been easy to predict, but it never makes predictions — other than purely nominal ones that can be explained anyway if wrong and therefore never falsified — for any specific or particular pending or future cases, in particular it never gives any axiom, rule, formula, or anything that can be applied to make falsifiable conceptual predictions for pending or future legality or illegality questions. It never gives any predictions or conceptual means for making predictions, because it cannot. There is no way to go from what anything "is" including what is the law to what ought to be: that is what is legal or illegal in anything but a nominal way; it is always possible for a Power make something legal or illegal by changing the intrepretation of what the law is. What prediction would this School have made for a law that states every violation "shall" be signed by the violator?

Being a Monday morning quarterback with no intent of playing in the next game is not science, it is simply being a spectator in the stands.

Though the Idiosyncracy Wing ephemerally argued that legality and illegality was not rationally predictable, it did so by arguing that it was predictable through psychology and even treated psychology as a science by taking out of context quotes of philosophers such as Willard Van Orman Quine using the word psychology in sentences dealing with epistemology. This latter attempt is outright nonsense. Even psychology never gives nor can it give any axiom, rule, formula, or anything that can be applied to make hypotheses that allow for parameter controlled, repeatable, falsifiable, testable predictions for pending or future legality or illegality questions. Any psychology other than behaviorism is a cult at best with no predictive value of anything and most definitively not of legality or illegality. Behaviorism is a science that has predictive value in the same way that marketing and advertizing have predictive value, it can be used to conform behavior to a desired behavior but not to predict it in anyway by statistically or probability. Even the Idiosyncracy Wing would not admit that legislators and judges are the equivalent of advertizing executives and marketing strategists though they should as this would be the closest to existential reality that mainstream philosophy of law could get.

Regardless, getting into the sophomoric attempts by schools of philosophy of law to incorporate philosophy of science and epistemology into their reasoning is unnecessary and should not be an issue relevant to our existential contemplation of a leap to morality opposing the law. The Realist School of jurisprudence and philosophy of law was never intended to be an existential critique of law and thus not of legality and illegality. From the beginning, as with most philosophies and schools of anything other than science, it was a wordgame by patrician Powers or want-to-be Powers assuming law to be a Good and seeking to foster and strengthen it as a moral and ethical social construct good. There was never any intention to oppose it as an equal normative power. In the end, the Realist School failed to make any substantive change in the nature of legality or illegality though law professors pretend it did. Its primary use and usefulness was to add to the aesthetics of the law by giving the false but aesthetically pleasing appearance of self-examination by the Powers — thus consistent with the best analogy for jurisprudence of it being marketing and advertizing for the law and its monopoly on violence.

Though the Realist school did lead to the nominal change in law school education of calling law books "case material" instead of simply "case books", calling such a purely aesthetic change that does nothing to oppose the unopposed normative monopoly on violence of the law "profound" shows the delusional nature of law school education. The 19th Century "science" of law was to be based on principles and rules derived from the logical study of case decisions only. Modern 20th Century and 21st Century "science" of law is to be based on principles and rules derived from the logical study of case decisions and related material. This difference sounds nice and is supposed to be aesthetically pleasing. Logically, it is simply another irrational attempt to get around the logical is/ought distinction that logic cannot get around. At least, 19th Century law school pedagogy taught its students to think logically, 21st Century law school pedagogy does not even do that.

Unfortunately, Legal Realism also served as a foundation for further wordgames adding to the aesthetics of the law by allowing future generations of patricians and their Inner and Outer Parties to develop wordgames such as Critical Legal Studies, Critical Race Theory, Critical Realism, Law and Economics, and other law school fad wordgames by which to market the law as caring about more than just maintaining the unopposed power of the Powers-that-be.

The opposition to American School of Realism by Logical Positivism further exhibits how the aesthetics of the law works to ignore the separate Will-to-Power truth of legality and illegality. Legal positivism through its prophet H.L.A. Hart asks Realism to assume a judge trying to decide whether a termination of a contract can be done within a certain amount of time. To make such a decision, the judge would look to the state's law on termination of a contract to make the decision. According to Realism, argued Hart and the logical positivists, the judge is searching the state's law to determine or with the thought "what do I think I will do" and this he stated is clearly not the case thus Realism must be inconsistent and not complete.

Why is it not the case? Hart does not say so and neither do any legal positivist. This supposed contradiction is simply accepted as obviously true, but it is not. What else would the judge be looking at other than for "what do I think I will do". The intentions of the legislature? The only meaning that could be given to their "intentions" is in the words they wrote. Looking for intentions in the words is no different than looking at the words, their only meaning as words is nominal and aesthetic. It is the reader who gives pragmatic meanings to words by how the reader uses and makes them useful not the writer. No reader has any clue as to what the writer thought, only what they wrote; the reader gives meaning to what they wrote. It is the reader of law and in the case of existentialism the absurd hero who by a leap to morality gives meaning to law other than its aesthetics. The absurd hero as with the reader of any purely aesthetic truth must give meaning to the law in the same way the Powers give it the meaning of power as an end in itself. It is the reader's intentions that matter and that can be perceived by the reader in terms of what we can speak about. As Wittgenstein established, there is no private language of the writer that is being translated into another private language of the reader. Any actions other than the words and thus any meaning given to those words other than their aesthetics would be given to them by the judge looking at them who is looking at them to decide what they as judge will do. So, the judge is in fact looking at "law" for the sole purpose of contemplating "what do I think I will do", but just does not want to admit to it in the use of the words eventually used fore execution upon the decision as to what to do.

For the nihilist dealing with legality and illegality, the only difference between "hard" cases and "weak" cases is the resources of the party arguing the case and the sympathy and empathy of the legislators, jury, judge, or judges hearing the case. That sympathy and empathy is in turn based on the social construct ethics and morality created by each individual's Will to Power. Thus individuals are condemned to death, jail, financial and personal ruin, and having their honor ruined by what are essentially and in substance decisions based on ignorance. Existentially, the absurd hero nihilist must accept this social construct decision-making of legality and illegality as a necessary aspect of social survival. As Judge Holmes stated in his <u>Common Law</u>: "[t]he first requirement of a sound body of law is, that it should correspond with the actual feelings and demands of the community, whether right or wrong. If people would gratify the passion of revenge outside of the law, if the law did not help them, the law has no choice but to satisfy the craving itself, and thus avoid the greater evil of private retribution" (Holmes, O.W. (1991). pp. 5, 37-38).

As an existentialist or nihilist, one will be battling against this necessary attribute of legality and illegality, thus one cannot expect to be accepted by the Powers-that-be as part of the Good in that reality. In fact, there is no Good in law, legality, or illegality other than that which gives power to the law.

B. To Counterbalance the Law, the Nihilist must be Rationally Opposed all Legality or Illegality in the Law not just Acceptable Opposition

"A man will be imprisoned in a room with a door that's unlocked and opens inward, as long as it does not occur to him to pull rather than push" (Wittgenstein. 1984. p. 42c.). Admittedly, the nihilism struggle against the tyranny of law is at best a rearguard action in the finest tradition of Thermopylae for one who makes the leap to morality to take on this struggle. This should not matter to a nihilist or to an existentialist, as Camus wrote in the *Myth of Sisyphus* "the struggle itself toward the heights is enough to fill a man's heart". (Camus. 1955. p. 91).

Communal creations of normative power are not created by agreement and peace but by struggle. Just as with scientific progress they are created by disagreement and struggle. In the absence of disagreement and struggle as equal but separate Powers between law and old school religion, the only option is first to use nihilism to create disagreement and struggle. From this forge of struggle between law and naturalized human existentialism, hopefully new school religion will rise to take on law as an equal but separate power. This leap to a faith the absurd hero wills in order to create a free and open society so as to avoid or minimize the effects on humanity's ability to discover, explore, and conquer the universe of the next step of the Platonic regime cycle

However, this struggle need not be suicidal. The strength and weakness of Technological Society is its rationality. It depends on logic to fight its battle against the universe. This is great except for the fact that the universe is not logical nor rational. Its master technicians varying from its lawyers and politicians onto Noah Chomsky, Marvin Minsky, and its other fanatic pundits varying from Richard Dawkins to Bill Maher can play as many fallacious wordgames as they want but they will never even be able existentially to define anything except pragmatic solutions to problems susceptible to solution by the scientific method. They will never provide any truth beyond pragmatic truth and never any solution to what ought to be other than irrational leaps to what ought to be. Despite the sophistication of modern physics, mathematics, and language techniques created to avoid paradoxes in the philosophy of language, none are able to give meaning to the simplest undisputable known fact of my existence consisting of "I am". Nor can they give non-contradictory answers to the simplest of paradoxes such as Thompson's Lamp Paradox or even any of the classical Zeno's Paradoxes establishing the irrationality of even the simplest of rational descriptions of reality when seeking anything other but pragmatic truth. "We feel that even when all possible scientific questions have been answered, the problems of life remain completely untouched. Of course there are then no questions left, and this itself is the answer" (Wittgenstein. 2009. Prop. 6.52, p. 81).

The law, legality, and illegality of Technological Society want to share rationality but cannot because they are all fundamentally irrational. Any nihilist opposition must do all it can to oppose the pretend rationality and to heighten the hidden irrationality of the law. As analogized before, the law is a fuel cell container trying to contain millions of interactions of moralities and ethics and legality and illegality. The cracks in the container are its irrationalities.

The only strength of existentialism and nihilism is its reliance entirely on the value and meaning of the individual life. To the law and to Technological Society, the individual is expendable. An analogy for imagining the nature of this struggle is to consider the aesthetic beauty of the nominalism of the law to be a beautifully sculptured blunt instrument engaged in brain surgery consisting of billions of random and arbitrary legalities and illegalities. Its strength is the toughness and weight of the unopposed beauty and bluntness of the sculptured tool; its weakness is that it cannot handle the simplest or most subtle of problems created by the most delicate of individual cells. Of course, it may solve these problems by simply banishing to death the entire brain, but existentially we know it will do that eventually anyway so we have nothing to lose by trying to get it to be partnered with an equal but more sophisticated surgeon so that the brain will live on and to continue its struggle with the universe.

It is impossible to give individual details of opposition acts because each individual life that leaps to this struggle is individual. Unfortunately, like Camus in the Myth of Sisyphus, the best that I can do is give examples and adages, but each individual must make their own leap to morality:

— Vote but do not vote for any listed candidate. My dream election would be one in which 90% of eligible voters vote but the listed candidates share at most 10% of the vote. It makes no difference who you vote for anyway, the party on the left or the party on the right. Existentially, they are all the same. Make a protest vote.

— Show no respect to any officer of the law of any kind, be it judge, police, or government official. Stop using a Walmart Greeter mentality to survive in life if you are not a Walmart Greeter.

— Oppose any new laws or legalities. Remember all laws no matter how benevolent they may appear at first will always, always eventually be simply another

means for power as an end in itself.
- Oppose all illegalities. Be a complete libertarian. You will never get it anyway. Go as far as you can.
- Answer aesthetics with the ugliness of science at work and technology. Law wants to create a unisex homogenous world by violence enforcing aesthetic diversity. Oppose its violence by creating the option of choosing or not choosing a unisex homogenous world through science and technology. The solution to material problems are material: robots, genetic engineering, whatever to create a Brave New World free of destructive battles including destructive battles between the sexes because there eventually may be no sexes only sexbots. Or, through technologically, there can be as much sex and gender as desired.
- Accept that the natural world of the universe is humanity's one true enemy and fight to discover, explore, and conquer it so as to create new economic wealth and power to raise materially all of society not just the richest of the Powers as the law does in order to maintain its power.
- Above all make honesty and empathy the ultimate virtues. Honesty in the sense of accepting and admitting the ever present Heart of Darkness. A Governor Rod Blagojevich type politician is not a criminal for honestly admitting he would be willing to give government appointments to his political friends and donors but not actually doing it — if you do not like it, vote against him. All other politicians who do in fact give government appointments to their political donors but are silent about it so as to pretend the appointments are based on merit, varying from Presidents Bush and Obama to the lowest hack maintaining a local civil service list, they are the true criminals.

The law and the Powers live in fear of losing their power, this fear is their only weakness in Technology Society. It must be used against them to control them. Power is an end in itself for them; they will always return to power and be in power regardless of what happens. Any option to practice and be scientific while also creating rationally and intentionally irrationality opposing the patrician Hegelian state worship that is Law is an option for nihilism to counterbalance the unopposed monopoly on violence that is Law.

"God is Power", thus the Powers have God on their side and they seek the infinite to discover, explore, and to conquer it so it is one with themselves through aesthetic truth. Plebeian nihilism wants pragmatically to discover, explore, and conquer the universe to survive and prosper; we have finite ambitions. This irrationality is our weakness but irrationality is the only weakness there exists in the aesthetic container of the law. We must use this weakness to constantly cause leaks in the container, these are the only battles that should concern us and that we can win. The war is lost.

XI. Legal Duty is a Gun Pointed at Your Head

"If you must break the law, do it to seize power: in all other cases observe it".

— Popularly attributed to Julius Caesar

As I have already contemplated, law and particular laws existentially exist in the universe of normative language in the same way that mathematics and numbers exist in scientific language: laws and numbers are as particular and as real as any bricks or stones thrown at us, yet law and mathematics are abstract universals. Just as mathematics becomes descriptive and particular through the use and usefulness of numbers in science to give predictive value and pragmatic truth, law becomes a descriptive and particular law by the use and usefulness of execution upon normative statements through determinations of legality and illegality: can the Powers get away with execution upon their normative statements through violence? All law and execution on particular laws will always act on behalf of maintaining the monopoly on violence of the Powers regardless of any initial appearance that it is helping the powerless.

Thus there is no obligation to comply with law or any particular law other than through its threat of violence. There is no non-legal obligation, moral, ethical, or any other duty or obligation to comply with law under than this threat. There is no legal duty or obligation created by law to comply with law distinct from law.

This does not justify committing physical or personal suicide to counterbalance the law. If the occasion arises to do an illegal act consistent with one's morality, there is no obligation to act legally other than a risk determination balancing one's irrational desire to act morally with the rational desire not to be killed by the law.

In disregard and in disrespect of the Honored Dead, Western Law is presently taking credit for Western Civilization being civilized. According to philosophy of law, jurisprudence, lawyers, law professors, and their worshipers, it is Law that ended slavery[46]; eliminated treatment of women as second class citizens; ended or is ending racism; protects workers from unfair employers; protects the poor from abuse by the rich; and is supposedly responsible for any advances made by the powerless and plebeian classes in becoming equal with the patricians above them. This marketing and advertising, which is all it is, is historically false. Almost all alleged social injustices for which the law claims credit for eliminating were social injustices because they were legal and enforced by law. Regarding quantitative improvements, almost all known monopolies of power and their ability to hinder invention and distort markets were able to do so solely with the aid of law. The advantage of the

---

[46] They do not even want to limit the credit for ending slavery to the laws of Western Culture but out of a need for political correctness give credit to the majesty of the Law. They do this despite the undisputed reality that slavery was legal in much of the Mideast and East and their Law until well into the 20th Century and into the 1970's.

wealthy in building further wealth while taking advantage of smaller companies and individual inventors is protected by the law. The division of society into an upper class 10% or 1% and even less of the population controlling as much as 60% - 80% of a society's wealth is the product of law.

Again, this is not a criticism, it is descriptive reality that must be accepted.

Throughout history, the opportunity for material progress was granted plebeians only through natural disasters or wars that forced patricians to deal with plebeians as equals for a limited amount to time. This path of opportunity is ridiculous and results in as much suffering to plebeians at the time as it creates material progress for the future. Now that Western religion is worthless in providing the necessary opposition to create opportunity, through nihilism and the disorder and chaos it creates among the Powers, existentialism can create the opportunity for material progress without natural disasters or wars.

XII. Am I Being Hegelian?

In that the supreme value for the animal is the preservation of life, consciousness should raise itself above the level of that instinct in order to achieve human value. It should be capable of risking its life. To be recognized by another consciousness, man should be ready to risk his life and to accept the chance of death. Fundamental human relations are thus relations of pure prestige, a perpetual struggle, to the death, for recognition of one human being by another.

At the first stage of his dialectic, Hegel affirms that in so far as death is the common ground of man and animal, it is by accepting death and even by inviting it that the former differentiates himself from the latter. At the heart of this primordial struggle for recognition, man is thus identified with violent death. The mystic slogan "Die and become what you are" is taken up once more by Hegel. But "Become what you are" gives place to "Become what you so far are not."

This primitive and passionate desire for recognition, which is confused with the will to exist, can be satisfied only by a recognition gradually extended until it embraces everyone. In that everyone wants equally much to be recognized by everyone, the fight for life will cease only with the recognition of all by all, which will mark the termination of history. The existence that Hegelian consciousness seeks to obtain is born in the hard-won glory of collective approval. It is not beside the point to note that, in the thought which will inspire our revolutions, the supreme good does not, in reality, coincide with existence, but with an arbitrary facsimile. The entire history of mankind is, in any case, nothing but a prolonged fight to the death for the conquest of universal prestige and absolute power. It is, in its essence, imperialist. We are far from the gentle savage of the eighteenth century and from the Social Contract. In the sound and fury of the passing centuries, each separate consciousness, to ensure its own existence, must henceforth desire the death of others. Moreover, this relentless tragedy is absurd, since, in the event of one consciousness being destroyed, the victorious consciousness is not recognized as such, in that it cannot be victorious in the eyes of something that no longer exists. In fact, it is here the philosophy of appearances reaches its limits. (Camus, A. 1991. p. 71).

Am I committing the ultimate existential sin of treating words as more real than reality? My one hope is that I am not. As an existentialist living in absurdity, reality may be made up of the mind and its ideas, but it is not made up of words — words are just intermediaries between what reality is and what we want it to be.

I must end by reminding myself of the questions and goals of this contemplation of an existential philosophy of law to determine if I have answered them. Also, I have to assure myself that I have not given in to the ultimate existential temptation of becoming Hegelian as has Legal Positivism and most of all other modern philosophy of law — in which they go further by being in delusional denial as to being Hegelian.

    The only valid objection to my reasoning is itself existential: my reasoning depends on a normative belief or intention that an existential and even nihilist struggle against the unopposed violence of the normative power of Western law will act as a rational Hegelian dialectical struggle of reason serving eventually to give meaning to the concepts of justice and fairness in law and thus in life. As always, intentions are one of those realities of which we cannot speak and of which we should be silent but of which we cannot be silent because their existential meaning is obviously affecting the fabric of my use and usefulness or non-existential meaning fabric of my words.

    I do not consider this Hegelian objection to be sound. For an existentialist or any absurd hero to contemplate philosophy of law, the individual by logical necessity must have first made a leap to a morality caring about social constructs, otherwise there is no reason to care about philosophy of law nor any social construct. I explicitly stated in the beginning of my contemplation, I made the leap to contemplation of the nature of law for the specific purpose of determining whether existentialism can oppose the present unopposed normative violent power of the law in Western Civilization in order to prevent or at least diminish the adverse effects of our eventual transition into anarchy and tyranny. I have specifically said that I do not want this transition to destroy Technological Society and its ability to continue to discover, explore, and conquer the universe. This is a challenging problem because Technological Society is its own worse enemy by wanting the law to be an unopposed normative violent power in order to avoid the inefficiency of having competing and struggling normative powers.

    I also explicitly stated that any existential truth must be pragmatic truth: it works to accomplish my existential goal or my Good. Otherwise, no one cares what the truth is. To further explain this pragmatic nature of truth, one final analogy between law and mathematics.

    What is the correct answer to this mathematical formula: $1 +$

1 + 1 + 1 + 1 x 0 = ? Depends on your semantics of numbers and the syntax of your mathematics. Until fairly recently in the history of mathematics, 0 was not a number just as nothingness was not something in language. In which case, the adding of "x 0" to this formula or in any formula was nonsense. Further, it is only in recent history that the syntax has been arbitrarily created that one must first complete the multiplication functions in any formula before completing the addition functions. Thus, based on the recent use and usefulness of numbers and mathematics, we first multiply the last 1 by 0 and then complete the remaining addition to get the correct answer to this formula of 4 — not as many conclude by adding and the sum by 0. This is normative rule following of a given wordgame made up of descriptive rules — similar to using and making useful the descriptive wordgame of chess. For us to use these normative and descriptive rules for pragmatic truth beyond their aesthetic and nominal meanings, the wordgame of mathematics must work to get rockets to the Moon. Failing at that, it is all just a game.

    Now, what is the answer to the question of whether it is legal or illegal not to sign a citation if the law requires "[s]uch citation shall be signed ... by the violator"? The answer is still an issue of semantics and syntax however the semantics and syntax is not descriptive in anyway, it is completely normative: the answer depends on the semantics of the ultimate normative values of the Powers who will decide execution upon this law and the syntax of their power to execute upon those semantics. In mathematics, beauty is power with the pragmatics of power as a side benefit; in the law, power is beauty with the pragmatics of maintaining power the only goal. At any given moment, those with the power to use and make useful this law — that is to decide its meaning — can give it whatever meaning they want; the only limitation is the ability to execute upon it which is the syntax of this law.

    It is correct to say that I have a normative intent and a pragmatic truth for this contemplation. For any existentialist to contemplate a philosophy of law, there must already be a leap to meaning and a morality — or at least a nihilist leap to opposing any normative power simply because it is a normative power or any power, otherwise there is no point to contemplating a philosophy of law. Any existentialist or nihilist who decides to become a *1984* O'Brien and join the law and its Will to Power as an end-in-itself also does not need a philosophy of law except as an aesthetic delusion to hide their Will to Power as is most of modern philosophy of law. As I have stated, even a nihilist fighting as an end-in-itself the power of law needs to know the opponent in order to make it a good fight. So, it is not a sound objection to my philosophy of law that I have such a normative intent. If I did not have this normative intent and its problems, I would need another one in order to serve as a basis for pragmatic truth. If I make no leap to meaning or morality, there is no need to contemplate any philosophy including any philosophy of law — I would simply live in the power of timeliness or commit suicide.

It is incorrect to say my pragmatic truth involves a rational Hegelian dialectical struggle of reason. The struggle is purely existential: Will-to-Power against Will-to-Power. Reason may be a tool in this struggle but only a tool. There is no ultimate rational consciousness coming to know itself in this struggle. If I want to exist and have made a leap to meaning other than that of a *1984* O'Brien, then the Will to Power for my meaning and its morality upon the meaningless universe will eventually find an opponent in the law as the final arbiter through violence of all morality and ethics. This struggle may be dialectical if my Will to Power is strong enough so that the Powers of the law will have to incorporate my leap into the aesthetic beauty of their normative statements: such as by legalizing abortion, changing the meaning of marriage, or making corporations equal to persons, or the exact opposite if that is my struggle and I win it. However, if my Will to Power is not that strong, the Powers will simply ignore me or kill me.

In the end, the individual and all morality and ethics is insignificant to the law except for its ethics: its pragmatic truth deals with the problems of maintaining its power as the final arbiter of all ethics and morality and thus by necessity to maintain its monopoly on violence for the social construct that created it. In the meta-language of Law, the law of the United States, France, Stalinist

Russia, North Korea, and even International law are all variables bound by its universal semantics and syntax. International law is presently only seeking a monopoly on violence and does not have it, so calling it law is inaccurate in a strict sense in the same way as calling quantum waves "waves" is strictly inaccurate, but it is used and useful for Law thus is part of the aesthetic truth of law.

It is not correct to state my pragmatic truth seeks eventually to give meaning to the concepts of justice and fairness in life. In the end, there is no justice or fairness in life. Concepts such a equal protection, due process, equality under the law, and so forth are aesthetical truths; they mean nothing empirically except what the law wants them to mean. In the law as with everything else in life, some are more equal than others and due process means what process those in power decide they want to process. As always, "you see, in this world there's two kinds of people, my friend: Those with loaded guns and those who dig. You dig" (Leone, S. 1966. [Film]). The law is the means by which the inequalities of any given social construct are not eliminated nor reduced but maintained as long as they can be maintained.

However, despite these attributes of the bound variables of laws that make up Law, the empirical reality is that material progress in life are worsened by giving such a universal as Law that can and will kill me an unopposed normative power to decide when the Powers can kill me. Humanity will always have a Heart of Darkness, but whether it is free enough from material wants and needs so as to have the time to contemplate it is other issue. Technological Society would give us such time if we can avoid serving such time in its Room 101 prisoning of the mind. If one has made a leap to a morality demanding collective power not be a god subsuming the individual search for God into its god of power, that leap must oppose the unopposed power of violence that is a necessary attribute of Law.

A. *Questions Asked and Answered*

"I may not be innocent in these events, but they are truly guilty" (Author Unknown). The existential questions about the nature of law that I have sought to answer and the answers that I have reached are as follows.

1. Does an existentialist absurd hero need a philosophy of law? Does it matter what law is? In an existentially meaningless universe, what difference does it make — one god is the same as any other as long as the gods and their worshipers leave me alone? No, unless one has made a leap of faith to caring about ethics and morality. What existentialist philosophy does not contemplate or does not want to contemplate is what are the right circumstances and the how of controlling both the individual and the social Heart of Darkness reality of humanity so that we do not kill each other into oblivion. If one is still contemplating suicide when viewing our Heart of Darkness, these circumstances and the how do not matter. However, once one passes that point and makes a leap to morality, the nature of law does matter and existentialism must make a leap of faith to social constructs such as law and its violence. At that point, the absurd hero begins to care about how that violence is used and made useful; the question of what is law need be answered.

Even the word "violence" is a social construct whose use and usefulness as a link to empirical reality changes as law changes and as the societies change of which it is a construct; in the present moment, even simple words of satire are often considered to be "violence" and illegal. Having grown up in a violent era, in a violent neighborhood, in a violent culture, and with family violence, the present world seems very peaceful to me and I fail to understand much of the need for "safe places" from violence. Historians seem to agree with me.[47] Given the five-fold growth in human population in the 20th Century, Technological Society is more than able to survive the Heart of Darkness that caused the World War (entitled or divided into versions I and II). The greater danger to humanity

---

[47] *See generally*, Gat, A. (2006). *War in Human Civilization*. Oxford University Press.

continuing to exist on earth is from non-technological threats such as the universe and its indifference and antagonism to us than the danger from technology. Yet, law because of its completely self-centered concern for power, in Technological Society, has lost contact with such greater danger. The tidal wave that damaged the Fukushima nuclear power plant drowned 16,000 to 18,000 individuals. The nuclear plant damage killed no one, injured six. Yet, the concern of the Powers is concentrated on the nuclear plant. I do not know whether global warming exists or not or whether it is or is not a threat caused by technology. If it exists and technology caused it, I know technology can solve the problem. I cannot control Yellowstone National Park becoming a massive volcano destroying the United States, but at least I know technology will save lives by moving those that can afford it out of the United States — or off the earth some day.

Again, the Powers care only about the present not the future: the threat of violence must involve their power or something that threatens their power of execution or it is not a concern to them. For the Powers of Technological Society, God is Power and thus is an end-in-itself. It is up to the absurd hero and their leap to faith in this life to give meaning to life if they want it.

In the end, as with most absurd existentialist concerns, nothing really matters. Irrationality is a necessary attribute of our existential Heart of Darkness. Our existence and our Will to Power is irrational, reason is just a tool to achieve the meaning for life to which we leap. The Powers are as justified in enjoying the aesthetics of the law as I am in enjoying the aesthetics of the rock band AC/DC — only difference is that my enjoyment does not seek to kill anyone nor does it need or have an exclusive power to kill anyone.

However, existentially, the Heart of Darkness is more than just the threat of individual humans killing each other. It is a subtle and deep existential truth of which we cannot speak that goes further than the sound bites of which we can speak. Just as Technological Society is its own worse enemy by wanting the efficiency of the law that will in turn kill it as a danger to its power, it is further its own worse enemy by its need for efficient sound bites to replace and negate the inefficiency of deep, subtle, and sincere historical analysis that would help it beat the power of the law trying to kill it. This is descriptive of the relationship of all Powers with all normative descriptions of the Heart of Darkness: regardless of whether they are called liberal, conservative, fascist, or democratic. So-called liberal individuals can readily dismiss any threat to their Will to Power by using the sound bite "nazism". Knowing and understanding the historical construct of Nazism beginning with The Seven Years War, The League of the Three Petticoats, The Miracle of the House of Bradenburger, The Franco-Prussian War, World War I, and The Treaty of Versailles is much more difficult and forgiving of opposing views. Similarly, so-called conservatives can readily dismiss any threat to their power by using the sound bite "communism". Knowing and understanding the historical construct of communism and the fact that even the worse of it under Stalin and Mao was and meant as hope for a better life for plebeians than did life under the tzar or emperor or even the Tibetan Dalai Lama is much more difficult and forgiving of opposing views and opinions on history. (For example, modern history seems to forget it was communism not Buddhism that in 1948 finally outlawed slavery in Tibet in 1949.)

Treating our Heart of Darkness as more than a sound bite, as contemplated earlier, leads to the Heart of Darkness being a necessary attribute of the individual Will to Power. Again, "'Everything is permitted' is not an outburst of relief or of joy, but rather a bitter acknowledgment of a fact." (Camus. 1955. p. 50). Once the leap to meaning in life is made, we are entitled to that meaning: there is no reason to let anyone or anything stop us from having that meaning including the law. We will probably never attain it but we can at least struggle for it.

However, many things can stop us both from having the meaning and from struggling for it: such as the law. If it stops the struggle completely, we might as well be in jail or dead. Our Technological Society and its law is bringing to life O'Brien and his Room 101, but it is not a room with a rat cage but a sterile, pleasantly decorated, warm, friendly room with surround sound of aesthetics. In many ways this Brave New World of the law in which our existential struggle is stopped and replaced by the tranquility of loving Big Brother with a tear in our eye may be the only accessible utopia of this world. If you agree, you can ignore the philosophical nature of law. If you do not agree or simply do not want a utopia, you have a problem that this contemplation is intended to help.

2.   What is "law" when used in its nonscientific sense? Is this word a universal something that has universal attributes true of all legal systems that can be philosophically studied and contemplated? If so, what are they? Are these attributes useful for anything other than nominal meaning? Is "law" a word used simply as shorthand for the millions of individual uses of the word "law" and determinations of what is "legal" occurring each day in courts and other government entities entitled to make useful the word "law"? Does this word "law" include "ethics" and "morality"? Law and its decisions of legality and illegality existentially exist in the universe of normative language in the same way that mathematics and numbers exist in scientific language: decisions of legality and illegality as are numbers are as particular and as real as any bricks or stones thrown at us, yet law as is mathematics is an abstract universal. However, unlike mathematics using rationality to go from aesthetics to particular and empirical pragmatic truth by its use and usefulness to science as descriptive predictive language, the aesthetics of the universal law becomes particular and empirical as a social construct by irrational decisions of legality and illegality: with their rationality running backwards from their pragmatic truth to aesthetics. The only descriptive "is" in law consists of the pragmatic truth of the empirical execution upon law through decisions of legality and illegality. The pragmatic truth of execution is dependent on whether the Powers, those that control the execution upon law, get away or can get away with execution upon their normative statements through violence.

   The universal law in the meta-language of Law is used and is useful as a universal to describe a social construct that is an unopposed normative language with a monopoly on violence to enforce its normative statements. It is the final arbiter through violence of all morality and ethics within the social construct that created it; it is essentially an unopposed ethics with a monopoly on violence whose goal is the survival of the social construct that created it in its struggle with the universe to survive. Thus, just as science does not care, the universal that is law does not care about the nature of the social construct that created it; regardless of whether it is the Republic of San Marino, the Democratic People's Republic of North Korea, the United States, or Stalinist Russia, the law has the same attributes as a bound variable with a monopoly on violence and will use its monopoly on violence to maintain and empower the social construct that created it.

Though the particular decisions of legality and illegality that execute upon the aesthetics of law are irrational leaps of morality and ethics, this empirical attribute is contingent upon the only necessary empirical attribute of these decisions: can the Powers get away with executing upon their morality and ethics through their decisions of legality and illegality by violence. Though some indeterminacy in decisions of legality and illegality are caused by indeterminacy of language, most of it is not actual indeterminacy but intentional and knowing determinacy by the Powers to maintain the aesthetics of law. Ultimately, all morality and ethics and the individuals whose Will to Power is advocating them are expendable and will be sacrificed to whatever violence is necessary to maintain the law and its Powers' monopoly on violence thus maintaining the meaning of the "Powers-that-be" as a used and useful universal itself. Law reaches perfection as a universal when it is a power whose power is an end-in-itself.

> We are the priests of power," [O'Brien] said. "God is power. But at present power is only a word so far as you are concerned. It is time for you to gather some idea of what power means. The first thing you must realise is that power is collective. The individual only has power in as far as he ceases to be an individual.... Every human being is doomed

to die, which is the greatest of all failures. But if he can make complete, utter submission, if he can escape from his identity, if he can merge himself into the party so that he is the Party, then he is all-powerful and immortal. The second thing for you to realise is that power is power over human beings. Over the body—but, above all, over the mind. (Orwell. 1977. p. 333)

3. **Is law a hindrance or an asset to allowing, fostering, and motivating Technological Society to discover, explore, and conquer the universe? Existentialism must either accept or respond to O'Brien, the modern conqueror of our Technological Society, to take a stand on the question of whether law is a hindrance or an asset to allowing, fostering, and motivating Technological Society to discover, explore, and conquer the universe. Which is it?** The Powers of the law will not and will never leave you alone once you reject suicide and make a leap to meaning in life. Even if you want to commit suicide but want to take others with you, the law will not leave you alone. Not because it cares about you or the others you will take with you, but because killing and violence is a monopoly of the law.

Law when allowed to make its necessary attribute of an unopposed monopoly on violence an empirical reality is a hindrance to all historical struggle and whatever progress it may have — material or otherwise. If it reaches its perfection as an unopposed power, it is a hindrance because its Will to Power is to maintain the present not the future. Any Will to Power looking toward the future — irrespective of its morality, ethics, or pragmatic truth, if it threatens the present power of the law then it will be an illegal Will to Power. If its status as an unopposed normative language with a monopoly on violence is a social construct work in progress for the law and its Powers because it has an equally powerful normative language opposing it that does not consider itself an end-in-itself, such as Western Christianity once was, then the law may be an asset to the existential Will to Power to discover, explore, and conquer the indifference and antagonism of the universe to the existence of the individual. It is the struggle between an illegal morality and the legality of the law that creates the future by winning the struggle, at least temporarily, thus forcing the law to amend its aesthetics to include this new morality.

None of this matter unless you want it to matter. If your conqueror hero that you endeavor to be is the Orwellian *1984* O'Brien, than law is your wordgame to do with as you want. If the law is allowed to reach its perfection as a power, which it might have already, with you being one of its O'Brien's, it is tyranny and the absurd hero is allowed to oppose it with all the hate that can mustered and replace the rule of law will be by alternatives such as the rule of honor:

> Whoever appeals to the law against his fellow man is either a fool or a coward. Whoever cannot take care of himself without that law is both. For a wounded man will shall say to his assailant 'If I live, I will kill you. If I die, you are forgiven'. Such is the rule of honor. — "Omerta" lyrics by the band *Lamb Of God* (Blythe, D.R., Campbell, J., Adler, C., Adler, W., & Morton, M. (2004). *Omerta* [Lyrics].)

4.   Are there existential alternatives to such a monopoly? Ought there to be? Yes, if the absurd hero existentialist wants there to be. With Christianity having become worthless as a normative opponent to the law, existentialism and even nihilism putting existence before essence is the only viable opponent to the law. However, it must be a pragmatic existentialism; its truth must be pragmatic. One cannot oppose a monopoly by joining it (unless one is acting as an insider solely to destroy it). One must create a successful competing wordgame or by using any available cracks in the container of the monopoly to break out. Existentialism that seeks to make law is a surrender to the law. All opposing morality to the law will be illegal by definition. Regardless of how existential or caring the law may appear to be at first, it is not. All law will put its essence before any individual or any individual morality.

5. Is law the Outer Party of our present and future Technological Society? Law and the Outer Party have the same meaning as long as Law is allowed to make a necessary attribute of its laws an unopposed monopoly on violence an empirical reality. In which case, the Powers are its Inner Party.

XIII. Conclusion
"To the last, I grapple with thee; From Hell's heart, I stab at thee; For hate's sake, I spit my last breath at thee" (Melville, H. 1999. p. 538).

God is Power. In the end, the artists of the aesthetics of law who give meaning to their lives by the aesthetics of unopposed normative power creating a world as it ought to be in their image may actually be empowered by divine and natural law after all. This would be the ultimate absurdity for the absurd hero who makes a leap to an existential philosophy of law.

Despite all my disagreement with Marx, there is only one descriptive certainty in history:

> The history of all hitherto existing society is the history of class struggles.

> Freeman and slave, patrician and plebeian, lord and serf, guildmaster and journeyman, in a word, oppressor and oppressed, stood in constant opposition to one another, carried on an uninterrupted, now hidden, now open fight, that each time ended, either in the revolutionary reconstitution of society at large, or in the common ruin of the contending classes. (Marx, K., Engels, F. 2014. p. 20).

Struggle is the source of truth and pragmatic progress not kindness, acceptance, and congeniality or whatever any present delusional social justice or cosmic justice safe place demands may be. Thus it was and thus it forever will be as long as there exist more than just isolated hermits in humanity — as long as social constructs exist. Even Christianity admits to such in its less known and less popular theology such as the Parable of the Workers in the Vineyard; Predestination; and even in Kierkegaard's Knight of Faith praising Abraham's willingness to kill his son Isaac upon God's command.

The entirety of American jurisprudence could be replaced by one statute stating: decide cases through your intuitive sense of justice as well as you think best, all things considered. This is what they do anyway. However, this does not mean that there is no pragmatic truth.

It is easy to fall into the modern self-absorbed versions of existentialism viewing and arguing about reality as if it can all be arbitrarily and randomly changed to fit self-centered moralizing and Will-to-Power shallowness. For the absurd hero who has made a leap to a morality that does not leave any fellow plebeians and the Honored Dead of all generations, races, and times behind in a world in which the end comes with a whimper created by patricians admiring their god-like images in the aesthetics of the law, the unopposed problem of the law with its violence seeking power as an end in itself is an existential problem. It is a problem for any leap to meaning in life that must either be accepted to enjoy its power or to be opposed so as to enjoy battling its power. With the law and its Powers having unopposed violent control of post World War II technology and science, I do not believe physical violence among humans is the substantive threat to humanity continuing to move into the future and the next step of historical progression — at least not in Western Civilization. The threat to Western Civilization is the destruction of the will to fight all humanity's joint enemy: the universe. With the destruction of this will to fight, a loss to the anarchy and tyranny of Eastern Civilization and of Plato's cycle of regimes is inevitable.

The Powers and the aesthetics of the law offer irrationality disguised as beauty; an existential absurd hero opposing philosophy of law offers irrationality in all its ugliness. The absurd hero must pick a side and give meaning to law other than its aesthetics. Again, "a work of art has no meaning at all that can be abstracted from it ..." (Fogle, R.H. 1958. p. 110). The absurd hero as with the reader of any purely aesthetic truth must give meaning to the law in the same way the Powers give it meaning: by its use and usefulness. For the law, the Will to Power is an end in itself and provides meaning and truth for its wordgame. For the absurd hero, power is only a tool to a chosen end of their leap to faith.

If the latter option is chosen, violent opposition is a fool's choice and suicide. An unopposed monopoly on violence is an unopposed monopoly on violence. The days of violent rebellion as a means for revolution are gone. Any such attempt will only serve to strengthen the unopposed monopoly of the law just as has the last few years of what will mostly be a never-ending war with "terrorism", drugs, and antisocial behavior. Remember, for law "War is Peace".

However, any other tools of opposition are allowed. Do not limit yourself to the well-marketed tools of love, acceptance, diversity, compassion, so on and so forth. There are alternatives such as the old school honor virtues of crusader warriors: faith, loyalty, courage, humbleness, fairness, mercy, and such. In the end, neither the Powers nor the law cares for any of these. They will kill physically or by other means any individual that is a threat to their violence. The plebeian and the absurd hero trying to give meaning to life and any leap to morality should be willing to do the same to the Powers or do not bother fighting.

Appendix

Why Tolerate Law?

Abstract

Initially when I started reading Brian Leiter's *Why Tolerate Religion*[48], my first impression was that I had found one of the rarest types of lawyers especially of the academic type: one with a sense of humor. As I continued, my impression of dark humor changed to his being factious, then he was gloating, but finally I was forced to conclude he was serious. The timid, cowardly, and fainthearted response by the American religious and legal culture in essence lamely trying to justify nonexistent toleration, "special" or otherwise, worsened the tragedy of his question and answer. In Western Technological Society, the law does not tolerate religion in any sense but a nominal one and most certainly not in any normative or pragmatic sense, the only senses that matter for either law or religion. Western Law has negated and displaced Western Religion to become the only normative power in Western Civilization. The realistic question that should be asked is why tolerate law *qua* law: what principled argument is there for tolerating law with its special monopoly on violence? If this special toleration for the law is really just a categorical demand unhinged from reason and evidence then by Leiter's own reasoning, it is a religion with its own morality and demigods not entitled to this special toleration. Realistically, without Western Law and Western Religion giving each other special toleration as separate but equal communal normative powers, the former violent and the latter nonviolent, either is a tyrant willing to kill the innocent for power and there is no principled argument to tolerate either.

I.   Prologue / the Nature of the Question

"One has to belong to the intelligentsia to believe things like that: no ordinary man could be such a fool" (Orwell, G. 2005. p. 1945).

---

[48] Leiter, B. (2012). *Why Tolerate Religion?* Princeton University Press.

Having grown up lower working class in which the only source of hope in life was through religion, and then working my way up through military service eventually into Harvard Law School, and then 25 years of solo-attorney trial practice in the miserable trenches of the American system of injustice, I am fully aware of the power and weaknesses of both religion and law. For all but a small minority of humanity, the existential question we should ask of law and religion is why we tolerate either. Neither should have the audacity to question the other's communal authority to which neither is rationally entitled. This reality should be undisputed in Western so-called "Realist" philosophy of law and jurisprudence that supposedly recognizes two separate but equal normative powers: the law is law and not morality; morality is morality and not law. Despite such existential and legal reality, a philosopher of law Brian Leiter gives fallacious answers that have little connection to reality to his question *"why tolerate religion"* while assuming that tolerating law is a given.

In asking his question, as easily could be predicted, as is true of most academics' myopic view of life, though Leiter and his school of philosophy readily make distinctions as needed between different word meanings, wordgames, legal systems, laws, rules, philosophies of law, philosophies, moralities, obligations, principles, and much more, to him and to Western Law, they consider all religions the same and assume they can be lumped into a bound variable called "religion" they can judge and give value as the law deems necessary in its wisdom. Then, using popular cliches lacking any philosophy of language, he gives the existential attributes or values of this bound variable "religion" to be: *"categorical demands that are unhinged from reason and evidence"*. Amazingly, despite philosophy of law having spent more than a hundred years unsuccessfully arguing about whether "law" is a universal, in a few pages he has no problem telling us not only the ontology of religion but doing so while leaving out its most important attribute: a communal social construct just as is law.

While Leiter digitally compresses the nature of religion to its supposed essence in order to contemplate toleration, he cannot be bothered to define and tell us in any analytic sense what he means by "tolerate".

Based on Leiter's ontology of religion, faulty logic, hidden premises, and a confusion of word meanings as necessary to reach his predetermined answer — an exemplification of jurisprudence at work — the answer to his question was also readily predictable. He answers that as a matter of *noblesse oblige* within "*limits* of religious toleration" as decided also by law, the law should not grant religion *qua* religion any special toleration or protection but simply place it alongside any other toleration the law in its wisdom decides to give to matters or liberty of "conscience". If and how this answer is to be enforced on society and pontificating on what "liberty of conscience" entails is left for another day.

The timid, cowardly, and fainthearted response by the American religious establishment to this *Why Tolerate Religion* essay is consistent with all of their other surrenders of the past hundred years to the power of law — that is supposed to be its equal in power — thus indicating the question and the answer to be facetious and gloating at best. In Western Technological Society, the law does not tolerate religion specially or in anyway; instead, as a secular religion with its own irrational disguised morality and demigods, law has negated and displaced religion to become the only normative power in Western Civilization. Realistically, in the law's path of displacement are all other moralities or matters of conscience with the intent being to have law reach perfection as a power no longer existing as a means but as an end in itself. As admitted in some of Leiter's other essays, this path is not governed by naturalized analytical thought but by elitist sympathies pretending to be Nietzschean existentialism that are really a Hegelian world view — the ultimate enemy to any existentialist free and open society.[49]

---

[49] Leiter, B. "The Truth is Terrible". *Journal of Nietzsche Studies* (7 April 2018). DOI:10.2139/SSRN.2099162 Corpus ID:

Leiter's question raises serious questions about the power of law that should be asked by both nonreligious and religious. Why is law allowed to pretend there is a universal thing such has "law" with nonlegal obligations — disguised morality — making categorical demands less "unhinged" from reason and evidence than the morality of a thing called "religion"? How is it that modern Western Law, itself a creation from the forge of Western Religion's power struggle within itself and with secular power to live on this earth with Christian morality but not of this earth, has the audacity to question its toleration of what is supposed to be its normative equal while Western Religion lacks the courage to ask likewise of its creation? How is it that Western Religion, Western Civilization's communal attempt to give not only metaphysical but physical meaning to the fire of time and space in which humanity burns, has become subservient to the secular religion of law created by a minority to force their power upon the majority through a monopoly on violence? How is it that philosophy of law though neither rational, analytic, nor scientific is allowed to continue to pretend it is all three? How is it that for modern American law school intelligentsia, elitists such as Nietzsche and their cowardly version of the existentialist view on reality, individual human life, and open society have greater value for philosophy of law as motivators then the courageous version of existentialism of an Albert Camus or Soren Kierkegaard or even of nihilism? Is it time for existentialism to step out of the shadows and create its own philosophy of law? Why tolerate law?

The answer to the last question will turn out to be relatively straightforward: there is no principled basis to tolerate law *qua* law but only because the law tolerates religion and *vice-a-versa*. If the reciprocity does not exist, no one has any obligation to tolerate either. Without such reciprocity, the dominant one is a tyrant, either a legal one in the Roman dictatorship sense or an illegal one — it does not matter, a tyrant is a tyrant to whom we owe no rational obligation to tolerate.

To contemplate these questions and to lay a foundation for an existentialist philosophy of law, one must first understand the elitist and mostly delusional history of modern philosophy of law and associated jurisprudence and the fork-in-the-road duality of existentialism in modern technological society that separates *hoi polloi* from those in its Orwellian Inner and Outer Parties such as Leiter and his colleagues. In order to understand how the law has gotten to the powerful position of being able to question its tolerance of religion without expecting a reciprocal question from religion and of the significance of such power; further, one must have a clear realist not Realist understanding of modern philosophy of law, the history of Western Civilization, and of the particular elitist school of existentialism hidden in modern law and modern Western academia pretending to deny the pragmatic value of all morality but its own — including its fraudulent wordgame pretending that its "nonlegal obligation" has a meaning other than morality. Such an understanding must not be solely an academic understanding intended to stand and be judged solely for its aesthetic value as is the case with most academic nonscientific work including all schools of philosophy of law but must be a pragmatic one.

A. The Unprincipled Reality of "Principled" Argument

Before getting to my question of "why tolerate law", one must understand the invalid and faulty reasoning, misleading and unsound premises, hidden premises, and unprincipled basis of Leiter's *Why Tolerate Religion* so that we do not repeat them and in order to understand the seriousness of my question "why tolerate law". The incredible fact that his fallacious argument and answer are taken seriously as "principled argument" requiring lame responses exemplifies the insignificant level of normative power to which Western religion has sunk essentially making his question meaningless in any pragmatic sense because there is nothing to tolerate. Thus, there is nothing to act as a control of the law as a monopoly on violence.

After defining "principled" as "reasons for toleration ... not based on self-interest, at least not directly" and then dividing "principled arguments" into two classes of "moral" and "epistemic",[50] the substance and essence of his argument are:

1. — the law is a thing that gives religion special toleration;
2. — there is no principled basis for special toleration of religion as opposed to other matters of conscience in "Kantian" and "utilitarian" theories of morality[51];
3. — sometimes religion is epistemic, sometimes it is not[52];
4. — religion is a thing that makes "categorical demands that are unhinged from reason and evidence"[53];
5. — no thing ought to conjoin "categorical demands" with "unhinged from reason and evidence"[54];

Therefore,

6. — there is no principled argument for law to give religion special toleration[55];
7. — the law ought not give religion special toleration.[56]

Even assuming all of the premises are sound and true, neither of the conclusions logically nor rationally follow even at the simplest level of logic. They would only logically follow with

---

[50] Leiter, B. *Why Tolerate Religion,* at n. 9 & p. 7

[51] *Ibid.* pp. 7 - 10.

[52] *Ibid.* pp. 10 - 14.

[53] *Ibid.* pp. 15 - 19.

[54] *Ibid.* pp. 20 -27.

[55] *Ibid.* pp. 28-34.

[56] *Ibid.*

hidden premises: 1) the law ought not give special consideration to any thing that conjoins "categorical demands" with "unhinged from reason and evidence"; 2) the moral and epistemic principles that Leiter considered are the only ones that matter.

The first hidden premise makes the argument invalid as obvious begging the question fallacy. Having defined religion as a thing that conjoins "categorical demands" with "unhinged from reason and evidence", this hidden premise is the same as saying, "the law ought not give special consideration to religion". Why not? Throughout the law, it gives special toleration to "ought not" conjunctions. For example, no government official ought to conjoin "negligent" with "doing their job" or "intentional" with "violation of law while doing their job" . Despite such seemingly universally agreed "ought nots", the law gives special toleration to government officials by giving them various types of immunity from such conjunctions including judges who have absolute immunity for liability for their judicial actions involving such conjunctions. Since there is no reason given for the first hidden premise requiring the law not to treat this particular "ought not" conjunction any differently than the others to whom it gives special consideration, it must be a "categorical demand unhinged from reason and evidence" and thus by his definition this hidden premise is religious — law, the religion of Western intelligentsia demanding a monopoly on violence to enforce its dogma.

The second hidden premise is irrelevant to the question; if he wants to use it, he should be principled about it and ask, "why tolerate religion pursuant to any principles I want to consider".

This is not logical or even rational argument. It is not principled argument in any sense including by his definition of "principled". It is simply reaching a predetermined conclusion by mistakenly or intentionally using invalid reasoning and changing the meaning of words as necessary to fit the predetermined conclusion — *i.e.*, it is jurisprudence.

Now, how about the premises? Are any unsound or irrelevant to either his question or his answers? Are the meanings of the words in his premises consistently used and consistent with each other and the answer? I will examine them one-by-one:

1.   The law is a thing that gives religion special toleration. It says so in the law and thus must be nominally true, but does it in reality in any descriptive sense or other sense? If the law forces meat eaters under threat of violence to live in a society where only vegetarian food is legal, is the law being tolerant or intolerant of the meat eater? The politically correct answer for now is "intolerant". According to Christian morality abortion is baby killing, corporations are not persons, and marriage is a covenant between a man and a woman. Yet, the law requires Christians under threat of physical punishment to accept the annual killing of one million babies as legal, corporations as persons, and homosexual marriage as an enforceable covenant. So, is the law being tolerant or intolerant to Christianity? Is the politically correct answer still "intolerant"? I expect not, the answer now would be "tolerant" because the law — for the present at least — agrees with the meat eater but not with the Christian morality.

So, ignoring the nominal, realistically through reasoning naturalized to science, the special toleration granted religion under the law is: do as the law orders when you morally or religiously or in anyway disagree with what the law orders, or you will be violently punished. What is so special about this type of toleration? It is realistically no different from any other toleration granted by the law. In fact, interpretively, it is the same toleration given by a sniper acting within legally recognized rules of engagement to the target within his sights; it lets the target live until the sniper concludes an act warrants execution.

Is not the substantive difference between morality, matters or liberty of conscience, and religion that religion is not an individual construct but like the law is a social construct or community with the same morality and conscience? Is not religion morality in action? If so, is not forcing religion to accept immoral communal acts an act of intolerance? Is not the substantive difference between Western religion and political ideologies such as Marxism and even Eastern religions such as Islam, Western religion's acknowledgment of "give to Caesar what belongs to Caesar, and give to God what belongs to God"? If so, should not Caesar return the favor in more than just a nominal sense?

2. There is no principled basis for special toleration of religion as opposed to other matters of conscience in "Kantian" and "utilitarian" theories of morality. This premise is sound but only because Leiter arbitrarily and randomly decided how to define "principled", what theories of morality to consider, and arbitrarily to fabricate classes of such theories. How are his arbitrary definitions relevant to the ultimate issue presented by the question of whether the law ought to give religion special consideration or even whether there is any — not just Kantian or utilitarian — principled basis for special toleration? Leiter defines "principled" as "reasons for toleration not based on self-interest, at least not directly". He then splits them up into "moral" and "epistemic" principles. Using his definitions, there are without doubt more principled and moral reasons for special toleration other than the only ones he considers consisting of Kant's categorical imperative and utilitarianism — these are just the present fad theories of morality among academics but they are definitely not the only ones.

Morality is simply a system through which a person determines right and wrong conduct. By his reference to the United States and Canadian constitutions,[57] it seems Leiter is contemplating law in a democracy, republic, or other form of free and open society. So, should we not consider the theories of morality held by *hoi polloi*; after all, the law is not a private club for the powerful and their intelligentsia trying to create a world in their image, right?

In a free and open society, there are millions of "principled" reasons for special toleration of religion. If one is a moral subjectivist, there are as many theories of morality as there are people. According to Gallup, 89% of Americans believe in God.[58]

---

[57] *Ibid.* pp. 1, 2, 14, 32.

[58] Newport, Frank. (2016). "Most Americans Still Believe in God." *Gallup Polls*.

There are hundreds of millions of individuals in the free and open societies of the Western world whose subjective moral theory says religion is entitled to special toleration as a virtue in life good for all of humanity because it gives hope that humans and their dogs will find happiness in another life. Divine command theory is a non-subjective moral theory held by hundreds of millions in Western free and open society: God says religion is entitled to special toleration thus as a matter of principle it is. Since Leiter is sitting in judgment of religion to determine if it is morally worthy of special toleration, as a matter of principle, should he not employ the religious virtue of empathy and view religion from the perspective of religion to see if religion provides a principled basis for special toleration — especially in a supposed free and open society? According to the *Summa Theologica* of Thomas Aquinas and most of Christian moral philosophy, religion is a special higher virtue and morality. All other virtues and morality deal with human will, not ability. A person can be virtuous and moral by good intentions though they lack the ability to act upon them; "[c]*um dilectione hominum et odio vitiorum*" (St. Augustine. 2015. p. 424) (Love the sinner but hate the sin). This is not enough for the virtue of religion. It requires acts actually done for the greater glory of God, thus as a special virtue requiring communal action, it requires special toleration.

      Of course, Leiter would consider the above religious theories of morality to be nonsense and as begging the question presented. For him, it is dogmatically obvious the law cannot allow religion to decide whether or not it gets special toleration, though he has no problem with the law deciding on its own that it will get special toleration for its monopoly on violence. He ignores Christian morality despite the historical fact of Western Law's assumption, some would say hijacking, of Christian theories and concepts of morality making Western Law the unique normative force it is in the

---

http://www.gallup.com/poll/193271/americans-believe-god.aspx

Western world: for example, the law assuming (or hijacking) the Sermon on the Mount and Beatitudes that forced the law to give up such legalities as chattel slavery for the first time in human history. Without its foundation in Christian morality, Western Law would not have the normative authority to now challenge the Christian morality it assumed or hijacked.

My arguments showing there are other available moralities providing the principled basis Leiter seeks is nonsense but not simply because Leiter says so. He wanted a "principled" basis for special toleration, one defined as not based on self-interest at least not directly, and I have listed some for him and could get more through numerous options in subjectivist and religious principles of morality even through secular ones such as Pragmatism — according to William James, "[o]n pragmatistic principles, if the hypothesis of God works satisfactorily in the widest sense of the word, it is true" (James, W. 1907. pp. 115). However, none of them would matter. The reality is that Leiter does not want to find any and asked his question never expecting to find a principled basis as he defined "principled". It is nonsense because morality is nonsense as Leiter has stated in his other writings: "... *moral* obligations – [that] do not really exist: when we speak of moral 'obligations' (or 'rights' or 'duties') we are expressing certain attitudes, often very intense and insistent attitudes, about what we feel other people should or should not do." (Leiter, B. 2017. p. 2). All moralities, including religious, Kantian, and utilitarian, eventually come down to some form of self-interest. As Leiter's beloved Nietzsche has established, in relation to the social constructs that are law and religion, "morality" is simply a means to hide one's Will to Power. This is consistent with the reality of the natural law of the universe: "might makes right" (I have no idea in what delusional reality Natural Law theorists live in) and consistent with the nature of the pure God of the ontological proof. As George Orwell said, "God is Power". (Orwell, G. 1977. p. 333). As the reason there is something instead of nothing, God can do whatever He wants with His reality. All is self-interest; even religious saints are saints because they want to go to heaven.

Once one defines "principled" as not involving self-interest, the definition can be rationally used to deny there is a principled basis for special toleration for anything — religion or the law.

All morality is self-interest and therefore there will never be a "principled" basis for special toleration of religion as Leiter defines "principled". By fabricating this definition, he was setting his reasoning up for the answer he wanted. As I will contemplate in the next section, to the extent "morality" is a meaningful word, it is a metaphysically real one about which I cannot talk or a private language whose translation is an issue behind the scope of this essay.

Regardless, morality is not relevant to my question and should not have been relevant to Leiter's question. Defining "principled" as "not based on self-interest" and then splitting it up into "moral" and "epistemic" classes guarantees we will never find any principled basis for anything including no principled basis for special toleration of religion nor of the law.

3. **Sometimes religion is epistemic, sometimes it is not**. This is a sound statement of everything in life. Seeking an epistemic "principled" basis for special toleration of religion is also nonsense unless one admits that knowledge of God is special knowledge — which Leiter does not and will never admit.

4. **Religion is a thing that makes "categorical demands that are unhinged from reason and evidence".** What categorical demands? Such as "love your neighbor as yourself"; "blessed are the poor in spirit for theirs is the kingdom of heaven"; "blessed are they that hunger and thirst after justice for they shall have their fill"; "blessed are the merciful for they shall obtain mercy"; "blessed are the clean of heart for they shall see God"; "blessed are the peacemakers for they shall be called the children of God"; "blessed are they that suffer persecution for justice sake, for theirs is the kingdom of heaven"; and other Beatitudes and Sermons.

Are these really "categorical" with no exceptions tied to reason or evidence? If so, how is Leiter able to descriptively accuse religion of hypocrisy between its categorical demands and the exceptions granted by religion in action? Without doubt the above quoted Christian demands are unhinged from reason and evidence, but is that not a good thing? If we were to hinge them to reason and experience they would convert: to the golden rule of "he who owns the gold makes the rules"; "might makes right"; "every rat for himself"; and "there are those with loaded guns and those who dig".

Unhinged from what "reason and evidence"? What he really means is "reason and evidence" not naturalized to the reason and evidence of science.

Before binding such values to the variable that is religion in his reasoning, I would think he should at least have the "principled" integrity to read the philosophical reasoning and evidence of an analytical philosopher such as Thomas Aquinas or similar Scholastic analytical philosophers and theologians upon whom much of the Renaissance and the Enlightenment was based including the rise of science, instead of intentionally limiting argument to the usual suspects and Nietzsche. What about the "ontological proof" that even in the post-modern world of philosophy has yet to be decisively refuted. What evidence is there on the question of "why is there something instead of nothing" that even science has given up on.[59] What Leiter really means in this premise is "categorical demands that are unhinged from reason and evidence with which I agree".

What about the historical evidence? Western religion as a historical fact has helped human progress much more than the law ever has. In history, law has never been on the right side of history because it has never been a historical force. It is simply an interlude between periods of lawlessness after which the lawless winners become the law and force upon the losers as law what were "nonlegal" moral obligations. At least religion throughout history until recently existed as a normative historical physical force both during interludes of lawfulness and in periods of lawlessness when

---

[59] *See generally,* Holt, J. (2013). *Why Does the World Exist?: An Existential Detective Story.* Liveright..

law was nowhere to be found.

The legal obligations of American law started with an armed revolution by a minority consisting of mobs of fanatical tax evaders, bootleggers, gunman, terrorists, and other criminal mobs against the majority loyalists and their law. If not for the hope in some of the "Founding Fathers" criminal mob of morality derived from religious obligations such as "all men are created equal, that they are endowed by their Creator with certain unalienable Rights, that among these are Life, Liberty and the pursuit of Happiness" and so forth, we might as well call ourselves United Mob Island. If the Legal Positivist Rules of Recognition, Rules of Change, and Rules of Adjudication were left to work on their own, we would still have chattel slavery in Western Civilization. It was Christian morality making its "tastes" powerful in Western Civilization that made and makes Western Law a unique power in history and at present — though maybe not in the future since according to Leiter Western Law need not give Western religion special toleration.

Regardless, I will assume as Leiter does that scientific "reason and evidence" is the true and only reason and evidence that matters. Though Realism, Real Positivism, and almost all other modern schools in the philosophy of law want to be a "science of law", one will find throughout their writings as is found with Leiter, terms such as "common sense", "intuitive", "obviously true", "any educated person would know", "as understood in other domains", "ordinary standards", and so forth indicating one has reached a dead-end in reasoning or one wants to start a chain of reasoning to a specific conclusion but lacks the foundation premise upon which to start. Though schools of philosophy of law very much want to be a science of law, this is a very unscientific reasoning process and is a wordgame anyone educated or uneducated can play with or without any sense. Strictly speaking in philosophy of language terms, when you reach a point in reasoning requiring the use of words such as this you have reached a point "whereof one cannot speak, thereof one must be silent"; however, no one ever is. This is especially true when Leiter and others use the word "common-sense" to describe their reasoning. As the popular adage goes, "Common sense is not so common".

I am not saying that scientists would never use such words as "common sense" and similar attempts to avoid reasoned premises. In fact, they probably care less about philosophy of language than almost any other area of thought and even less than they care about philosophy of science. Except for the heuristic limitations of Ockham's Razor, scientists will use whatever and any words necessary to successfully solve a problem in a predictive sense; that is to predict the future given what the past was and the present is. What a scientist cannot do is pretend that scientific words have any evaluative or perspective normative meaning: state what "ought" to be. Scientists can play with the semantics and treat an "ought" statement as shorthand for an action that "is". For example, one can say that when dropping a rock from my hand from a tall building on earth, its acceleration due to gravity "is" 9.8 m/s/s, thus after eight seconds its velocity "ought" to be 78.4 m/s. However, the "is" and the "ought" are being used in the same non-normative "is" sense. The physicist saying what velocity ought to be is not making an evaluative or perspective normative judgement of the velocity but simply stating what will be the empirical "is" measurement of that velocity.

Science makes no "*categorical demands* that are unhinged from reason and evidence" because it makes no categorical demands and only cares about reason or evidence when necessary to achieve predictive value; otherwise, it is willing to dump both or either as necessary to achieve a pragmatic truth distinct from any normative meaning. As described by modern philosophers of science and scientists, science is not even limited to reason and evidence for achieving its purposes but often begins with creative, theoretic anarchy, and through techniques such as zeta function regularization scientists are even willing to play with the meanings of numbers in order to give predictive pragmatic meaning to their wordgames. According to a popular adage attributed to Albert Einstein, "the true sign of intelligence is not knowledge but imagination". "Science is an essentially anarchic enterprise: theoretical anarchism is more humanitarian and more likely to encourage progress than its law-and-order alternatives" (Feyerabend, P.K. 2010. p. 9).[60] As one of Leiter's often cited philosopher of science Willard Van Orman Quine stated:

> [p]hysical objects are conceptually imported into the situation as convenient intermediaries -- not by definition in terms of experience, but simply as irreducible posits comparable, epistemologically, to the gods of Homer. ... But in point of epistemological footing the physical objects and the gods differ only in degree and not in kind. ... The myth of physical objects is epistemologically superior to most in that it has proved more efficacious than other myths as a device for working a manageable structure into the flux of experience. (Quine, W.V.O. 1980. p. 44).

It is to scientific "reason and evidence" that Leiter wants all categorical demands hinged. That is, all demands are to be hinged to the reason and evidence that does not care whether it exists in the United States or North Korea; in a fascist, communist, Stalinist, democratic, free, republican, or tyranny state; in a concentration camp or in a free and open society; or anywhere as long as its words have predictive meaning and are allowed to reach a pragmatic truth without normative meaning. Apparently, he does. How is this categorical demand of amorality by Leiter that everything be naturalized to science in any way hinged to reason and evidence, particularly historical evidence? If not, is it his religion? Given the reality of historical evidence, if anyone or thing is going to have a monopoly on violence over me and my community as does the law now and as naturalized law would, as a matter of my will to power as his beloved Nietzsche would say, should I not want it

---

[60] *See generally,* Hanson, N. R. (2010). *Patterns of Discovery*. Cambridge University Press; Kuhn, T.S. Kuhn, T.S. (2012). *The Structure of Scientific Revolutions* 4th ed. University of Chicago Press.

counterbalanced by an equal but separate normative nonviolent power — at least for pragmatic reasons?

5.   No thing ought to conjoin "categorical demands" with "unhinged from reason and evidence". Again Leiter is playing with the meaning of words here as he did most clearly in the previous premise but did to some extent in all of them. What he really means is that "no thing ought to conjoin 'categorical demands with which he disagrees'", "unhinged from reason and evidence with which I agree", or "be hinged to reason and evidence with which I disagree". He has no problem with law making a categorical demand unhinged from reason and evidence for a necessary unchecked monopoly on violence to enforce its dogma.

6.   There is no principled argument for law to give religion special toleration. This is an invalid conclusion. The only conclusion that validly follows from his premises is that none of the usual suspects and evidence he cites have a principled argument. There are libraries of principled argument and evidence out there for law to give religion special toleration if one actually wants to find them varying from Scholastic philosophers such as Aquinas on to pragmatic philosophers such as William James and to all of history. This is an invalid, predetermined conclusion that is more jurisprudence than principled thought.

7.   The law ought not give religion special toleration. This is an invalid, predetermined conclusion even assuming the law does give religion special toleration in anything but a nominal sense. It is a normative "ought" statement that logically follows from none of his mixed descriptive, interpretative, predictive, and mixture of "is" meanings for words changed as necessary to reach this conclusion. This is the unprincipled basis by which philosophy of law argues and the technique by which jurisprudence hides its morality as "nonlegal obligation".

Leiter's "principled" reasoning that he defines as not based on "self-interest" is entirely based on self-interest. Though Leiter's argument and answer are logically invalid and really not even reasoning let alone "principled" reasoning, what Leiter as a philosopher of law and law professor has given us by his question and answer is the reality of jurisprudence. Even Leiter admits such in some of his writings such as "The Truth is Terrible"[61], "American Legal Realism"[62], "In Praise of Realism (And Against 'Nonsense' Jurisprudence)"[63], and "The Roles of Judges in Democracies: A Realistic View"[64]. In the former he is not referring to his nonsense jurisprudence; in the last one, it is so entitled though it is not very realistic as it too assumes the law's monopoly on violence is a given to be absolutely tolerated with no consideration of the effects of such a monopoly on a free and open society. As with Leiter, judges and other law givers view the facts, then based on their beliefs, assumptions, intuitions, and personal or universal prejudices and bias and outright bigotries decide an answer. They then go on to use or fabricate facts, word meanings, and wordgames as necessary to justify their predetermined answer they then call "law".

---

[61] Leiter, B. "The Truth is Terrible". *Journal of Nietzsche Studies* (7 April 2018). DOI: 10.2139/SSRN.2099162 Corpus ID: 170211129

[62] Leiter, B. (2005). "American Legal Realism". *The Blackwell Guide to the Philosophy of Law and Legal Theory* [Martin P. G., William A. E., Eds.). Blackwell.

[63] Leiter, B. (2012). "In Praise of Realism (and Against "Nonsense" Jurisprudence)". 100 Georgia. L.J. 865, 867 (2012).

[64] Leiter, B. (2017). "The Role of Judges in Democracies: A Realistic View". *University of Chicago Law School Chicago Unbound Working Papers.* https://chicagounbound.uchicago.edu/cgi/viewcontent.cgi?article=2105&context=public_law_and_legal_theory

Realistically, based on my 25 years as a trial attorney handling about a thousand cases in the miserable trenches of the legal system, a world never experienced by Leiter because it is unclean, what Leiter's question and deceptive irrational process to his answer show us is how jurisprudence reasons — that is, how judges and other lawgivers think.

So, why tolerate law?

II. The Unprincipled Reality of Principled Argument

As I try to answer my question "why tolerant law", unlike Leiter, I will be up-front as to what I am doing. I will only consider descriptive, normative, and pragmatic meanings as relevant because none other are. The descriptive fact that creates my rational or irrational concern, belief, or whatever you want to call it that begins my chain of normative reasoning is the law's unchecked and uncontrollable by anyone but itself monopoly on violence to enforce itself. I do not like violence; no one should be entitled to use violence on me nor my community without good reason; and most definitely no one or thing should have a monopoly on violence over me or my community. The sound historical evidence is that such a monopoly leads to humanity destroying itself through tyranny; I do not want anyone or thing having a monopoly of violence over my life and community — including God, but I have no other option with him; hopefully I do have options with the law. I am seeking those options; my question is normative. I want to know what ought to be. The truth of my answer is to be pragmatic: making what ought to be workable so that I can live life without the law (or religion) destroying me and my community. So, in essence, I am not looking for "principled" argument for tolerating law as Leiter defined "principled" since that was a joke; he only made that up knowing that he would never find any. As a matter of self-interest, I want to find a normative and pragmatic argument for special toleration of the categorical demand unhinged from reason and evidence of law *qua* law having a monopoly on violence. If the only reason for such toleration is to avoid its physical violence upon me, it is time to look for other options.

In this writing I will use the assumptions made by Leiter that there are values for a bound variable in reality called "law", "religion", and "toleration".

Eventually if not in this essay but in other writings, I will hopefully get to contemplate whether or not there really are such universals. It may be there are only particular laws and worse: no competent or incompetent attorney has a serious clue as to what they are; clients do not care what they are; and judges only care to the extent they can or cannot get away with execution upon any particular law. It may be there are only particular religions: Christianity, Islam, Aztec, Buddhism, so forth, that at best can be divided into Western and Eastern with significant overlap such as between Christianity and Buddhism.

The material attribute for a religion for the question at issue is whether it is not simply a matter of conscience but a communal morality of action that recognizes a necessary separation between "give to Caesar what belongs to Caesar, and give to God what belongs to God".

In asking why tolerate law, it is important not to repeat the logic errors and what may be intentional sleight-of-hand with meanings and logic used by Leiter to answer his question of why tolerate religion that allowed him to use unsound and hidden premises and invalid reasoning to reach a predetermined conclusion.

The use of language is crucial to any morality or legal system as it is to any religion. In my reasoning and in any philosophical reasoning on law and religion, there needs to be an understanding or at least an agreement as to the meanings of the words we will be using for this purpose. Specifically in this essay, we need an understanding or agreement on the meanings of "tolerate", "law", and "religion" and of the wordgame "why tolerate law"? This requires some understanding of the meaning of words. What is language? More specifically, what is the meaning of a word in language? What is the meaning of meaning? Is it meaningful to contemplate language using language? If so, to what extent is such contemplation meaningful? What is the relationship between words and truth, if any? Are science and its pragmatic truths the king of the mountain to which all else must be naturalized? These are serious questions whose answers result in paradigm shifts in any philosophy of anything, philosophy of law and morality included, and even cast doubt on whether "philosophy" is anything other than an analytic contemplation of language thus making philosophy of law, morality, metaphysics, and everything seeking non-pragmatic truth rationally meaningless wordgames.[65]

Luckily, philosophies of law and any attempt by its preachers such as Leiter to engage in discussion of morality are extremely sophomoric as philosophy and do not ask the important analytical questions about language before they start their pontificating, so we do not need to get into great analytical detail on a philosophical contemplation of language nor into any of its major paradoxes. However, we must have a basic understanding of how language is used and abused relevant to the questions at issue of "why tolerate religion" and "why tolerate law". As I stated previously, any philosophical use of words such as "common sense", "intuitive", "obviously true", "any educated person would know", "as understood in other domains", "ordinary standards", and so forth indicate one has reached a dead-end in reasoning or one wants to start a chain of reasoning to a specific conclusion but lacks the foundation premise upon which to start. In philosophy of language analysis, when you reach a point in your reasoning requiring you to use words such as this you have reached a point "whereof one cannot speak, thereof one must be silent"; however, no one ever is silent but I will try to be.

A. *Philosophy of Language Relevant to the Question*
The meaning of a word either is a "thing-in-itself" existing independent of our use of the word or is dependent on our use of it.

In the former, my question would involve asking whether

---

[65] *See generally*, Wittgenstein, L. (2009). *Philosophical Investigations* (G.E.M. Anscombe, Trans.). Wiley-Blackwell.

there is true "law" or "religion" that I must tolerate in the same way that I must tolerate my existence or in the same way that Christians must follow the true God.

In the latter, law and religion are social constructs tied to experience at one end and to theory at another end.

The former concept of meaning is called metaphysical realism and is completely absent from mainstream philosophy of law (philosopher of law Michael S. Moore of the University of Illinois School of Law is the only one I know of) and secular morality. It is absent for dogmatic reasons and not because of any rational proof making it unsound or invalid. A majority of professional mathematicians — the purest of logical minds — are metaphysical realists who believe numbers are just as real or more real than sense experience and they "discover" numbers in their reasoning in the same way that one discovers a stone.[66] Some of the greatest logical minds of the 20th Century were metaphysical realists such as Kurt Godel, Erwin Schrödinger (in his later years), and Sir Roger Penrose. Examples of everyday words that appear to have metaphysically real meanings independent of their use are words such as "I", "consciousness", and either the Cartesian or existentialist version of thought ("I think therefore I am"; "I am therefore I think" or "existence precedes essence"). These common words seem to have a true meaning as things-in-themselves in the world that are discovered and guide our actions and dealings in the world everywhere and anywhere in all possible worlds in which we exist, they are not contingent on social or even private use. In does not matter these words cannot be defined other than by reference to themselves nor refuted and thus logically should be meaningless since they cannot be interpreted either by the user privately or publicly; they mean existence and necessarily mean so in all possible worlds.

Without doubt, Leiter is not a metaphysical realist, nor am I.

---

[66] *See* Holt, J. (2013). *Why Does the World Exist?: An Existential Detective Story*. Liveright.

If he were, he would have phrased his question as "why tolerate false religion" or "why not just tolerate true religion". These are questions that he not only would never ask but that no lawyer in Western legal culture would ever think of asking as a meaningful question. With due respect to the truly great minds who are metaphysical realists, I am not a metaphysical realist because I agree with Wittgenstein that "[t]he limits of my language means the limits of my world" (Wittgenstein, L. 2009. Prop. 5.6, p. 63) and thus "whereof one cannot speak, thereof one must be silent" (Wittgenstein. 2009. Prop. 7, p. 82). I am willing to be silent about it. Any questions that may imply or implicate metaphysical realism such as "what is the meaning of 'meaning'"; "how can we use words of unknown meaning to contemplate meaning"; the Wittgenstein Private Language Argument; and the Wittgenstein Rule Following Paradox are irrelevant to the question at hand since no one who is reading this, if anyone, will be a metaphysical realist. Therefore, instead of asking "why tolerate [true] [or] [false] law", I also only ask "why tolerate law".

So, for pragmatic simplicity, I will accept that the meanings of words are dependent on their use and their usefulness to that use. This does not make all words arbitrary and random creations. A language or wordgame is a fabric of intertwined words — a "social construct" is the present popular phrase — that must at some point even if only at the periphery have some contact with factual sense experience or empirical observation, but language is not completely reducible to sense experience or empirical observation. Language is laden with theory that often decides what facts we experience, observe, and use. Such attributes are true of all language even our Technological Society's beloved scientific language. "Whether you can observe a thing or not depends on the theory which you use. It is the theory which decides what can be observed." (Salam, A. 2005. Quoting Albert Einstein, p. 85).

Forgetting to anchor a language to both ends, to fact and to theory, makes it lose its meaning but not its power; in fact, in many ways both in law and in religion, language becomes more powerful as it becomes more meaningless. Both the tragedy and comedy of such reality are readily apparent everywhere around us at the modern world constantly arguing about "social constructs" as if they can be randomly and arbitrarily changed without concern for facts or pragmatics. The power of meaningless words is obvious in the last hundred years of writings in the philosophy of law. The most obvious example is the wordgame in which some philosophers of law pretend there is other than just a nominal difference between "moral" obligations and "nonlegal" obligations in the philosophy of law.

Making the meaning of words be their use creates sets of meanings whose quantity and whose set members increase as necessary for academia to justify its daily generating of libraries of verbiage: nominal, legal, predictive, pragmatic, normative, descriptive, epistemic, interpretative, hermeneutical, deontological, consequential, and much more that I cannot remember for the moment and do not want to spend time trying to remember or looking up. It is at this point that philosophy of language and analytic philosophy in particular finds its meaning in life. "Philosophy is a battle against the bewitchment of our intelligence by means of language" (Wittgenstein. 2009. ¶109, p. 52)

In dealing with these various uses, there is almost no limit to what meanings can be created. Except for predictive meanings and wordgames such as science, none will have a useful meaning for the word "true" or "truth" that can be falsified; so it does not matter pragmatically whether any of these meanings have any contact with sense experience except for contact with other words. "'When I use a word,' Humpty Dumpty said in rather a scornful tone, 'it means just what I choose it to mean — neither more nor less'" (Carroll, L. 2009. p. 50). The only limitation is their usefulness to the use to which the words are being put. If the same word has different uses, it will have different meanings. For example, "wave" has multiple different meanings varying from use at the beach to use in quantum physics. If different words have the same use or usefulness, they will have the same meaning. "A rose by any other name would smell as sweet". This process is often called wordgames. This concept does not mean however that the same word used in one wordgame can be moved to a different wordgame and retain in its meaning by assumption; it retains its meaning if it retains its use and usefulness. Also, words cannot change meaning within their usefulness. So, for example one cannot take the words of a descriptive wordgame supposedly stating "what is" then to state an interpretative conclusion stating the relationship between "what is" using the same words by assuming they will retain the same meaning.

An example of the latter intertwining is Leiter's wordplay with "tolerate" and "toleration" that he fails either inadvertently or intentionally to define analytically despite the fact it is the substance of his question and argument: *Why Tolerate Religion*. Instead, as a judge would, he plays with these words as necessary to reach his pre-determined answer. At some points he uses "toleration" and "tolerate" to describe how persons treat each other, *i.e.*, they do not act adversely against neighbors who are empirically different from themselves. The words are then used in an interpretive and hermeneutical sense, *i.e.*, in order for persons to tolerate each other they cannot be indifferent to each other. (This interpretation is false. I have dealt with many cold-blooded killers who are indifferent to my existence but tolerate it anyway until the day they randomly or for a reason may decide to stop tolerating it.) Finally, it becomes normative, *i.e.*, we ought not give special toleration to religion.[67]

As you can infer already, much of these wordgames are arbitrary creations and often overlap in practice for aesthetic reasons — for words or wordgames with no predictive value, aesthetic value is as good a value as any other. Nothing is more aesthetically pleasuring to the rational mind than listening to itself talk or reading its words. This is true of even the simplest of descriptive meanings. As any reasonably experienced trial attorney will tell you, if you ask a hundred people to describe the same event, you will get a hundred different descriptions because each person's interpretation of the event affects what they will describe — and what they see in the

---

[67] Leiter, B. (2012). *Why Tolerate Religion?* Princeton University Press. pp. 2-3, 32-33.

first place. This is one of the reasons that led the philosopher Willard Van Quine to describe knowledge as a "man-made fabric which impinges on experience only along the edges" (Quine, W.V.O. 1980. pp. 43-44).

There are at least two relevant wordgames however that are logically independent and must not be allowed to overlap in meaning even for aesthetic reasons if you are to have a logical contemplation on why tolerant anything: "is" statements and "ought" statements. The nature of this logical reality is known by names such as "is-ought", "open question", Hume's Law, or Hume's Guillotine named after the philosopher David Hume who described it best and as follows:

> In every system of morality, which I have hitherto met with, I have always remarked, that the author proceeds for some time in the ordinary way of reasoning, and establishes the being of a God, or makes observations concerning human affairs; when of a sudden I am surprised to find, that instead of the usual copulations of propositions, is, and is not, I meet with no proposition that is not connected with an ought, or an ought not. This change is imperceptible; but is however, of the last consequence. For as this ought, or ought not, expresses some new relation or affirmation, 'tis necessary that it should be observed and explained; and at the same time that a reason should be given, for what seems altogether inconceivable, how this new relation can be a deduction from others, which are entirely different from it. But as authors do not commonly use this precaution, I shall presume to recommend it to the readers; and am persuaded, that this small attention would subvert all the vulgar systems of morality, and let us see, that the distinction of vice and virtue is not founded merely on the relations of objects, nor is perceived by reason. (Hume, D. 1739. pp. 469-70).

Despite centuries old Hume's Law and a century of modern philosophy of language, all modern schools of philosophy of law without explanation and without any attempt at analytical justification assume they can infer from statements about experience, from what "is", to evaluative or perspective normative statements, to what "ought" to be. Jurisprudence has gotten away with such dogma for millennia. One can play as many wordgames as one wants such as calling "ought" statements nonlegal obligations or economics instead of morality, but no matter how you change your syntax or semantics, there is no way to deduce nor induce from predictive, descriptive, epistemic, interpretative/hermeneutical, or any other fabricated categories of statements of what "is" to conclusions expressing a new relation of an evaluative or perspective normative "ought". Logically and rationally, no matter how well hidden the meanings may be by the fabrication of words to hide what is going on, one can only go from evidence of "is" statements to other "is" statements and from "ought" statements to other "ought" statements.

Eventually, to avoid an infinite chain of ought statements to justify one's evaluative or perspective normative statements of what ought to be, one must start at the beginning by foundation premises relying on beliefs, assumptions, and intuitions using words as Leiter does in his essays such as "common sense", "intuitive", "obviously true", "any educated person would know", "as understood in other domains", "ordinary standards", and so forth to hide the transition from "is" to "ought". All rational normative argument is founded upon and begins with irrationality. In law and economics, the sleight-of-hand is done by calling the "ought" statements economics. In Legal Positivism, the switch is done by calling them "non-moral obligations". These are all attempts to avoid Hume's Law.

To the extent "morality" is a meaningful word and wordgame, it is either as Leiter states a rational structure of personal "tastes" or a metaphysically real one about which I cannot talk or a private language whose translation is an issue behind the scope of this essay. Regardless of which it is, it is irrelevant to my question.

Leiter, as do most academics, jumps around without acknowledging the change in meanings of his words hoping no one will notice as necessary to reach a predetermined result. He starts out concerned with the legal meaning of his question in the wordgame of the law: its "special treatment" in the "American and Canadian constitutional law". At that point, his question should have been phrased: "why tolerate religion in a legal sense". This is a boring question that is meaningless in any sense but nominal giving an answer that cannot be refuted: because the law says so. Similarly, if I phrase my question as "why tolerate the law in a legal sense", it too would answer itself, cannot be refuted, and thus would be meaningless except nominally.

In both our questions, we are really asking for a normative answer. He is asking whether the law ought to give religion special toleration. I am asking whether religion or anyone ought to allow law a special monopoly on violence.

After ignoring the legal meaning of his question, Leiter goes on to various forms of wordgames — in a very unscientific manner though he wants everything to be naturalized to science — involving and varying from descriptive, interpretive, and normative or moral meanings through epistemic meanings (all of which he calls principles) and ends with what are predetermined disguised normative or morality statements as answers to his question. He starts out with meaning in a legal sense and through a thought process using different meanings ends with normative meaning: the law ought not single out religion for special protection. Can he switch from initial meaning to other meanings to a completely different meaning from words taken from completely different wordgames? No, this is an invalid fallacious combination of different meanings and wordgames to give the appearance of valid argument and contradicts the entire concept of meanings being dependent on their use and usefulness to a given wordgame in which the words are used.

To what use and wordgames are my words "law", "religion", and "tolerate" useful?

1. What is "law" relevant to the toleration being questioned? Modern philosophers of law have been arguing for about a hundred years over the meaning of "law" and have fabricated all sorts of aesthetically pleasing wordgames for it. (In classical philosophy, any contemplation of law was considered a branch of ethics or moral philosophy as it should be.) They even have been arguing over whether their theories of law are descriptive, interpretative, normative, hermeneutical, descriptive/interpretative (whatever that means), and so forth apparently for no other reason than to listen to themselves talk. Again, as I stated before, since none of these meanings are predictive as a scientific wordgame would be, the intelligentsia can make up as many meanings as they want to fit into whatever wordgames they make up. In the end, it does not matter and no ones should care except for tenure committees.

Supposedly, they all want to make a "science of law" in which its wordgame is a social construct that possesses certain attributes by its very nature or essence as law whenever and wherever it happens. They disagree as to whether or not the essence of this social construct "law" includes morality. If it does not, according to Legal Positivism it only has legal obligations, rights, and duties created by a social process involving Rules of Recognition, Rules of Change, and Rules of Adjudication that by a Separability Thesis are separate from moral obligations but that allows lawgivers to consider other nonlegal "obligations" that according to Leiter cannot be "understood as *moral* obligations" (Leiter, B. 2017. pp. 2-3). If it does not include morality, then law is law regardless of whether it is democratic, fascist, or whatever. For those philosophers of law who argue law must consider moral obligations, what morality would that be? Unclear, except they all agree it is not any type of religious morality; usually they mean the morality as decided by Oxford, Harvard, or Yale academia. How are nonlegal obligations different from moral obligations? (They are not, it is simply different words with the same meaning.) How does one make a "science of law" if the law is not a predictive wordgame concerned only with pragmatic truth that can be tested and falsified? (You cannot.)

I do not know and do not care about these academic

questions and their academic answers because none of these issues with "law" as a universal are relevant to my question nor should they matter to any working class person nor anyone in any but the highest of social classes or their intelligentsia. The only descriptive universal attribute or value of the bound variable "law" is the one it possesses by its very nature and essence as a social construct whenever and wherever it happens: its special monopoly on violence to enforce itself. The realities of any law be it contract, tort, probate, estate, civil, criminal, tax, inheritance, administrative, and whatever, the unique and omnipresent feature of all law is that eventually even in the absence of any other obligation or in opposition to other obligations such as religion and matters of conscience, the law will violently enforce obedience as a matter of normative right.

    The Legal Positivist H.L.A. Hart however was correct that this monopoly on violence as an attribute of law is not the same as a gunman's threat. It is in reality the same as a social group of gunmen's or a mob of gunmen's threats because law is a social construct; there is no such thing as private law just as there is no such thing as a private language. Though these days I should phrase it as a mob of gunpersons since women are now made-men in the mob that is law. If a criminal mob takes over an island and begins to enforce its oaths, code of conduct, contract rules, pragmatic obligations of care, rules of inheritance, family rules of care, and rules for maintenance and distribution of wealth on the island, with a little time and with the help of philosophers of law such as Leiter, it eventually becomes the government of Mob Island with its mob rules becoming its criminal law, contract law, tort law, estate law, probate law, and so forth. One of the purposes in life for philosophers of law is to assist a mob of gunpersons in transforming themselves from a mob to being law; they essentially act as the mob's *consigliere*.

    Philosophers of law ignore this necessary value or attribute in their philosophizing most likely unintentionally so as not to demean the meaning of their lives and because with few exceptions most have never actually practiced law so they do not know what they are describing nor how its different aspects work with each other; in fact, they consider practice as something beneath them, as something with which it is not worth getting their hands dirty. As trial attorneys describe appellate judges, they like to watch from on high the legal battle fought below, and when the dust and smoke of the battle clear they come down out of the hills and shoot the wounded.

Just as the meaning of science for philosophers of law everywhere has the same meaning, it is the intent of naturalized law everywhere to be the same wordgame wherever and whenever it is found: United States, Stalinist Russia, Great Britain, North Korea, wherever. According to naturalized law, law is law; it is has nothing to do with moral obligations because even if it did, they do not really exist in any sense other than the lawgiver's personal beliefs, opinions, "tastes", bias, and so forth — their morality, deceptively called nonlegal obligations to hide the same meaning of the words and the is-ought transition.

The only limit on these nonlegal obligations and the law's monopoly on violence is the physical reality of execution: how far will the law's enforcers or hitmen go before the one with the gun pointed at their head becomes suicidal.

As I stated up-front, I dislike and disapprove of this descriptive reality granting law a normative monopoly on violence and believe it ought not to be. Based on historical evidence and life experience, power corrupts; the unchecked power of law "ought" not to be in order to maintain a free and open society. There ought to be something to counterbalance it other than an opposing mob who wants its own monopoly on violence. America can now claim to be the oldest continuing modern democracy or republic — depending on how you define those terms. However, it is not the first of either; democracies and republics have come and gone before and were a well-known form of governance even in the ancient world among tribes and then on to city states. So much so that the philosopher Plato whom Leiter loves to criticize became history's first known sociologist by studying their rise and fall then developing a descriptive and interpretive theory allowing for predictions that have yet to be falsified by time. According to Plato, all states begin with kingship then evolve into timocracy or plutocracy; then oligarchy; then democracy; then anarchy; finally tyranny.[68]

George Orwell in *1984* accurately and succinctly described the new school tyranny that is presently the law and destined to be our future under the law:

> As compared with their opposite numbers in past ages, the new aristocracy is less avaricious, less tempted by luxury, hungrier for pure power, and, above all, more conscious of what they were doing and more intent on crushing opposition. This last difference was cardinal. By comparison with that existing today, all the tyrannies of the past were half-hearted and inefficient. The ruling groups were always infected to some extent by liberal ideas, and were content to leave loose ends everywhere, to regard only the overt act, and to be uninterested in what their subjects were thinking. Even the Catholic Church of the Middle Ages was tolerant by modern standards. Part of the reason for this was that in the past no government had the power to keep its citizens under constant surveillance. The invention of print, however, made it easier to manipulate public opinion, and the film and the radio carried the process further. With the development of television and the personal computer, and the technical advances which made it possible to receive and transmit simultaneously on the same instrument, private life came to an end. Every citizen, or at least every citizen important enough to be worth watching, could be kept for twenty-four-hours a day under the eyes of the police and in the sound of official propaganda, with all other channels of information closed. The possibility of enforcing not only complete obedience to the will of the State, but complete uniformity of opinion on all subjects, now existed for the first time.

---

[68] Plato. *Republic, Book VIII.*

Nothing the citizen does is indifferent or neutral. His or her friendships, hobbies, behavior towards his or her spouse or lover, facial expressions, gestures, characteristic movements, tones of voice, words muttered while asleep -- all are jealously scrutinized. Not only any actual misdemeanor, but any eccentricity, however small, any change of habits, any nervous mannerism that could possibly be the symptom of an inner struggle, is certain to be detected. Endless purges, arrests, tortures, imprisonments, and disappearances are inflicted both as punishments for crimes which have been actually committed and as the systematic wiping-out of any persons who might perhaps commit a crime at some time in the future.

And so today the determining factor in perpetuating a totally obsolete hierarchical society is the mental attitude of the ruling class itself. The problem, that is to say, is educational. It is a problem of continuously molding the consciousness both of the directing group and of the larger executive group that lies immediately below it. Skepticism and hesitancy among the ranks of the rulers must be prevented. (As will be seen in Chapter 3, the best method of molding consciousness is continuous warfare.)

The consciousness of the masses (the "proles"), by contrast, needs only be influenced in a negative way. The masses could only become dangerous if the advance of industrial technique made it necessary to educate them more highly: but, since military and commercial rivalries are no longer of primary importance, the level of popular education is actually declining. What opinions the masses hold, or do not hold, is looked upon as a matter of indifference. They can be granted intellectual liberty because it is thought that they have no intellect. In a member of the ruling elite, on the other hand, not even the smallest deviation of opinion on the most unimportant subject can be tolerated.

All the beliefs, habits, tastes, emotions, mental attitudes that characterize our time are really designed to sustain the mystique of the rulers and prevent the true nature of present-day society from being perceived. A member of the elite is required to have not only the right opinions, but the right instincts. Many of the beliefs and attitudes demanded of him or her are never plainly stated, and could not be stated without laying bare the contradiction at the heart of modern-day hierarchical society. To maintain this regime, a continuous alteration of the past is necessary. Both the elites and the masses will tolerate present-day conditions because they have no standards of comparison. Everyone must be cut off from the past, as well as from other countries, because it is necessary for one and all to believe that everyone is better off than his or her ancestors and that the average level of material comfort is rising. But by far the most important reason for the constant readjustment of the past is to safeguard the validity of the system itself. It is not merely that speeches, statistics, and records of every kind can and must be constantly brought up to date in order to show that the fundamental principles of society are sound. No change in these basic principles -- work, commodity production, private property, the State -- can ever be admitted. For to change one's mind is a confession of weakness, and weakness cannot be tolerated in a "perfect" system.

...

From the point of view of our present rulers, therefore, the only genuine dangers are the splitting-off of a new group of able, under-employed, power-hungry people, and the growth of liberalism and scepticism in their own ranks. The problem, that is to say, is educational. It is a problem of continuously molding the consciousness both of the directing group and of the larger executive group that lies immediately below it. The consciousness of the masses needs only to be influenced in a negative way.

In principle, membership [in the Party] is not hereditary. The child of Inner Party parents is in theory not born into the Inner Party. ... . Nor is there any racial discrimination, or any marked domination of one province by another. Jews, Negroes, South Americans of pure Indian blood are to be found in the highest ranks of the Party, and the administrators of any area are always drawn from the inhabitants of that area. ... Its rulers are not held together by blood-ties but by adherence to a common doctrine. It is true that our society is stratified, and very rigidly stratified, on what at first sight appear to be hereditary lines. There is far less to-and-fro movement between the different groups than happened under capitalism or even in the pre-industrial age. Between the two branches of the Party there is a certain amount of interchange, but only so much as will ensure that weaklings are excluded from the Inner Party and that ambitious members of the Outer Party are made harmless by allowing them to rise. Proletarians, in practice, are not allowed to graduate into the Party. The most gifted among them, who might possibly become nuclei of discontent, are simply marked down by the Thought Police and eliminated. But this state of affairs is not necessarily permanent, nor is it a matter of principle. The Party is not a class in the old sense of the word. It does not aim at transmitting power to its own children, as such; and if there were no other way of keeping the ablest people at the top, it would be perfectly prepared to recruit an entire new generation from the ranks of the proletariat. In the crucial years, the fact that the Party was not a hereditary body did a great deal to neutralize opposition. The older kind of Socialist, who had been trained to fight against something called 'class privilege' assumed that what is not hereditary cannot be permanent. He did not see that the continuity of an oligarchy need not be physical, nor did he pause to reflect that hereditary aristocracies have always been short-lived, whereas adoptive organizations such as the Catholic Church have sometimes lasted for hundreds or thousands of years. The essence of oligarchical rule is not father-to-son inheritance, but the persistence of a certain world-view and a certain way of life, imposed by the dead upon the living. A ruling group is a ruling group so long as it can nominate its successors. The Party is not concerned with perpetuating its blood but with perpetuating itself. Who wields power is not important, provided that the hierarchical structure remains always the same. (Orwell, G. 1977. pp. 259-264).

Given law's monopoly on violence that makes it essentially a new school Technological Society form of tyranny consisting of a few wearing judicial robes instead of one or a few wearing a military uniform, why tolerate law?

2. What are the usefulness and use of the word "religion"? Unlike Leiter, I am not going to make up words describing religion while pretending my description is independent from my normative and pragmatic concerns. One can use the made-up words Rules of Recognition, Rules of Change, and Rules of Adjudication used by philosophers of law describing the communal social construct "law" just as easily to describe the communal social construct "religion" except for the Separability Thesis that would be changed to requiring religion to be distinct from law and legal obligations but allowing it to consider moral and "non-moral" obligations. For purposes of my question, I only care about religion as a social construct possessing by its very nature and essence as a social construct whenever and wherever it happens: 1) a belief in a morality of how a community ought to be distinct from the obligations of law; 2) recognizing the distinction "give to Caesar what belongs to Caesar, and give to God what belongs to God". For something to be a religion, it must have these attributes. Anything else is either a political movement or a matter/liberty of conscience.

Leiter completely ignores these two religious attributes that separate religion from morality and matters and liberty of conscience: religion is communal, a social construct just as law is communal and a social construct.

Obviously, my definition excludes many social constructs that are commonly considered religion and may include some that are commonly not considered religion, but this is my intention. An Eastern religion such as Islam requiring the state and religion to be one or an ancient religion of state worship such as Roman or Greek worship of the *polis* or Aztec unity of state and religion is useless to my normative goal of evenly counterbalancing law's monopoly on violence. They would simply be the new mob in town.

Existentially, one can no more have a private religion than one can have a private law. One can have a morality and matters of conscience as to how one ought to live life but religion is a communal or social construct of how a community ought to live life or how an individual within the context of a community ought to live life. Once the communal "ought" is lost, religion existentially becomes just another morality or matter of personal "conscience" just as law would become just another rule. A purely private religion is not existentially a religion in the same way that a purely private law is not a law — such private concepts are meaningless words as would be a private language.

Further, at least in Western Civilization, religion has a unique descriptive attribute that makes it distinct from any political movement seeking a normative power to enforce its morality: it recognizes a separation of normative power between religious power and the state, "give to Caesar what belongs to Caesar, and give to God what belongs to God" (Mark 12: 17).

Religion, unlike matters of conscience and political movements, can be and once was in the Western World a powerful check on the power of law as a normative power "in the world but not of the world" (John 17:15-21).

Thus the usefulness of the word "religion" to my wordgame and question is its pragmatic usefulness to check the tyranny of law. At least Western religions such as Christianity begin with the belief and hope of a loving God and use Rules of Recognition, Rules of Change, and Rules of Adjudication to develop what they admit to be a "morality" of what society "ought" to do. Religion fails miserably sometimes in acting on its morality but law has done no better and usually much worse. Without Western law's assumption — again, some would say hijacking — of the "tastes" of Western religion's Sermon on the Mount and Beatitudes and the power struggle within itself and with secular law as to the pragmatic requirements of such "tastes", there would be no Rules of Recognition, Change, and Adjudication different from those used in Aztec, Islamic, or ancient states.

That Leiter is clueless about the essential nature of morality and the essential difference between morality, matters of conscience, and religion is evident from his statement: "no one needs a moral theory, after all, to know whether they are against racism or in favor of racial equality, against chattel slavery or in favor of human freedom, against cruelty or in favor of treating people in a dignified way, against human misery or in favor of human happiness" (Leiter, B. 2017. p. 5). Of course they do, that is what morality is. They do not need a religion — unless they want to apply their morality to the community — but by definition they need a morality to evaluate the meaningless indifference of the universe and then evaluatively and perspectively to conclude how it ought to be. Morality is simply a system through which a person determines right and wrong conduct. It may not be a rational morality that goes beyond the initial irrational belief or opinion foundation or premise necessary to build a rationally explicit morality but so what? Morality by its nature begins as irrational, not only as an existentialist protest (in the non-Nietzsche sense) against the meaningless of the universe but also in order to avoid an infinite chain of "ought" statements. One must start with an initial irrational belief, opinion, conclusion, or something to make meaningful normative statements. If one is amoral, one does not care about any of the issues in Leiter's statement, and one is free to enjoy and share in the clarity, beauty, and power of the indifference of the universe. Only if one has a morality are the words of the stated beliefs meaningful in a normative sense.

Where was Leiter's beloved Nietzsche when he made this absurd statement about not needing a moral theory for the issues stated? In any naturalized view of reality, words such equality, freedom, cruelty, dignified, misery, and happiness are empirically meaningless. No one is equal or free. The universe by its essential nature is cruel. There is no dignity in life — life is miserable and then we die. Only the empirically delusional are happy. We cannot eliminate chattel or wage slavery by saying that all humans are empirically equal. Not only is no one empirically equal by any empirical measure of equality but such issue should be irrelevant to the issue of one person owning another legally as chattel or as a wage slave. In theory, if humans are unequal in any naturalized sense — that is based on sense experience and empirical observations — the law could justify slavery as it did in all social constructs throughout history based on such sense. Slavery in any form "ought" to be illegal because it is immoral regardless of what is said or rationally concluded by Leiter's beloved naturalized "evidence and reasons [as] understood in other domains concerned with knowledge of the world ... ordinary standards of evidence and rational justification ... common-sense and in science" (Leiter, B. 2012. p. 19).

A bunch of individuals with "matters of conscience" opposing law's monopoly on power is always at least economic suicide and usually physical suicide. A political movement opposing law is simply a mob of gunpersons trying to be the new mob controlling the neighborhood. Is religion the only option?

3. What is the meaning of my question's "toleration"? The word "toleration" has as many uses and therefore meanings as there are things to tolerate and people to tolerate them. Prison guards tolerate prisoners as long as the prisoners do what they are told; under such toleration, prison is a very peaceful and orderly existence but not a free and open society. At present, I can honestly say that during my 4 ½ years of sea duty on three boats that the old school Navy tolerated more freedom of speech among its submariners and other sailors than anyone does in the legal profession or in law school academia or even in the civilian world among its attorneys, students, and civilians. Neither is now a free and open society for speech but at least the Navy is not supposed to be.

I do not mean nominal toleration as the law means of religion.

The law in its demand for toleration of law is at the other end: absolute toleration of law — follow orders, do not cause trouble, or else. It even has the audacity to call this type of toleration "diversity". There are no exceptions except those law creates. Using this meaning leads to a very straightforward and simple answer to my question. Why tolerate law in the sense of absolute toleration of its demands? There is no reason for such toleration other than fear. It is the same toleration due a mob of gunpersons. I must tolerate them until I can oppose them.

The meaning I seek for "toleration" in my question is normative and pragmatic, so its meaning is not as simple as that which the law requires of itself. To give "toleration" useful meaning as a normative word in relation to law and religion, I begin with a rejection of the law's demand for absolute toleration based on historical reasoning and evidence that power corrupts and absolute power corrupts absolutely. Once I do that, my question becomes one of asking: why I must I accept the law's absolute power of violence if it does not work for a free and open society and there are alternatives? In a way, this seems to be word-playing, just replacing "tolerate" with "accept" plus a phrase. Unfortunately, there seems to be no way around it. The added phrase sufficiently describes the normative and pragmatic basis of my concerns to differentiate "toleration" from its nominal and absolute meanings, and thus is useful for the question at hand.

III. Why Tolerate Law?

In answering my question, since it is essentially normative and pragmatic, as I have admitted, I accept as a given that anything with a monopoly on violence to enforce itself upon me and my community does not work for establishing, maintaining, or fostering a free and open society. It has never worked in the past, thus there is no reason to believe it will in the future absence the law's categorical demand unhinged from reason and evidence that we so believe and have faith in its nonlegal obligations in the same way religion demands faith in its moral obligations. Such monopoly does not work to promote a free and open society in the present consisting of a Technological Society well on its way to achieving Orwellian *1984* reality. In our Orwellian present and future, however, the Room 101 of our O'Briens will not be a room with a rat cage but a sterile, pleasantly decorated, warm, friendly room with a surround sound of aesthetically pleasing legal verbiage convincing everyone slavery is freedom negating substantive diversity of thought and conscious and complex and empathetic comic and tragic thought. Meanwhile, outside our Room 101, the law will be busy denying the truth that $2 + 2 = 4$ using as justification law and economics.

Not that religion is any better if given its own monopoly on violence. The essence of the historical battle for separation between church and state in Western Civilization first comes to life with his Honor Judge Pontius Pilate (a hero of Nietzsche) condemning to death a man he knew to be innocent by asking *"quid et veritas"* (John 18: 38)? Christianity condemns the act as immoral or amoral conveniently ignoring it is Christianity's dogma that it was necessary. Both law and religion will kill the innocent if for them need be especially if unchecked by other power.

So, I am left with determining whether there are alternatives to such special monopoly on violence for law. Historically, the alternatives going back to antiquity — when the state and religion were one — consist of finding either an internal or external armed mob willing to take on the armed mob that is law. The external means war. The internal requires civil war based on a communal unity of purpose established by tribal, class, family, ethnic or race, religious, or some other form of social bonding or loyalty strong enough to take on the law or religion.

War is not much of an alternative and I will give the benefit of a doubt to law on this issue because I do not see any legal cultures out there having any less of a monopoly on violence than American law if they militarily conquered us. I include Islam in this as an external force. As a warrior religion founded for the specific purpose of military and commercial conquest not recognizing the separation between church and state, Islam is not a religion but a state relative to the normative and pragmatic answer I am seeking to my question.

As far as the internal alternatives remaining, civil revolt based on class loyalty is the only one that has worked successfully for any considerable period of time without consequences that were as bad or worse than the law it was fighting. An example is The Conflict of the Orders or the Struggle of the Orders in the Roman Republic between Plebeians (commoners) and Patricians (aristocrats) in which the Plebeians sought political equality with the Patricians. It materially affected the Constitution of the Roman Republic and kept the Republic a viable free and open society relative to the ancient world for 400 years. However, the United States has always and still does deny the reality of social classes, and it is too late now to accept such reality. In our modern Technological Society, even if individuals were to acknowledge social class allegiance it is no longer possible to do anything about it as the law would technologically quickly notice it and put a stop to it by violence as it has done to the other listed social loyalties and bonds.

As to the other listed social bonds and loyalties, it was not enough for the law simply to abrogate the laws that converted them into violent "ism's" such as racism. Acting as a monopoly should act, the law through law with the aid of modern technology has by law abrogated those social bonds and loyalties themselves to assure a sterile world lacking in any social bonds or loyalties outside of the law and thus assuring its racism and its other -ism's to be part of its monopoly. It even has the audacity to call cultural stagnation "multi-cultural" and its lack of substantive diversity "diversity".

In prior historical periods of social struggle against the violence of law, individuals always had at least one alternative other than the law for social and moral support such as these listed loyalties or at least family support to fight the law's monopoly on violence. Except for those in United States upper social classes and their intelligentsia who need no family support but have plenty of it, even family support is fairly quickly becoming meaningless now that the majority of American workers have never been married; and given that for those workers who have children and try to support them, of these children at least 40% and rising will be raised most of their lives by single parents with neither extended nor nuclear family support. (Pew Research Center. 2014. p. 1) (Pew Research Center. 2019. p. 1). It is fine and encouraged by the law since it intends to be a new school substitute for all old school concepts of marriage and family anyway by becoming our Big Brother who we will eventually learn to love — or else. It is only a matter of time before the majority of workers are single and childless and children are either a luxury for the few that can afford them or a necessity manufactured under government regulation as needed by the law's Brave New World. New school racism and wage slavery of individuals is the new norm beloved by law with the same social and political effects as old school racism and chattel slavery only this type around it is not limited to any particular class.

Western religion for centuries has worked to control the law. Beginning with the Battle of the Milvian Bridge, on to Pope Leo saving Rome from sacking by Attila the Hun, on to the Battle of Vienna, and further, the power of Christianity has civilized Western law not the other way around. Though law school professors continually preach of the Magna Carta as the foundation of modern "rule of law" constitutional jurisprudence, they all seem to forget that it was Archbishop Stephen Langton of the Catholic Church who in 1215 incited and gathered the Barons together to create this document in an attempt to force even the King to admit submission to Divine Law. There would not have been a Renaissance or Enlightenment without the equal but separate struggle for power between church and state. Such examples are omnipresent throughout Western history. Whatever good is in Western law is there either because of Western religion or because of Western religion struggling with law as a counterbalance to their respective desires for a monopoly on violence.

These above descriptions are hinged to reason and evidence.

Unfortunately, religion has surrendered the battle. Though historians disagree, I view the paradigm shifting surrender as happening in the 20th Century World Wars as with so much else that shifted. Though the center to right Christian political parties in Germany kept the Nazi Party as a minority electoral party through successive elections despite the violence it used to intimidate voters, once they passed the Enabling Act of 1933 and legally took over as a tyranny, religion gave up the struggle and did as legally required — they tolerated law absolutely.

This surrender continued and has become complete in the last few decades. It is at the point now where millennia-old Christian communities in the Mideast have been eliminated through intentional and knowing genocidal application of Islamic law, yet the best Christianity can muster in defense is having its Pope stand at a balcony and waive the peace sign. "How many divisions does the Pope of Rome have" (Churchill, W. 1986. Vol. 1, ch. 8, p. 105 *quoting* Stalin)? None, it no longer has any normative power having surrendered it to the law during the World Wars just as it surrendered its crusading powers centuries ago.

Leiter in the asking of the following question shows his pragmatic ignorance of what should be the most important attribute of religion by his critical comment finding "the devoutly religious among those who bomb abortion clinics". (Leiter, B. 2012. p. 19). From the Christian perspective, this criticism is the equivalent of complaining that we find "the devoutly religious among those who bombed legal human extermination camps in Germany", if they had done so which they did not. To any religion that believes regardless of whether it is by divine revelation or by rational beliefs, intuitions, or assumptions that life begins at conception and thus that abortion is infanticide and it "ought" not to be legal, such beliefs morally justify bombing legal abortion clinics in the same way such beliefs would morally justify bombing legal extermination camps to prevent the killing of six million adults. The fact that religions with such beliefs did not do so when extermination camps were legal is an argument for denying special toleration to both religion and law and not just one or the other. The fact that modern Western religion, despite the fact that they believe abortion is infanticide, is not bombing abortion clinics because they are legal in the same way that they did not call for a crusade to bomb German extermination camps because they were legal is undisputed evidence that it has surrendered to law.

Since the World Wars, it has been all down hill for Western religion acting as a counterbalance to law's monopoly on violence. Western religious have become more like Nietzsche than our intelligentsia who love him. The religious just want to meet once a week, hold hands, sing *Kumbaya*, hug the Turin horse and cry, and then go back to the real world of following orders, doing as told, and not making trouble for the law. From abortion to equal legal rights for corporations, to gay marriage, to secular control of religious education, to forced association by the religious with immoral acts, to meaningless toleration, and on to any legal battle one can name between law and religion, religion has lost — all the while law pontificating that it gives religion nonexistent special toleration. Not only has religion lost, but it lost its battles timidly and cowardly without a serious fight. It is a meaningless, worthless opponent to the monopoly of violence held by the law.

A.   *The Answer to the Question of Why Tolerate Law?*

The law makes a categorical demand unhinged from reason and evidence that by necessity it must have a special monopoly on violence. By Leiter's definition, it is a religion and therefore by his own argument it ought not have this special toleration.

As far as my contemplation goes, if Western religion were the law's equal opponent in power, my answer would be: only tolerate the law's special monopoly on violence if it tolerates a separate by equal non-violent force of normative religion to counterbalance it, otherwise there is no normative or pragmatic reason to tolerate it. Law is just another mob to be feared and given only the usual toleration given any mob of gunpersons until we can find a better option. Unfortunately, modern Technological Society does not at present allow for any other option, so we are stuck. Political opposition would simply be another mob. Individual opposition through matters or liberty of conscience is ineffective as a surrender to the mob's protection or as economic or physical suicide.

Since Western religion has surrendered the battle, we have no choice but to tolerate law so that it does not kill us while we look for and hopefully find an equal opponent. I submit the opponent must be a naturalized version of existentialism and even nihilism if need. Just as scientific thought when necessary begins with anarchy, we may have to begin developing a counterbalancing force with nihilism. We must develop a naturalized existential philosophy of law founded upon a courageous human existentialism not a cowardly one founded on the aesthetics worship of Nietzsche that can only lead to a Hegelian world view destroying individual freedom and free and open societies.

IV. The Philosophy Behind Philosophy of Law

Given that all normative statements including religious morality and the disguised morality of the law it calls non-moral obligations must begin with essentially irrational beliefs, opinions, or conclusions, what is the philosophy behind Leiter's normative conclusion that the law ought not give religion special toleration? According to Leiter's *The Truth is Terrible*[69], it is the philosophy of Frederick Nietzsche. This means there is no God; if there is, He is dead. "[A]ll of us are destined for oblivion" (Leiter, B. 2018. p. 9-10). In contrast to the 89% of American *hoi polloi* who believe in God,[70] Leiter has been "cleansed of theological superstitions"(*Ibid.*)

---

[69] Leiter, B. (2018). "The Truth is Terrible". *Journal of Nietzsche Studies* (7 April 2018). DOI: 10.2139/SSRN.2099162 Corpus ID: 170211129

[70] Newport, Frank. (2016). "Most Americans Still Believe in God." *Gallup Polls*. http://www.gallup.com/poll/193271/americans-

and the "fake immortality" (*Ibid.*) of a nonexistent spiritual union with those that have struggled before us and that hopefully will struggle in the future against the indifference and outright hatred of us by the universe. Oohs! Should not have mentioned hope. Hope is an illusion; all is meaningless suffering. The only reason to prefer life to nonexistence in answer to "Schopenhauer's challenge" (*Ibid.*) is the aesthetic creations of "the spectacle of genius, a spectacle incompatible with the triumph of ascetic moralities over the past two thousand years". (*Ibid.*) I assume Leiter and his work are one of these aesthetic creations of genius that give life meaning.

In *The Truth is Terrible*, Leiter praises the "Dionysian" (*Ibid.*) perspective on life as life affirming compared to the life threatening perspectives of Plato, Socrates, the "crucified", and the Stoics (*Ibid.*). He seems to miss entirely the irony that Dionysus was a god while the others — including the "crucified" — were all human. This is not nihilism, nor was Nietzsche a nihilist. It is a cowardly attempt to defeat nihilism no better than the cowardice of modern Western religion.

Nietzsche? Really? Schopenhauer's challenge? In an age of science, with a whole universe waiting out there for us to discover, explore, and conquer, this is the best modern intelligentsia can come up with as a foundation for the normative "non-moral" obligations of its philosophy of law? That Western religion has trouble being equal in power to this nonsense further shows how low it has gotten.

I know Leiter is serious and expects to be treated seriously, but the image of academic dons in their bow tie suits after having led risk-adverse sheltered lives in which their only motivation and concerns were for success in their professional career; who now lead a sheltered exclusion from reality consisting of life-tenure positions in academia; standing at a classroom podium shaking their fist (metaphorically only of course, never physically) at heaven; and crying God is dead is a comical image at best and usually a very farcical image. They have not killed God, they have simply replaced

---

believe-god.aspx

Him with self-worship of themselves as demigods — just as the patrician Schopenhauer did of himself and his patrician class. Every time I imagine this image or read academic pontificating on Nietzsche, I can hear the song "Wanna be a Gangsta" by the band *Body Count*. (Cunningan, E.T., Marrow, T.L., & Dennis, V. (2014).

The story of Nietzsche and the Turin horse and the movie *Turin Horse* by Bela Tarr (Tarr. 2011. Hungarian: *A torinói ló*) based upon that story say much about the dangerous hypocrisy of Nietzsche and the cowardly followers of his brand of existentialism and any philosophy of law they create. Their image of the suffering artist crying about suffering horses then going back to his apartment safe-place luxuries to have his mother take care of his delicate sensibilities while the *de facto* slave human owners of the Turin horse and the horse itself go back to work epitomizes the Technological Society intelligentsia view of reality. This concept that aesthetics and the genius of art are the only possible source of meaning in a meaningless universe explains why the intelligentsia creates so much beautiful verbiage that says nothing; after all, there is nothing more atheistically pleasing to reason then listening to itself talk or reading its words even if they do not say anything. However, if such philosophy is truly the *Terrible Truth* of the law as Leiter claims, it only serves as a further reason not to tolerate law *qua* law; not only because it is a mob of gunmen but it is a mob with certain tastes in art it wants to force me to buy with my taxes.

The tragic terrible truth is that this comical philosophy is a real source of meaning and brute normative force through law among our Outer and Inner Parties. It gives their lives meaning and a need to create a world in their image by a monopoly of force. Their aesthetic meaning goes on to admit treason to the existentialist struggle by raising Hegel to praise judges such as Richard Posner as a Hegelian "'Owl of Minerva', who has captured the moral ethos of his time and place" (Leiter, B. 2012. p. 24). Again, Leiter seems oblivious to the fact that Hegel's initial World Spirit and Owl of Minerva were the glory of the Prussian military state and the absolute rule of its Frederick William III.[71] Thus, though pretending to have an existential faith to the freedom of a Nietzsche, it is really to the tyranny of Hegelian state worship that is the foundation for modern law's nonlegal obligation demanding an unchecked monopoly on violence to enforce the law's World Spirit morality.

As if it were not bad enough that the law hides its morality as nonlegal obligations, it also wants to hide it as "economics". With the likes of judges such as Leiter's beloved Posner, it now also uses the word "economics" to hide its morality and its is-ought transition. The present fad of law-and-economics allows life-tenured judges in the secret of their chambers to arbitrarily decide what is the best economic goal for society; then in court spend a few minutes and a few pages of briefs pretending to let lawyers and their clients, for whom they hold nothing but contempt, argue law; and then back in the secrecy of their chambers fabricate law and facts without any input from actual economists to achieve their arbitrarily chosen result. All the while, as would the Wizard of Oz, they tell the *hoi polloi* "pay no attention to the man behind the screen". Such terrible truth is not only reality for sophisticated con artists such as Posner, but even of the simplest and unsophisticated of con artists of the Inner Party. Present Supreme Judge Sonia Sotomayor stated in an Associated Press interview that she wanted to be a judge by age ten after watching a Perry Mason episode at which point she "realized that the judge was the most important player in that room".[72] If anyone is reading this, ask what were you dreaming about at age 10?

---

[71] *See generally,* Popper, C. (1994). *The Open Society and Its Enemies.* Routledge.

[72] Associated Press. (2009). "Sotomayor wanted to be a judge since age 10." *Today.* (May 26, 2009).
http://www.today.com/id/30940443/ns/today-today_news/t/sotomayor-wanted-be-judge-age/#.WOasLWe1uyo

At age 10, I was just trying to survive until the next day. If I did dream, it was about having love and a happy family; about the girl sitting next to me in class; to become an astronaut; an explorer of the world and the universe; to cure cancer; to become a military hero; or doing something great to help my fellow humans. The few times I watched Perry Mason, I sympathized with the innocent defendant being railroaded through the system by the powers — including the moron judge — miraculously saved from imprisonment or worse only by the hero Perry Mason. Supreme Sotomayor despite having a loving extended family supporting her path not only to survive but to prosper in life instead was dreaming of being the judge simply because the judge has the most power in the room. At age ten, she wanted to sit in judgment of fellow humans and jail them, ruin their families, ruin them financially, or do whatever else is necessary to have the powerful stay in power. This is the will to power mentality that demands absolute toleration to its monopoly on violence.

For the United States, inevitably falling into anarchy and eventual tyranny may be unavoidable if the law is our only technique to avoid such transition. The law has never in history stopped such a transition and often is the instrument for its occurring. As legal "enabling acts" start and continue, we cannot expect a legal culture willing to give a handful of judges a monopoly on violence to enforce their personal morality upon all of society simply because they wear judicial robes and call their morality nonlegal obligations and economics to stop tyrants wearing military or lab uniforms from doing the same. Such a categorical expectation is unhinged from reason and evidence and is religion as Leiter defines it.

V.   The Hope of an Existentialist Philosophy of Law

Western Religion having surrendered the struggle, our one hope for an equal but separate normative power to counterbalance the soul crushing and mind numbing monopoly on power the law demands is not a godly Dionysian existentialism but a human and naturalized existentialism and the religious passion that a human communal normative existentialism would create. There is an entire universe out there waiting to be discovered, explored, and conquered. If the law has its way, as it has done throughout history, instead of acting to discover, explore, and conquer it, we will all be slaves to the small minority that are its Outer and Inner Party wasting precious time and resources on stupid arguments over whether Rule of Recognition, Rules of Change, and Rules of Adjudication are descriptive or interpretative; what pronouns to use; what gender is; and whether nonlegal obligations are different from moral obligations. Forget Nietzsche and our present religious and all sycophants and cowards that make categorical demands unhinged from reason and evidence for unchecked monopolies on violence. If God is to be found, He is out there somewhere because He is definitely not here. Let us all go look for him together. Let sycophants such as Leiter stay in their room or whatever safe place they have for hugging, whining, and admiring their self-centered aesthetic arbitrary verbiage regardless of whether they call it economics or nonlegal obligations.

  Recognize that we cannot fight the universe and any tyranny of law individually, such is a suicidal struggle regardless of how well intentioned may be our individual liberty or "matters of conscience". Politics is simply an opposing mob of gunpersons. We can oppose a social construct with a monopoly on violence such as law only by an equal but separate social construct normative power whose essence is nonviolent. The struggle of life requires a communal act of hope and a normative belief of what ought to be including a morality of nonviolence: a religion. As it has done throughout history, the law rather than have a free and open society would rather see much of humanity stuck in slavery in order to maintain a status quo of law and order — only this time around it is wage slavery instead of chattel slavery. In order to defeat the inevitable violent tyranny of the law's demand for absolute toleration of it, with religion gone, it appears we must first embrace nihilism not avoid it. Communal creations of normative power are not created by agreement and peace, just as with scientific progress they are created by disagreement and struggle. In the absence of disagreement and struggle as equal but separate powers between law and old school religion, the only option is first to use nihilism to create disagreement and struggle. From this forge of struggle between law and naturalized human existentialism, hopefully new school religion will rise to take on law as an equal but separate power to create a free and open society.

To bring existential religion back to life or to give it life, we most certainly should not join in condemnation of the dead universally done by our Outer and Inner Parties through the likes of Leiter on the right equaled by the likes of a Ta-Nehisi Coates on the left — neither of which are the great minds and genius the intelligentsia worships them as. Instead, maintain your humanity and do not replace God with yourself as demigod. We should join both our Honored Dead and dishonored dead in a leap-of-faith struggle by continuing the struggle. The struggle is not "between the world and me", it is between the world and us:

> Take up our quarrel with the foe
> To you, from failing hands, we throw
> The torch: be yours to hold it high
> If ye break faith with us who die,
> We shall not sleep, though poppies grow
> In Flanders fields
>   — *In Flanders Fields* by John McCrae[73]

In this conclusion to my essay, I am only trying to lay a foundation for further contemplation and development of a naturalized existential philosophy of law. I hope to develop further details at a later date. Is there a universal thing called "law"; are there not just particular laws? How about religion? Is there a universal thing called "religion"; are there not just particular religions? I want to leave emphasizing that such development need not reject analytic philosophy, being naturalized with scientific

---

[73] McCrae, J. (1918). *In Flanders Field*. Poets.org. https://poets.org/poem/flanders-fields

thought, nor the philosophy of language as is done by so many continental especially nihilist philosophers. Existentialism begins with three basic analytical premises commonly shortened to the colloquialism of "existence precedes essence". In this colloquialism, there are three analytical premises that reverse the successful portion of Cartesian criticism of skepticism: "I am"; "I am therefore I think"; "I am and I will". Accepting these three premises as true existentially gives the rational mind the minimum of three variables it needs to create logic and use it to fight against the universe and its will to kill us and our community and for humanity to engage in the struggle that is life: $x, x \to y, x \wedge z$. Binding these variables by values is the beginning of all the complexities of logical thought.

The problem faced by existentialism is talking about the existential truth of the initial three premises. This seems to be a situation of "whereof one cannot speak, thereof one must be silent" (Wittgenstein, L. 2009. Prop. 5.6, p. 63). However, this warning only applies to logical thought. One can still talk about the reality of these three premises illogically in the same way that one begins normative speech by beginning with irrational premises: by such language techniques as analogy, fiction, dialectical reasoning, (reasoning that rejects the classical law of non-contradiction), emotion, and anything else that works to get a meaning across.

The power of scientific language is its firm anchoring to both ends of fact and theory successfully using the past to predict the future. Existentialism is firmly anchored in fact; the problem is theory. As with any language or wordgame, the details of this firm anchoring are much disputed among philosophers of science. The line between non-science, pseudo-science, and science is difficult to establish and they often overlap. Luckily, again, philosophy of law is as sophomoric about philosophy of science as it is about language and thus avoids most of these disputes. However, there are three agreed upon universal attributes of scientific wordgames that make scientific language unique that existentialism must remember and understand for creation, attraction, and development of a philosophy of law: the use of Ockham's Razor at least as a heuristic technique if not an ontological one; its goal of using the past to predict the future; and thus by its falsifiability when its predictions fail.

In addition, regardless of one's morality, for studying philosophy of law, one must accept that none of these scientific attributes apply to the other end of the language wordgame spectrum consisting of morality: Ockham's Razor is useless for any purpose other than marketing — *i.e.*, "thou shall not kill" is good marketing but the books of exceptions are the real substance; it seeks not what is but what ought to be either now, in the future, or in both; and thus can only be falsified by assent — either by the individual or community whose morality it is. Regardless of whether this existential reality is good or evil, the existential reality is that scientific wordgames are rational processes that may have an irrational foundation in existential creativity or imagination but morality is an irrational process from start to finish that avoids being an infinite chain of "ought" statements only by starting either with Divine revelation or by individual or communal will to power beliefs, feelings, intuitions, or hopes.

The admission of irrationality as a foundation and substantive force is the keystone to making existentialism a force equal to religion for counterbalancing the tyranny of law. It must not in anyway condemn nor ignore the factual reality of history. It is what it is. "A slave begins by demanding justice and ends by wanting to wear a crown. He must dominate in his turn" (Camus, 1991, p. 25). It is an existential fact of reality.

These analytic and existential considerations at this point are contingent upon what we used to call in the military: a will to fight. Have *hoi polloi* given on up continuing the struggle as have religion and intelligentsia? If so, we are not only destined to live in a Technological Society in which war is peace, freedom is slavery, ignorance is strength, stagnation is multi-cultural, and sameness is diversity, but, more significantly, we will lack the meaning in life and sense of community created by fighting and struggling against it. I love to paraphrase George Patton's comment on a future of technological wonder weapons that will soon, if not already, be applicable to law: "My God, I do not see the wonder in them. Killing without heroics. Nothing is glorified, nothing is reaffirmed.

No heroes, no cowards. No humanity, no emotion, and no soul involved. Only those that are left alive and those that are left dead" (Schaffner, F.J. 1970. [Movie]).

I end not with the Dionysian cowardice of a Nietzsche or Schopenhauer. I end first with an existential prediction of what will happen if the special toleration giving the law a monopoly on violence is not removed. I then leave with words of courage involving existential humans from the crucified to Camus with whom we can create a social construct religion as a separate but equal nonviolent normative power to counterbalance the present and inevitable tyranny of law and its violence — thus provide the only pragmatic justification for tolerating law:

> Power is not a means; it is an end. One does not establish a dictatorship in order to safeguard a revolution; one makes the revolution in order to establish the dictatorship. The object of persecution is persecution. The object of torture is torture. The object of power is power. (Orwell, G. 1977. p. 332).

> It requires courage not to surrender oneself to the ingenious or compassionate counsels of despair that would induce a man to eliminate himself from the ranks of the living; but it does not follow from this that every huckster who is fattened and nourished in self-confidence has more courage than the man who yielded to despair. (Kierkegaard, S. 1992. p. 239).

> I leave Sisyphus at the foot of the mountain! One always finds one's burden again. But Sisyphus teaches the higher fidelity that negates the gods and raises rocks. He too concludes that all is well. This universe henceforth without a master seems to him neither sterile nor futile. Each atom of that stone, each mineral flake of that night filled mountain, in itself forms a world. The struggle itself toward the heights is enough to fill a man's heart. One must imagine Sisyphus happy. (Camus, A. 1955. p. 91).

Detailed Summary of an Existential Meta-Ethics: Nihilism as a Morality[74]

    Meta-ethics seeks to know whether there are properties or attributes common to all instances of the words "good" and "evil" in all their forms as normative universals of ultimate value. The term "normative" as are all words is vague and indeterminate with many uses and usefulness. Meta-ethics deals with the conceptualization of evaluative and perspective normative good and evil. It does not deal with the normative in a descriptive rule-following or descriptive predictive sense (though rule-following will be an issue in meta-ethics) such as for example: "to play chess, one cannot move the pawn more than two spaces"; "to get to manhattan quickly, one ought to take the subway"; "to help your plant live, give it more sun"; "to get to the moon, follow classical physics". Meta-ethics deals with good and evil in terms of ultimate value: "honesty is good"; "robbery is evil"; "killing is evil"; "all humans have equal human rights".

    The conceptual problems raised by various meta-ethics proposed properties and attributes for the words "good" and "evil" in all their forms as normative universals is well known — varying from the famous Hume's Guillotine and Moore's Open Question Argument to J.L. Mackie's error theory and Susan Neiman's history of philosophy as an inquiry into the nature of good and evil. Though it is important to seek theories of knowledge that can naturalize morality and ethics or at least by Rawlsian style rationalism link them to knowledge about the world, in many ways this problem in meta-ethics is simply irrelevant to modern society. In Technological Society, because its power of propaganda exists independently of any epistemic worth other than for power as an end in itself (as

---

[74] Diviacchi, V. (2019). *An Existential Meta-ethics: Argument for a Return to Its Roots in Nihilism as a Morality.* Available on Amazon.com and at bookstores in the U.S. and Great Britain.

Orwell wrote in *1984*, "God is Power"(Orwell, G. 1977. p. 333)), it is morality and ethics that now often decide not only what ought to be the state of affairs but what actually is the state of affairs — not just as theory-laden language but ontologically as the language of fact and truth. For example, "gender is a social construct" is no longer a question of fact but of ethics; the Powers want it so, it is so. Thus, given this state of affairs, nihilism not only acts as individual morality but also as a theodicy in which God is the ultimate nihilist.

A.   *Basic Concepts*

Thus the following are now all ontologically true, not just linguistically true as a matter of language based on there being "nothing outside of text" or a similar philosophy of language, but ontologically objectively true — to the extent these words can have meaning — for the concepts of evaluative and perspective normative ultimate valuation of good and evil:

1)   In the language wordgames of ethics and morality, there are no objective foundational prescriptive or evaluative values for good or evil in a normative sense though these wordgames always assume objective foundational absolute values. Saying there is no truth is a contradiction and nihilism does not require such inconsistent skepticism toward descriptive reality and truth especially toward scientific truth and this is not the nihilism that I will be contemplating. Saying there are no objective values for ultimate normative good and evil is not a contradiction. Nihilism accepts this lack of value as factual truth.

2)   Good is anything that one approves as giving meaning to one's life. Evil is anything of which one disapproves because it opposes or threatens that meaning.

3)   Morality and ethics are distinct conceptual forms of life or wordgames. Morality consists of rules by which an individual analyzes compliance with their Good. Since all rules are talked about by public language, morality seems to be public but ontologically it is an individual construct that exists ontologically only as action. Ethics is a set of rules by which a social group defines what is good for the group. Because groups cannot act

except through individuals, ethics is ultimately decided by the most powerful of any social group and thus ethics is always ontologically ruling class ideology.

4) A necessary and final ontological attribute of all morality and ethics is violence. If an individual is unwilling to enforce their morality upon the Other by violence then it is simply habit. An ethics unwilling to enforce its ideology by violence upon the Other is simply etiquette or custom. Ethics reaches perfection as ruling class ideology with a monopoly on violence: that is by becoming law. The more a society is dependent upon ethics and law for its social cohesion, the more a society is dependent upon violence for its social cohesion. To paraphrase the philosopher Willard Van Orman Quine's comments on science, the language fabric of normative language impinges on experience only at the edge of the dagger hidden beneath the fabric: acting upon its attribute of violence.

5) There is no interpretative language that can logically derive normative language from descriptive language and thus neither moral nor ethical beliefs need be based upon true assertions of fact: one can rationally say without contradiction "it is snowing but I do not believe it is snowing" or "Trump is President but I do not believe him to be President". Epistemically, the foundation of ethics and morality is having norms that are not based on descriptive reality but on what reality ought to be. This gives ethics and morality the power of being the only descriptive wordgame in which a concept of non-pragmatic truth is more than just a deflationary assertion of what is: one can rationally say "there is no objective basis for rape (murder or whatever) to be wrong but I believe it to be objectively wrong". However, this creates the weakness that pragmatic truth — that is whether an ethics or morality actually works to solve a problem — and descriptive assertions of what is or exists are irrelevant to ethics and morality. For example, for those of a certain ethics, "Trump is not President" becomes a true assertion of fact regardless of whether he is or is not President because according to the norms of such speakers Trump ought not to be President — and similarly the same could have been said by certain

speakers of Clinton if the election results had been different.

6) Modern Technological Society ruling class ideology will by necessity seek through ethics to have power and control over all individual morality including religious morality just as it needs control over everything else in reality. This necessary methodology serves humanity's needs as a form of life to discover, explore, and conquer the universe trying to kill both the individual and humanity and requires a building of collective knowledge at the expense of individual knowledge (C.S. Pierce's "colony of insects" with the individual and their morality expendable if not subservient to ruling class ideology).

7) The early religious existentialist Kierkegaard saw hope for individual meaning for the individual living even in necessary servitude to the arbitrary and random Fates through three ascending stages of what are now called phenomenological experiences: aesthetic, ethical, and religious. The incomplete work of Camus reversed the ascending experience: religious, ethical, and aesthetic. I want to begin anew the early thought of the work of Camus by dissolving all three stages into nihilism as a morality based on action not words for the individual trying simply to find meaning in the unavoidable incapacitating ruling class ideology — its ethics — of Technological Society. An opposition struggle to Technological Society so as to continue historical struggle cannot derive from ethics or even from socially acceptable morality but only from nihilism as a morality.

B. *Foundational Conclusion*

Meta-ethics as a Wittgensteinian "form of life" language must use both logical analytic reductive analysis and the holistic nature of storytelling to come to life. Thus by necessity my meta-ethics *Masters* essay and any further work developing and applying its concepts will first require some contemplation and agreement on a philosophy of language and of a wordgame descriptive methodology for use in such contemplation. An existential philosophy of language is necessary for this contemplation not only because it also will give us a hint and guidance as to how language confuses — especially by its power of aesthetics — our conceptual understanding of meta-ethics but also because, as with everything in modern Technological Society, there must be some common language for our contemplation. Just as language is necessary for creating aesthetically pleasing verbiage, a common language is necessary to differentiate between such verbiage and actual knowledge and meaningful beliefs. Achieving this common language in meta-ethics is much simpler than in metaphysics generally because we need not worry about a social construct and ontology distinction. In morality and ethics, the social construct/ontology distinction is worthless because the Wittgensteinian form of life that is the normative language of morality and ethics by necessity assumes a universal ontology of good and evil. The only reality of morality and ethics consists of its written and spoken words and the use and usefulness of those words that is their meaning — not their deconstruction, but what they actually say.

Sound Generalization or Unsound Stereotype

This is a short essay to assist in understanding the meaning of universals in language by differentiating between generalizations and stereotypes.

Originally, the Greek "ism" began life in the English language as a suffix means of forming action nouns from verbs or nouns and did not imply anything evil (i.e., baptize, baptism; real, realism; existence, existentialism; Darwin, Darwinism). Unfortunately, since "communism" and especially now with "terrorism", using an "ism" to describe an individual's acts or ideas has become an easy and instinctive way to ridicule the acts or ideas. Intellectualism, sexism, racism, heterosexualism, barbarism, despotism, plagiarism are modern obvious omnipresent examples as is classism though the latter is little acknowledged or used in the United States that falsely claims and wants to be classless. This easy and in the modern world instinctive method of argument uses the same supposed evils of which it accuses the proponent of the bad "ism": generalization and stereotype. Is there a difference between generalization and stereotype? If there is, at what point if any does a generalization become a stereotype or the other way around? Is either one or both inherently logically unsound or evil?

Throughout known history, any human coming in contact with another human has differentiated him or herself from the other. There is no way around self-consciousness; I am, therefore I think. Even a solitary hunter/gatherer meeting another solitary hunter/gatherer in the middle of nowhere will have to make a decision as to what to do about this other. If the decision is made irrationally or reflexively, by that I mean without going through a conscious process of induction or deduction, it will be made upon instincts created by life experience — instincts resulting from prior successful or unsuccessful inductions or deductions. If the decision is a conscious one, it will be made by a process of induction or deduction based on prior successful or unsuccessful inductions or deductions. Either way, in the absence of a pure altruistic instinct (assuming such exists) or a purely malevolent instinct (assuming such exists) fully controlling the individuals, the process will unavoidably involve such generalization or stereotype about the other individual.

Thus, in human consciousness, there is no way around the use of generalization and it is not evil nor logically unsound. All statements of fact or truth require some generalization. Generalization is the foundation of science. All inductive reasoning infers from a finite set of observations and experiences to a generalization claiming to hold true for a larger set of observations and experiences, even for those in the larger set that have not been seen or experienced. These generalizations, if not proven false, are then the premises for deductive reasoning, including for scientific deductive reasoning. Generalizations offer a theory about how things are in general. Thus the statement "all ravens are black" is a useful generalization, though no one person has ever been able to validate it by inspecting every raven on earth or every raven that has ever existed, and no one knows what ravens will be like in the future. Without such inductive reasoning, we would not be able to survive the day, survive life, nor would we have the modern world of science and technology. For purposes of the present contemplation, I will not challenge the soundness of inductive reasoning. If any one person has a firm belief in the rationality of inductive reasoning as somehow being better than instinct or faith, I suggest that they contemplate the Raven Paradox also known as Hempel's Paradox. (Hempel, C. G. 1945. pp. 1–26.)

In my philosophy of law, I have accepted my prior arguments for a pragmatic concept of truth and with that comes the further concept that the meaning of a word is its use and usefulness. In common use and usefulness, a "generalization" refers to a rational effort to categorize or describe facts, while a "stereotype" refers to an irrational effort to categorize or describe facts. Ideally, then, neither is a subset of the other but are distinct means of consciously categorizing or describing reality (unless you want to define the set as a collection of such means). Practically, however, how does one differentiate between a "rational" and an "irrational" effort? This is not as easy as it seems it should be. Both generalization and stereotypes involve inductive reasoning to reach a conclusion and then deduction to test or to live based on that conclusion. Often they are impossible to differentiate except based on a polemic reason: we want a statement to be one or the other.

When the differentiation is possible, it involves examination of the speaker's intent in combination with an examination of the quantitative basis for the induced inferences. The deductions made from those inferences do not matter because in the real world, simply as a result of pure luck, true deductions may result from completely false inferences and bad intent. A stereotype should not become rational and thus a generalization as a result of pure luck.

Intent is one part of the criteria for differentiation and often is dispositive of the question. The function of the generalization "all ravens are black" is to understand and to allow people to understand and to work better with ravens not to harm or to oppress ravens. If the intent was purely to harm or oppress ravens for one's benefit, we would have some doubt about it being a purely rational process and may call it a stereotype until we get an almost certain basis for the induction. We can never get certainty because it is induction. Is observation of one raven enough or do we need 100,000 observations when you are trying to harm all ravens based on the generalization that all ravens are black? For general statements made by a person with an obvious intent to categorize an entire class of people for oppression such as "all women are delusional" or "all black men are criminals", the evil intent is so clear that unless they are supported by an observation of every individual woman and every individual black man — which is impossible — they would be called irrational and thus stereotypes regardless of the factual basis.

However, intent is not the sole basis for differentiation. What if the latter statements were made by an isolated person observing women in a large psychiatric ward and while observing black men in a prison? In these latter examples, there may be no evil intent but the statements would still be called stereotypes because the latter statements involve a set of observed facts that are too small for making inferences about the large quantity of members in the larger class or, based on simple experience, would clearly result in false inferences, thus they are stereotypes regardless of intent. The quantity covered by the generalization must be compared to the quantity of the observations upon which it is based. If the comparison leads to a ratio that experience indicates is too high, it is usually called a stereotype.

Sometimes, these two elements are ignored or hidden. Even simple scientific generalizations are not free of some subjective perhaps evil intention by the speaker that is often ignored for practical purposes. In science's case, the intent many would say is to manipulate nature to human ends. In the absence of this intent for power, I doubt much if any scientific knowledge would have ever occurred, but again, this issue is beyond this essay. Regardless of this hidden malevolent intent that may be present in all scientific generalizations, they are still called generalizations and not stereotypes if the inferences are based on an acceptable quantity of facts and lead to deductions that can be tested and proven false in such test. Again, since we are dealing with induction, no generalization can ever be proven true because it is impossible to test all of reality. Similarly, if there is acceptable or politically correct intent, inferences based on insufficient or unsound observations are readily called generalizations. This happens all the time in economics and politics whose practitioners almost as a matter of routine assume A causes B simply because A correlates with B. (For an interesting analysis of such assumption, please see David Hume's famous critique of cause and effect in his *A Treatise of Human Nature and An Enquiry Concerning Human Understanding*.)

In areas of non-economic human interaction, the differentiation is much more difficult and usually impossible to make. A person listens to a fishing story from a black man or woman and assumes that they are lying about the size of the catch because they are black or a woman. Such would be irrational and thus stereotype because even basic life experience leads to the conclusion that everyone lies when they want to lie regardless of sex or skin color — thus this stereotype can also be described as evil sexism and racism. However, what if the person does not believe the story simply because based on 25 years of life experience with fishing and dozens of fishing stories they have honestly made the generalization that "all fishermen exaggerate the size of their catch"? We cannot simply say that such is stereotype because it is based solely on one person's experience but has never been scientifically tested. The vast majority of our generalizations by which we survive the day and life have never been and will never be tested scientifically and are based solely on our experience. In this latter situation, the statement about fishing cannot be formally or practically stated to be either a generalization or a stereotype and may be either, and no conclusion can be made as to whether it is inherently good or evil; any such moral conclusion would depend on the circumstances of its use. Some people make this conclusion about fishing, use it to survive in life, and it is simply an unfortunate reality of human nature that it needs generalization and stereotype to survive in life.

Logically therefore, there is a difference between generalization and stereotype. However, in practice, it is often difficult and sometimes impossible to make this differentiation. In the difficult cases, if there is any hope of making the differentiation, it would require a logical but open mind, life experience with the facts at issue, and empathy to make the differentiation — traits entirely lacking in most popular pundits on racism or classism, either for or against. Without this combination of traits, outside of science and technology where generalizations actually can be empirically tested, a generalization becomes a stereotype or the other way around when the individual making an argument wants to make the change. A generalization though logically sound can be either good or evil. A stereotype is logically unsound and not good but not necessarily evil. What about specifically racism and classism? What are they? Good or evil? Are either a necessary part of social and cultural interaction, arbitrary creations of the human will, or both depending on the situation?

On an individual level, classism and racism when acting as stereotypes are equally evil. They each will result in a situation of one person acting upon or toward another irrationally for purposes of oppression. When acting as generalizations, that is resulting from a rational basis, each is equally good. However, when individual generalizations or stereotypes some time join and some time conflict in a social fabric of almost infinite interactions serving as a basis for social and cultural power distribution and normative principles, classism not only is the greater evil but unfortunately it is a necessary evil. As the Good Book says, the battle is not always to the strong nor the race to the swift but that is the way to bet. Through the science of genetics and cosmetic surgery, we may eventually live in a world without racism because eventually there may be no races. We will never live in a world without classism. As even Christianity admits, "[y]ou will always have the poor among you ..." (Matthew, 26: 11; Mark 14: 7).

Why this is true is a question of why God hates the poor.[75]

---

[75] Diviacchi, Valeriano. (2020). *Why Does God Hate the Poor?* Available on Amazon.com and in bookstores in the U.S. and in Great Britain.

Bibliography (References)

Adams, J. (1814). From John Adams to John Taylor, 17 December 1814. *National Archives Founders Online.* https://founders.archives.gov/documents/Adams/99-02-02-6371.

Adams, A., Adams, J., & Ellis, J. J. (2007). My Dearest Friend: Letters of Abigail and John Adams (M. A. Hogan & C. J. Taylor, Eds.). Harvard University Press. https://doi.org/10.2307/j.ctvt9k62m

Arendt, H. (1963). Eichmann in Jerusalem (The original version - from the 'a reporter at large' series). *The New Yorker.* (16 February 1963) https://www.newyorker.com/magazine/1963/02/16/eichmann-in-jerusalem-I.

Associated Press. (2015). "Judge Removed for Deciding Case with Coin Toss". *AP* (13 January 2015). https://www.foxnews.com/story/judge-removed-for-deciding-case-with-coin-toss.

Associated Press. (2000). "Jury Flips Coin to Decide Murder Case". *AP* (26 April 2000). https://apnews.com/article/2c7dd9f60106fe05b63e37b81ef7fe7b

Associated Press. (2009). "Sotomayor wanted to be a judge since age 10." *Today.* (May 26, 2009). http://www.today.com/id/30940443/ns/today-today_news/t/sotomayor-wanted-be-judge-age/#.WOasLWe1uyo

Austin, John. (1998). *The Province of Jurisprudence Determined and The Uses of the Study of Jurisprudence.* Hackett Classics Publishing.

Austin, J.L. (2018). *How Do Things with Words.* Martino Fine Books.

Ayer, D., Dir. (2014). *Fury* [Film]. Columbia Pictures Corporation.

Bailey, R.H. (1981). *Prisoners of War (World War II)*. Time-Life Books.

Barrett, W. (1990). *Irrational Man: A Study in Existential Philosophy*. Random House.

Basboll, T. (2017). "Kate Clancy Gets James Watson Disinvited". *Research as a Second Language* [Blog]. http://secondlanguage.blogspot.com/2017/05/kate-clancy-gets-james-watson-disinvited.html

Bennett, M.R. & Hacker, P.M.S. (2014). *Philosophical Foundations of Neuroscience*. Blackwell.

Bennett, M.R., Bennett, D., Hacker, P.M.S., & Searle, J. (2007) *Neuroscience and Philosophy*. Columbia University Press.

Bergmann, M., Moor, J., & Nelson, J. (1990) *The Logic Book*. McGraw Hill.

Berkowitz, P. (1995). *Nietzsche: The Ethics of an Immoralist*. Harvard University Press.

Bretall, R., Ed. (1973). *A Kierkegaard Anthology*. Princeton University Press.

Bix, B. (2003) *Law, Language, and Legal Indeterminancy*. Clarendon Press.

Blair, W.G. (1982). "Flip of Coin Decides Jail Term in a Manhattan Criminal Case", *New York Times* (2 February 1982). https://www.nytimes.com/1982/02/02/nyregion/flip-of-coin-decides-jail-term-in-a-manh-attan-criminal-case.html.

Blythe, D.R., Campbell, J., Adler, C., Adler, W., & Morton, M. (2004). *Omerta* [Lyrics].

Boeckel, J. (1993). *The Betrayal by Technology, A Portrait of Jacques Ellul* [Film]. ReRun Produkties. English transcript: https://archive.org/details/JacquesEllul-TheBetrayalByTechnology-EnglishTranscript.

Bogen, J. (2014): "Theory and Observation in Science". *The Stanford Encyclopedia of Philosophy* (Summer 2014 Edition) (E.N. Zalta, Ed.).

Browning, C.R. (2017). *Ordinary Men: Reserve Police Battalion 101 and the Final Solution in Poland*. Harper.

Buchanan, Anne V., Sholtis, Samuel; *et al.* (2009). What are genes "for" or where are traits "from"? What is the question?". *Bioessays,* (February 2009), p. 4. DOI: 10.1002/bies.200800133.

Burgess, A.G. & Burgess J.P. (2011). *Truth*. Princeton University Press.

Burgess, A.G. & Burgess J.P. (2009). *Philosophical Logic*. Princeton University Press.

Camus, A. (1956). *The Fall* (J. O'Brien, Trans.). Vintage Books.

Camus, A. (1955). *The Myth of Sisyphus & Other Essays* (J. O'Brien, Trans.). Vintage Books.

Camus, A. (1965). *Notebooks* (P. Thody, Trans.). Modern Library.

Camus, A. (1991). *The Plague* (S. Gilbert, Trans.). Vintage.

Camus, Albert. (1991). *The Rebel: An Essay on Man in Revolt* (A.

Bower, Trans). Vintage Books.

Camus, Albert. (2020). *Reflections on the Guillotine* (O'Brien, J. Trans.). Penguin Books.

Camus, Albert. (1954). *The Stranger* (S. Gilbert, Trans). Vintage Books.

Carroll, L. (2009). *Through the Looking-Glass.* The Floating Press. ebook https://openlibrary.org/publishers/The_Floating_Press.

Chang, R. (2015). Resolving to Create a New You. *New York Times,* 3 January 2015, https://www.nytimes.com/2015/01/04/opinion/sunday/resolving-to-create-a-new-you.html?_r=0.

Chastenet, P. (2019). *A Biography of Jacques Ellul (1912–1994).* International Jacques Ellul Society. https://ellul.org/life/biography/

Churchill, W. (1986). *The Second World War, Vol. I.* Mariner Books.

Cimino, M., Dir. (1978). *The Deerhunter* [Script]. EMI. http://www.cinefile.biz/script/hunter.pdf

Collins, Francis S. (2006). *The Language of God*: *A Scientist Presents Evidence for Belief.* Free Press.

Conrad, J. (2016). *Heart of Darkness.* W. W. Norton & Company.

Coombs, M. I. (1993). The Case of the Speluncean Explorers: Contemporary Proceedings. *George Washington Law Review*, August 1993. http://faculty.law.miami.edu/mcoombs/documents/speluncean.pdf.

Copelston, F., S.J. (1963). *The History of Philosophy.* Volumes 1-9. Doubleday.

Crick, F. (1988). *What Mad Pursuit, A Personal View of Scientific Discovery.* Basic Books.

Cunningan, E.T., Marrow, T.L., & Dennis, V. (2014). "Wanna be a Gangstar" [Lyrics]. *Body Count.* https://www.songfacts.com/lyrics/body-count/wanna-be-a-gangsta

Derrida, J. (1977). *Limited Inc.* Northwestern University Press.

Dostoyevsky, F. (1983). *The Brothers Karamazov* (D. Magarshack, Trans). Penguin Classics.

Dostoyevsky, F. (2017). *Crime and Punishment* (C. Garnett, Trans.). Digireads Publishing.

Dostoyevsky, F. (2017). *The Demons* (C. Garnett, Trans.). Digireads Publishing.

Dribble, H. (2004). "A View from the Asylum". *Philosophical Investigations from the Sanctity of the Press.* Iuniverse.

Durant, W. (1942) *The Story of Civilization - Part I, Our Oriental Heritage.* Simon & Schuster.

Dworkin, R. (1977). *Taking Rights Seriously.* Harvard University Press.

Dworkin, R. (2013). *Religion without God.* Harvard University Press.

Ellis, J. & Guevara, D., Ed. (2012). *Wittgenstein and the Philosophy of Mind.* Oxford University Press.

Eliot, T.S. (2014). *The Idea of a Christian Society.* Houghton Mifflin Harcourt.

Ellul, J. (1964). *The Technological Society.* Vintage Books.

Enoch, D. (2013). *Taking Morality Seriously: A Defense of Robust Realism.* Oxford University Press.

Essays in Honor of Hans Kelsen: Celebrating the 90th Anniversary of His Birth. (1971). The California Law Review, Ed. Fred B. Rothman & Co.

Feser, E. (2008) *The Last Superstition, A Refutation of the New Atheism.* St. Augustine's Press.

Feyerabend, P. (2010). *Against Method.* Verso.

Field, H. (1980). *Science Without Numbers: A defense of nominalism.* Blackwell.

Field, H. (2009). What Is the Normative Role of Logic? *Proceedings of the Aristotelian Society,* 83, Suppl., 2009.

Finnis, J. (2011). *Natural Law and Natural Rights.* Clarendon Press.

Foley, R. (2018). *The Geography of Insight: The Sciences, the Humanities, How they Differ, Why They Matter.* Oxford University Press.

Fogle, R.H. (1958). "Billy Budd—Acceptance or Irony". *Tulane Studies in English*, viii (1958), 109–110, 112.

Ford, J. (1962). *The Man Who Shot Liberty Valance.* John Ford Productions.

Frankfurt, H. G. (2005). *On Bullshit.* Princeton University Press.

Frankfurt, H. G. (2013). *On Truth*. Alfred A. Knopf.

Frye, N. (2000). *Anatomy of Criticism, Four Essays.* Princeton University Press.

Fuller, L. (1949). The Case of the Speluncean Explorers. *Harvard Law Review*, Vol. 62, No. 4 (February 1949). http://www.nullapoena.de/stud/explorers.html.

Gat, A. (2006). *War in Human Civilization*. Oxford University Press.

Gefter, A. (2016). The Evolutionary Argument Against Reality. *Quanta Magazine*, April 21, 2016. https://www.quantamagazine.org/the-evolutionary-argument-against-reality-20160421/

Gershgorn, D. (2018). California just replaced cash bail with algorithms. Quartz, Sept. 4 (2018). https://qz.com/1375820/california-just-replaced-cash-bail-with-algorithms/

Gerstein, M.B., Bruce, C., Rozowsky, J.S., *et al.* (2007). What is a gene, post-ENCODE? History and updated definition. *Genome Res.,* Vol. 17, (2007), p. 670. DOI: 10.1101/gr.6339607.

Gibson, C. (2021). Actual Pennant Winners Versus Pythagorean Pennant Winners, 1901–2020. *Baseball Research Journal.* Spring (2021). https://sabr.org/journal/article/actual-pennant-winners-versus-pythagorean-pennant-winners-1901-2020/

Godfrey-Smith, P. (2014). *Philosophy of Biology*. Princeton University Press.

Goldhagen, D.J. (1997). *Hitler's Willing Executioners: Ordinary*

Germans and the Holocaust. Vintage.

Goldstein, R. (2005). *Incompleteness, The Proof and Paradox of Kurt Godel*. W.W. Norton.

Gray, J. (2009). Jim Grey on eScience: A Transformed Scientific Method. *The Fourth Paradigm* (T. Hey, S. Tansley, & K. Tolle, Eds.). Microsoft Research.

Hanson, N. R. (2010). *Patterns of Discovery*. Cambridge University Press.

Hacker, P.M.S., Baker, G.P. (1984). *Language, Sense and Nonsense*. Blackwell.

Harman, G. (1986). *Change in View: Principles of Reasoning*. MIT Press.

Hausman, D.M., Ed. (2008). *The Philosophy of Economics: an anthology*. Cambridge University Press.

Hart, H. L. A. (2012). *The Concept of Law*, 3rd ed. Clarendon Press.

Hempel, C. G. (1945). "Studies in the Logic of Confirmation I". *Mind* 54 (13): 1–26. doi:10.1093/mind/LIV.213.1. JSTOR 2250886.

Healey, R. (2007). *Gauging What's Real*. Oxford University Press.

Hegel, G.W.F. (2005). *Philosophy of Right* (S.W. Dyde, Trans.). Dover Philosophical Classics.

Hegel, G.W.F. (1977). *Phenomenology of Spirit* (A. V. Miller, Trans.). Oxford University Press.

Heidegger, M. (1969). *Discourse on Thinking* (J.M. Anderson, E. H. Freund, Trans). Harper.

Heinlein, R.A. (1973). *Time Enough for Love*. G.P. Putnam's Sons.

Heisenberg, W. (1971). *Physics and Beyond.* George Allen & Unwin Ltd. https://www.edge.org/conversation/science-and-religion

Hess, R. (1946). *Testimony of Rudolf Hoess, Commandant of Auschwitz*
[Testimony on Monday, April 15, 1946].
http://law2.umkc.edu/faculty/projects/ftrials/nuremberg/hoesstest.html

Hey, T., Tansley, S., & Tolle, K., Eds. (2009). *The Fourth Paradigm, Data Intensive Scientific Discovery.* Microsoft Research.

The History Place, Genocide in the 20th Century: Rwandan Genocide Facts. (1999). The History Place.
http://www.historyplace.com/worldhistory/genocide/pol-pot.htm, http://www.softschools.com/facts/history/rwandan_genocide_facts/857/.

The Holy Bible Saint Joseph Textbook Edition. (1963). Catholic Book Publishing Co.

Holmes, O.W. (1991). *The Common Law*. Dover Publications.

Holmes, O.W. (1897). "The Path of Law". *Harvard Law Review.* 10 Harvard Law Review 457 (1897).

Holocaust Encyclopedia. *United States Holocaust Memorial Museum.*
https://www.ushmm.org/wlc/en/article.php?ModuleId=10005144

Holt, J. (2005). Say Anything, three books find truth under cultural and conceptual assault. *The New Yorker,* 22 August 2005.

Holt, J. (2013). *Why Does the World Exist?: An Existential Detective Story.* Liveright.

Horgan, J. (2016). "Was Philosopher Paul Feyerabend Really Science's 'Worst Enemy'?". *Scientific American* (24 October 2016). https://blogs.scientificamerican.com/cross-check/was-philosopher-paul-feyerabend-really-science-s-worst-enemy/#:~:text=Feyerabend%2C%20who%20defended%20astrology%20and%20creationism%2C%20denied%20that,was%20no%20more%20valid%20than%20astrology%20or%20religion.

Hume, D. (1739). *A Treatise of Human Nature.* Wikisource. https://en.wikisource.org/wiki/Treatise_of_Human_Nature.

Hume, D. (1896). *A Treatise of Human Nature, 1896 reprint edition.* Clarendon Press.

Hunt, T. (2014). Reconsidering the logical structure of the theory of natural selection. *Communicative and Integrative Biology*, 2014, Oct 30, Dec, 7(6), e972848. DOI: 10.4161/19420889.2014.972848.

Hunter, D. (2010). *Essentials of Discrete Mathematics.* Jones and Bartlett.

Hut, P., Alford, M., & Tegmark, M. (2006). On Math, Matter and Mind. *Foundations of Physics*. 36 (6): 765–94 (2006).

Hutson, M. (2017). Artificial intelligence prevails at predicting Supreme Court decisions. *Science,* May 2, 2017. https://www.sciencemag.org/news/2017/05/artificial-intelligence-prevails-predicting-supreme-court-decisions.

Huxley, A. (1989). *Brave New World.* Harper Collins.

Hylton, P. (2010). *Quine*. Routledge

James, W. (1907). "Lecture 8 in Pragmatism: A new name for some old ways of thinking." *Pragmatism and Religion*. Longman Green and Co.

Jaschik, S. (2017). "Nobel Laureate's Talk Called Off Over His Racist Comments". *Inside Higher Ed.* (May 17, 2017). https://www.insidehighered.com/news/2017/05/17/u-illinois-calls-james-watson-lecture-over-his-racist-comments

Jugrin, D. (2016). AGNŌSIA: The Apophatic Experience of God in Dionysius the Areopagite. *Teologia*, 67 (2), (2016), pp. 102-115. ISSN 2247-4382

Kant, I. (2015). *Critique of Practical Reason* (M. Gregor, Trans.). Cambridge University Press.

Kant, I. (1999). *Critique of Pure Reason* (P. Guyer, A.W. Wood, Trans.). Cambridge University Press.

Kant, I. (1980). *Lectures on Ethics* (L. Infield, Trans.). Hackett Classics.

Keys, D. (2014). Saharan remains may be evidence of first race war, 13,000 years ago. *The Independent,* July, 2014. https://www.independent.co.uk/news/science/archaeology/saharan-remains-may-be-evidence-of-first-race-war-13000-years-ago-9603632.html

Kenny, A.J.P. (1984). *The Legacy of Wittgenstein*. Blackwell.

Kierkegaard, S. (1974). *Concluding Unscientific Postscript* (D. Swenson, Trans). Princeton University Press.

Kierkegaard, S. (1992). "Irony as a Mastered Moment: The Truth of Irony," pt. 2. *The Concept of Irony* [H. V. Hong & E. H. Hong, Trans. & Eds.]. Princeton University Press.

Kierkegaard, S. (1993). *Kierkegaard's Writings, XV, Volume 15: Upbuilding Discourses in Various Spirits* (H. V. Hong & E. H. Hong, Trans. & Eds.). Princeton University Press. http://www.jstor.org/stable/j.ctt1d2dm7b

Kiernan, Ben. (2009). *Blood and Soil: A World History of Genocide and Extermination from Sparta to Darfur*. Yale University Press.

Klesius, M. (2009). Neil Armstrong's X-15 flight over Pasadena: Here's the truth. *Air & Space Smithsonian Magazine.* 20 May 2009. https://www.airspacemag.com/daily-planet/neil-armstrongs-x-15-flight-over-pasadena-59458462/.

Knappman, P. (1973). *Watergate and the White House*. Facts on File Publishing.

Kreeft, P. (2020). *Socrates Meets Kierkegaard.* St. Augustine' Press.

Kreeft, P. (2014). *Socrates Meets Sartre.* St. Augustine' Press.

Kreeft, P., Ed. (1993). *Christianity for Modern Pagans: Pascal's Pensees.* Ignatius Press.

Kripke, S. (1982). *Wittgenstein on Rules and Private Language.* Harvard University Press.

Kuhn, T.S. (2012). *The Structure of Scientific Revolutions* 4th ed. University of Chicago Press.

Leeson, P.T. (2014). *Anarchy Unbound, Why Self-Governance*

Works Better Than You Think. Cambridge University Press.

Leeson, Peter. (2009). *THE INVISIBLE HOOK, The Hidden Economics of Pirates.* Princeton University Press.

Leibniz, G.W. (1991). *Philosophical Essays* (D. Garber, R. Ariew. Trans.). Hackett Classics.

Leiter, B. (2005). "American legal realism". *The Blackwell Guide to the Philosophy of Law and Legal Theory* [Martin P. G., William A. E., Eds.). Blackwell.

Leiter, B. (2012). "In Praise of Realism (and Against "Nonsense" Jurisprudence)". 100 Georgia. L.J. 865, 867 (2012).

Leiter, B. (2017). "The Role of Judges in Democracies: A Realistic View". *University of Chicago Law School Chicago Unbound Working Papers.* https://chicagounbound.uchicago.edu/cgi/viewcontent.cgi?article=2105&context=public_law_and_legal_theory

Leiter, B. (2018). "The Truth is Terrible". *Journal of Nietzsche Studies* (7 April 2018). DOI: 10.2139/SSRN.2099162 Corpus ID: 170211129

Leiter, B. (2012). *Why Tolerate Religion?* Princeton University Press.

Leone, S. (1966). *The Good, the Bad, and the Ugly* [Film]. Produzioni Europee Associate
United Artists.

Lewis, C.S. (1972). *God in the Dock: Essays on Theology and Ethics*. Wm. B. Eerdmans Publishing.

Lewis, C. S. (1987). The Humanitarian Theory of Punishment. *Issues in Religion and Psychotherapy*, Vol. 13, No. 1, Article 11 (1987). https://scholarsarchive.byu.edu/irp/vol13/iss1/11.

Linklater, R., Dir. (2001). *Waking Life* [Film]. Twentieth Century Fox.

Linnebo, O. (2017). *Philosophy of Mathematics*. Princeton University Press.

Lord, D. (1935). *"Hoi Polloi"* [Film]. *Three Stooges*. Columbia Pictures.

Lottman, H.R. (1979). *Albert Camus, A Biography*. DoubleDay & Co.

Lynn, Jonathan. (1992). *My Cousin Vinny*. 20th Century Fox.

Mackey, R., Ed. (2019). *#Accelerate#: the accelerationist reader*. MIT Press.

Mackie, J.L. (1990). *Ethics: Inventing Right and Wrong*. Penguin Books.

Marvell, A. (2015). To His Coy Mistress. *The Poems of Andrew Marvell*.
The University of Adelaide Library ebook web edition: https://ebooks.adelaide.edu.au/m/marvell/andrew/poems/complete.html#poem21.

Marx, K., Engels, F. (2014). *The Communist Manifesto*. International Publishers.

Maudlin, T. (2019). *Philosophy of Physics*. Princeton University

Press.

McCrae, J. (1918). *In Flanders Field*. Poets.org. https://poets.org/poem/flanders-fields

Melville, H. (2017). *Billy Budd, Sailor*. Dover.

Mellville, H. (2022). *Poetry, Vol. 3*. Columbia.

Melville, H. (1999). *Moby Dick*. Wordsworth.

Mill, J.S. (1904). On Nature. *Nature, The Utility of Religion and Theism*. Rationalist Press. Lancaster E-text prepared by the Philosophy Department at Lancaster University: https://www.marxists.org/reference/archive/mill-john-stuart/1874/nature.htm.

Morison, W. L. (1982). *John Austin*. Stanford University Press.

Morris, E., Dir. (1991). *A Brief History of Time* [Film Script]. Anglia Television, Channel Four Films, Elstree Studios, Tokyo Broadcasting System.

Nagel, E. (1979). *The Structure of Science: Problems in the Logic of Scientific Explanation*. Hackett Publishing.

Nagel, T. (1997). *The Last Word*. Oxford University Press.

National Conference of State Legislatures Press Release. December 27, 2011. https://www.ncsl.org/press-room/new-laws-ring-in-the-new-year.aspx

Neiman, S. (2002). *Evil in Modern Thought, An Alternative History of Philosophy*. Princeton University Press.

Newport, Frank. (2016). "Most Americans Still Believe in God." *Gallup Polls*. http://www.gallup.com/poll/193271/americans-believe-god.aspx

Nicholls, M., Kean, M., Malia, L., Fish, J., & Sykes, O. (2013). "Bring Me the Horizon" [Lyrics]. *Antivist*. https://genius.com/Bring-me-the-horizon-antivist-lyrics

Nietzsche, F. (2017). Beyond Good and Evil, The Genealogy of Morals (H. Zimmern, H.B. & Samuel, Trans). *The Essential Nietzsche*. Chartwell Books.

Nietzsche, F. (2008) *Human, All Too Human* (H. Zimmern, P.V. & Cohn, Eds). Hertfordshire.

Neiman, S. (2002). *Evil in Modern Thought*: an alternative history *of philosophy*. Princeton University Press.

Nozick, R. (2013). *Anarchy State and Utopia*. Basic Books.

Numbers, R.L. (2003). *Science without God: Natural Laws and Christian Beliefs. When Science and Christianity Meet* (D.C. Lindberg, R.L. Numbers, Eds.). University Of Chicago Press.

Orwell, G. (1977). *1984*. Signet Classics Penguin Group.

Orwell, G. (2009). *All Art is Propaganda: Critical Essays* (G. Packer, Ed.). First Mariner Books.

Orwell, G. (2005). *George Orwell: The Collected Essays, Journalism and Letters: IV Volumes* (Sonia, G., Ian A., Eds.). Nonpareil Books.

Peirce, C.S. (1958). *Collected Papers of Charles Sanders Pierce* (C. Hartshorne, P. Weiss, & A. Burks, Eds). Harvard University Press.

Peterson, M.L., Vanarragon, R.J., Eds. (2004). *Contemporary Debates in Philosophy of Religion*. Blackwell Publishing.

Pew Research Center. (2014). *Record Share of Americans Have Never Married*. Pew Research Center (24 September 2014). http://www.pewsocialtrends.org/2014/09/24/record-share-of-americans-have-never-married/

Pew Research Center. (2019). *U.S. has world's highest rate of children living in single-parent households*. Pew Research Center (December 12, 2019). https://www.pewresearch.org/fact-tank/2019/12/12/u-s-children-more-likely-than-children-in-other-countries-to-live-with-just-one-parent/

Pevney, J., *Dir*. (1967). *Star Trek. A Taste of Armageddon* [Film]. Desilu Productions. http://www.chakoteya.net/StarTrek/23.htm

Plato. (2004). *The Republic* (C.D.C. Reeve, Trans.). Hackett Publishing.

Popper, C. (2009). *The Logic of Scientific Discovery*. Routledge.

Popper, C. (1994). *The Open Society and Its Enemies*. Routledge.

Porn, Ingmar. (1970). *The Logic of Power*. Blackwell.

Poscher, K. (2016). *Vagueness and the Law*. Oxford University Press.

Potter, M. (2012). Frege, Russell and Wittgenstein. *Routledge*

Companion to the Philosophy of Language (G. Russell & D.G. Fara, Eds.). Routledge.

Pseudo-Dionysius. (1987). *Pseudo-Dionysius: The Complete Works* (C. Luibheid, Trans.). Paulist Press.

Putnam, H. (1982). Why Reason Can't be Naturalized. *Synthese Vol. 52,* 1982.

Quine, W.V.O. (1980). *From A Logical Point of View.* Harvard University Press.

Quine, W.O. (1969). *Ontological relativity and other essays.* Columbia University Press.

Quine, W.V.O. (1986). *Philosophy of Logic.* Harvard University Press.

Quine, W.V.O. (2013). *Word and Object.* Martino Publishing.

Rabin, R.L., Sugarman, S.D. (2003). *Torts Stories.* Foundation Press.

Rawls, John. *Political Liberalism.* Columbia University Press: N.Y., N.Y. (1993).

Rawls, J. (1971). *A Theory of Justice.* Harvard University Press.

Rectenwald, M. (2018). *SPRINGTIME FOR SNOWFLAKES, Social Justice and Its Postmodern Parentage.* New England Review Press.

Reed, C. (1950). *The Third Man.* London Films.
https://genius.com/Orson-welles-cuckoo-clock-speech-annotated

Rhees, R., Ed. (1981). *Ludwig Wittgenstein: Personal Recollections*. Blackwell.

Ricoeur, P. (1976). *Interpretation Theory: Discourse and the Surplus of Meaning*. TCU Press.

Roberts, P.C., (2008). *The Tyranny of Good Intentions: How Prosecutors and Law Enforcement Are Trampling the Constitution in the Name of Justice*. Broadway Books.

Roederer, C. (2003). Negotiating the Jurisprudential Terrain: A Model Theoretic Approach to Legal Theory. *Seattle University Law Review*, 27 (385), 385–451, 2003.

Roosevelt, T. (1910). *Speech at the Sorbonne, Paris, April 23, 1910*. Theodore Roosevelt Conservation Partnership. https://www.trcp.org/2011/01/18/it-is-not-the-critic-who-counts/ .

Rose, S. (2001). *Nihilism: The Root of the Revolution of the Modern Age*. St. Herman Press.

Rosenberg, S., Dir. (1967). *Cool Hand Luke* [Film]. Warner Brothers.

Rumble, W.E. (1985). *The Thought of John Austin: Jurisprudence, Colonial Reform, and the British Constitution*. Athlone Press.

Russell, B. (1998). *The Philosophy of Logical Atomism*. Carus Publishing.

Russell, B. (1901). "Recent Work on the Principles of Mathematics". International Monthly, Vol. 4 (1901).

Saint Augustine. (2015). *The Letters of St. Augustine* [John G. C.,

Trans.). Jazzybee Verlag.

Salam, A., Bethe, H.A., Dirac, P., Heisenberg, W., Wigner, E.P., Klein, O., & Lifshitz, E.M. (1989). *From a Life of Physics*. World Scientific.

Salam, A. (2005). *Unification of Fundamental Forces*. Cambridge University Press.

Schaffner, F.J. (1970). *Patton* [Movie]. 20th Century Fox.

Senensky, R., Dir. (1967). *Star Trek. Metamorphosis* [Film]. Desilu Productions. http://www.chakoteya.net/StarTrek/31.htm.

Shapiro, S.J. (2007). *The Hart-Dworkin Debate: A Short Guide for the Perplexed*. (2007) SSRN 968657.

Silvergate, H. (2011). *Three Felonies A Day: How the Feds Target the Innocent*. Encounter Books.

Sinclair, U. (1925). Mammonart - an Essay in Economic Interpretation. *Who Owns the Artists?* Self-published.

Soames, S. (2010). *Philosophy of Language*. Princeton University Press.

Sokal, A., & Bricmont, J. (1999). *Fashionable Nonsense*. Picador.

Sontag, S. (2005). Plato's Cave. *On Photography*. Rosetta Books. First electronic edition published: www.lab404.com/3741/readings/sontag.pdf .

Sosa, E (2017). *Epistemology*. Princeton University Press.

Sovell, T. (2008). *Applied Economics, Thinking Beyond Stage One*. Basic Books.

Stambaugh, J. (1994). *The Other Nietzsche*. State University of New York Press.

Stein, B., Steinberg, A. (2015). "No, You Cannot Catch An Individual Photon Acting Simultaneously As A Pure Particle And Wave". *Inside Science* (2015).
https://www.insidescience.org/news/no-you-cannot-catch-individual-photon-acting-simultaneously-pure-particle-and-wave

Steinbeck, J. (2008). *The Acts of King Arthur and His Noble Knights*. Penguin Classics.

Strohman, R.C. (1997). Epigenesis and Complexity, The Coming Kuhian revolution in biology. *Nature Biotechnology,* Vol. 15, March 1997, p. 195.

Tarr, B. (2011). *The Turin Horse* (Hungarian: *A torinói ló*) [Movie]. T. T. Filmműhely.

Todd, O. (1997). *Albert Camus, A Life* (B. Iury, Trans.). Alfred A. Knopf.

Tolstoy, L. (2008). *War and Peace* (R. Pevear, L. Volokhonsky, Trans.). Vintage Classics

The Trolley Problem. (2016). *YouTube*.
https://www.youtube.com/watch?v=-N_RZJUAQY4 .

The Trolley Problem — Thug Life. (2016). *YouTube*.
https://www.youtube.com/watch?v=NfZOwgW14zY&list=LLvhYzZy4TCqtgrwDJqB2euw&index=3&t=0s.

Townsend, P. (1971). "Won't Get Fooled Again" [Lyrics]. *The Who.* https://genius.com/The-who-wont-get-fooled-again-lyrics

Remarque, E.M. (1987). *All Quiet on the Western Front* (A W. Wheen, Trans.) Ballantine Books.

Whitehead, A.N. (1958). *An Introduction to Mathematics.* Oxford University Press.

Wanna be a Gangsta. (2014). *YouTube.* https://www.youtube.com/watch?v=Cp5RPaMcnWs.

Wikipedia. *World Population.* https://en.wikipedia.org/wiki/World_population.

Wilshire, B. (2002). *FASHIONABLE NIHILISM, A Critique of Analytic Philosophy.* State University of New York Press.

Wilson, A.N. (2001). *Tolstoy: A Biography.* W. W. Norton & Company.

Wittgenstein, L. (1965). *The Blue and Brown Books.* Harper and Row.

Wittgenstein, L. (1984). *Culture and Value* (P. Winch, Trans.). University of Chicago Press.

Wittgenstein, L. (2002). *Lecture on Ethics Delivered in November 1929 to the Heretics Society.* Cambridge University. http://sackett.net/WittgensteinEthics.pdf.

Wittgenstein, L. (2009). *Major Works.* Harper Collins.

Wittgenstein, L. (1944). *Nachlass: The Bergen Electronic Edition.*

The Wittgenstein Archives at the University of Bergen.
http://wab.uib.no/transform/wab.php?modus=opsjoner

Wittgenstein, L. (2009). *Philosophical Investigations* (G.E.M. Anscombe, Trans.). Wiley-Blackwell.

Wittgenstein, L. (1993). *Philosophical Occasions: 1912-1951* (J. Klagge & A. Nordmann, Eds.). Hackett Publishing Co.

Wittgenstein, L. (1984). *Recollections of Wittgenstein* (R. Rhees, Ed.). Oxford University Press.

Wittgenstein, L. (1998). *Tractatus logico-philosophicus* (C. K. Ogden, Trans.). Dover Publications.

Woese, C.R. (2004). A New Biology for a New Century. *Microbiology and Molecular Biology Reviews*, June, 2004, p. 175. DOI: 10.1128/MMBR.68.2.173-186.2004.

Wolfgram, H. (1993). *The Roman Empire and its Germanic Peoples*. U. of CA. Press. p. 193

World Population. (2022, August 25). In *Wikepedia*. https://en.wikipedia.org/wiki/World_population

www.ingramcontent.com/pod-product-compliance
Lightning Source LLC
Chambersburg PA
CBHW030942240526
45463CB00016B/1217